THE PRACTICAL METHODOLOGY OF

FORENSIC
PHOTOGRAPHY

SECOND EDITION

CRC SERIES IN
**PRACTICAL ASPECTS OF CRIMINAL
AND FORENSIC INVESTIGATIONS**

VERNON J. GEBERTH, BBA, MPS, FBINA *Series Editor*

THE PRACTICAL METHODOLOGY OF

FORENSIC PHOTOGRAPHY

SECOND EDITION

DAVID R. REDSICKER

Peter Vallas Associates
Endicott, New York

CRC Press
Boca Raton   London   New York   Washington, D.C.

Library of Congress Cataloging-in-Publication Data

Redsicker, David R.
    The practical methodology of forensic photography / David R. Redsicker, with
contributions by Gurden Gordner ... [et al.].— 2nd ed.
        p.   cm.
    Includes bibliographical references and index.
    ISBN 0-8493-2004-6
    1. Legal photography. I. Title. II. CRC series in practical aspects of criminal and
forensic investigations

    TR822.P73 2000
    363.25—dc21

                                                                    00-041367
                                                                    CIP

Visit the CRC Press Web site at www.crcpress.com

© 2001 by CRC Press LLC

No claim to original U.S. Government works
International Standard Book Number 0-8493-2004-6
Library of Congress Card Number 00-041367
Printed in the United States of America   2 3 4 5 6 7 8 9 0
Printed on acid-free paper

Dedication

Regardless of your chosen profession or field of expertise, at some time during your career, you will have the privilege of meeting and working with other individuals from whom you have gained new knowledge and/or experiences. It has been my privilege to have worked with a number of these individuals who have, unfortunately, passed before their time. To them, I dedicate this second edition. In memory of and sincere appreciation:

Gurden (Bud) Gordner
Rex G. Whitman
Anthony C. Laws, Sr.
Harold Glass
Alton Lewis
Gene Bricault

Editor's Note

This textbook is part of a series entitled "Practical Aspects of Criminal and Forensic Investigation." This series was created by Vernon J. Geberth, New York City Police Department Lieutenant Commander (Retired), who is an author, educator, and consultant on homicide and forensic investigations.

This series has been designed to provide contemporary, comprehensive, and pragmatic information to the practitioner involved in criminal and forensic investigations by authors who are nationally recognized experts in their respective fields.

Preface

A truth that does not understand becomes an error.

– Dezbarolles

Photographic documentation of evidence for presentation of an argument in a court of law is *forensic photography*. Unfortunately, the truth can be obscured by the advisorial protesting of the parties involved. It is, therefore, imperative that the photographic evidence be a fair and accurate representation of what was depicted at the scene.

The purpose of this text is twofold; first, to bring together in one readily available resource all the latest methods of photographic documentation, including the old tried and true methods with cameras, film, and lighting sources as well as new procedures involving video and thermography. Second and most important, the format of the text is a practical step-by-step application of forensic photography. Students and professionals alike will be capable of using any camera together with the aid of this methodology in producing their own photographic documentation.

The introduction to each chapter addresses the subject of forensic photography from the basics of "how to," with a wide variety of equipment, to proper and accepted court presentation of the photographic evidence. The application of the subject matter is then presented in text and illustration with many examples for practitioners to compare their work against.

The glossary of terms provided at the end of this book will be beneficial to the forensic photographer in the preparation of reports and courtroom testimony.

The Practical Methodology of Forensic Photography is both a learning tool for the student of this specialized field and a necessary reference manual for the professional community. It will be as useful in the classroom, laboratory, and attorney's library as in the field during an investigation.

David R. Redsicker

Introduction

Regardless of the type of investigation, be it fire or other crime, classroom theory is needed for background, but actual experience is necessary to round out an individual's knowledge, for intelligence and proficiency in the subject.

Years ago, when the investigation of fires and arson became a major concern, one of the basics stated in nearly every textbook and taught in every class was, "the origin of a fire is at the point of deepest char." It did not take involvement in many fire investigations to realize that this statement, along with many others, was far from being the all-time gospel truth. The theory was good but did not always ring true. At that time, the state of the art was new and actual field experience was minimal. Those who knew better were not about to tell others; they had found out the hard way, and the rest of us could do likewise.

The field of fire and crime scene investigation has long been in need of a forensic photography book written with a fresh, new approach to the subject. Most publications available are either basics already known by most investigators or highly technical beyond the everyday crime scene requirements. Herein, the author and additional contributors have deliberately bypassed the preliminaries and eliminated the highly technical aspects. Routine film developing, print making, and other photographic aspects that are covered extensively in other publications are also not included. This could very well be called a middle-of-the-road book; a guide for the beginner as well as the everyday investigator.

The additional contributors, each an expert in his field, provide insight from different sources, views, and knowledge based on years of personnel experience. Taking advantage of this experience advances the reader's knowledge in less time with less effort and expense.

As a textbook for new inductees in any of the fields covered, such a book is long overdue. Experienced personnel may, upon reading, find a better way of doing their job. Those individuals not directly responsible but who serve in related functions will be assisted in becoming familiar with and obtaining a better understanding of the fields covered herein. This book should be a required addition to every fire and crime scene investigator's library.

G. Gordner
Fire Investigator

Contributors

David R. Redsicker
Peter Vallas Associates, Inc.
Endicott, New York

Gurden Gordner
Peter Vallas Associates, Inc.
Endicott, New York
(Deceased)

Stuart H. James
James and Associates,
 Forensic Consultants, Inc.
Fort Lauderdale, Florida

Anthony C. Laws, Sr.
President, Nondestructive Testing Corporation
Manville, New Jersey
(Deceased)

Aaron D. Redsicker
Peter Vallas Associates, Inc.
Hackensack, New Jersey

Acknowledgments

Times have changed since the initial publication of the first edition in 1991. But as in life, change is inevitable and change is good. The initial contributions by Gurden "Bud" Gordner and Anthony C. Laws, Sr., may have changed, but their unfortunate passings have had no less an influence on my efforts in updating the second edition.

In addition to the contributors in the first edition, I would like to acknowledge the efforts of my Administrative Assistant, Amy J. Hilker, in the preparation of the new manuscript. I would also like to thank my son Aaron, Brian Johnson, John Russ, and Leonard Govern for their input in the new chapter on digital photography. Also, thank you to my daughter-in-law (pilot) Kerri Redsicker and New York State Police Investigator Ken Sosnowski for their assistance in updating aerial photography. My apologies to George Keyes for the misspelling of his name in the first edition. His advice was nevertheless invaluable in Chapter 4. Grateful appreciation is also extended to Peter R. Vallas, Peter S. Vallas, and staff for their support and encouragement.

Finally, a heartfelt thanks to my wife Patti for her continued support and encouragement.

David R. Redsicker

Table of Contents

3   Videography for Fire/Crime Scenes

9 Legal Aspects of Visual Evidence

10 Digital Photography

Principles of Photography

1

In the field of forensic photography, you will find that your work is scrutinized not for its artistic content but rather the accuracy with which it depicts the topic of interest. Therefore, a basic knowledge of the principles of photography is necessary, both from the standpoint of creating your photographic work and of being capable of intelligently defending its accuracy.

Whether this is your first step into the field of forensic photography or simply a review of its context and methodology, this chapter will prepare you for the photographic techniques described in the following text.

What is Photography?

The word photography is a derivative of two Greek words, *phos*, which means "light," and *graphos*, meaning "write." For our purposes photography best translates to "write with light." Therefore to document, record, or write with light we need an instrument with which to write or record the images, and second, we need a medium on which to permanently record the images. Our instrument is a little more complex than the commonplace pencil or pen; it is the camera and associated equipment necessary to capture the light (reflect light images) on the recording medium, light-sensitive film. Thus, we have the two basic requirements for our photographic needs; a camera and the film. Accessories such as auxiliary lighting, special lenses, and filters will be discussed later in this chapter.

Camera

The camera, no matter which type, is used to collect the reflected light images and record them on light-sensitive film. For this process to work properly, the camera must be light-proof except for the controlled light that is allowed to strike the light-sensitive surface (film plane) of the film. The light enters the camera through an opening called a *lens aperture*. The lens, whether it is fixed, telephoto, or zoom, collects the reflected light images to be recorded in focus on the film. A focused image of a subject is one that is clear, sharp, and accurately depicts the subject and its contents, color, and detail without distortion. Remember, the primary purpose of *forensic photography* is a true and accurate representation of the subject. Focusing is therefore a very important basic function of forensic photography. Depending on the camera being used, the lens and therefore the focusing capabilities may be limited. Lenses that are found on many instant cameras are preset by the factory for a sharp focus of a subject usually between 3½ feet and infinity. Other lenses are the adjustable type (close-up to zoom), many of which are very suitable for forensic photography. These lenses can be focused for distances as close as several inches or as far as infinity. Again, the versatility of a specific lens and its application in forensic photography will be addressed in subsequent chapters.

Lens

The lens is made up of several individual lenses which, in essence, form a compound lens. Located between the front and rear lenses is the aperture opening. Adjusting the aperture controls the amount of light entering the camera to be recorded on the film. The aperture setting (lens opening) is referred to as the *f-stop* or *f-number*. This f-number is calibrated to the size of the lens opening, much the same as gun ammunition is sized according to gauge. In other words, the smaller the number the larger the opening for light to pass through (see Figure 1.1). You will note that f-2 is the largest opening and f-22 is the smallest opening. Referring to Figure 1.2, you will note that as you increase the opening one stop *f* for example, from f.8 to f.6 — you double the amount of light allowed to enter through the aperture (lens opening). However, if you "stop down" — for instance, go from f-8 down to f-11 — you decrease the amount of light allowed to enter the lens opening by one-half. Remember, each time you open the lens from one stop to another, you double the amount of light and, and when you stop down you decrease the amount of light allowed to enter the lens opening by one-half.* Most lenses today are also capable of half-stops, which are settings half-way between the primary f-stops.

Shutter

Another equally important part of the camera for the control of light entering is the shutter. The purpose of the shutter is to control the amount of time the

---

* Some lenses' f-stop capabilities may be greater or less than that shown in Figure 1.1. The f-numbers are determined by the formula $f = F/d$, where F is the focal length of the lens and D is the diameter of the lens opening. This information is calculated by the manufacturer and provided on the front of the lens.

Figure 1.1 The *f*-stop or aperture opening is shown as it is typically found on most camera lenses.

light is allowed to focus on the film. The shutter is generally activated by depressing a shutter release button. Again, like the aperture/f-stop setting, the speed of the shutter may be fixed or adjustable. Usually the less expensive Instamatic and instant-print cameras have shutter speeds preset by the manufacturer.

Obviously, the adjustable-speed shutter is the one of choice for our purposes. Shutters come in two basic styles: leaf and focal plane (see Figure 1.3). The speed of the shutter is in increments of fractions of a second, ranging from a slow speed of 1 second to the fastest at 1/2000 of a second (see Figure 1.4). There is also a setting referred to as *bulb* (B), which is found on most variable shutter-speed cameras just below the 1 second setting. This refers to the early days of photography, when the shutter was activated by a squeeze bulb. When the bulb was depressed, the shutter remained open until the bulb was released. Essentially, the same effect is achieved when the shutter release button is depressed and held. This feature facilitates timed exposures, which will be addressed in Chapter 2.

You will note that shutter speeds, also known as *exposure times*, are in increments similar to aperture/f-stop openings. A 1-second speed or exposure allows twice as much light through the lens to the film as 1/2-second at the same f-stop. Likewise, 1/1000 second lets in half the amount of light that 1/500 second allows at the same f-stop. You will note that I specified the difference in the amount of light allowed by the shutter *at the same lens opening/f-stop*. If the exposure is the amount of reflective light allowed to expose the film, then we can control it by different combinations of lens

F-2

Figure 1.2 Illustrates the difference in lens/aperture openings from the largest (*f*2) to the smallest (*f*-22).

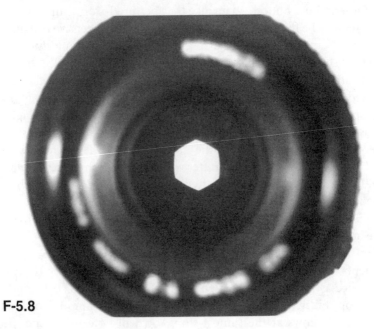

F-5.8

Figure 1.2b

F-8

Figure 1.2c

F-22

Figure 1.2d

Figure 1.3 The two basic types of shutters are shown above with the leaf shutter above and the focal plane shutter below.

openings and shutter speeds. If we allow too much light to be focused on the film, it will be overexposed. Likewise, insufficient light will result in underexposed film. Given this information, you can accomplish correct exposures with several different combinations of f-stops and shutter speeds. This will be particularly helpful in forensic photography, when the subject matter, light source, or distance may affect a correct exposure (see Figure 1.5). As

Figure 1.4a The shutter speeds are shown as they are most commonly found on the top right side of the camera.

Figure 1.4b The newer autofocus cameras display a variety of data on LCD (liquid crystal displays).

Figure 1.5 The top photograph is produced with an aperture setting of *f*-11 and shutter speed of 1/500 second. The bottom photograph was shot with an aperture of *f*-16 and 1/250 second.

you can see from the illustration, the same exposure (amount of light) can be obtained with various combinations of shutter speeds and f-stops. Learning these basic principles of exposure will help you in situations where it may be difficult to obtain the proper exposure with the newer, "programmed" cameras. It is convenient to be able to fall back on the manual capabilities of your equipment to obtain the accurate photographic documentation.

The flexibility of choice for the proper exposure is most evident in the documentation of evidence that requires "stopping" an object in motion. For this purpose, you will chose a faster shutter speed to stop the movement without blurring the object of interest (e.g., cast-off or trajectory of blood spatter). Some additional examples will be addressed in the following chapters.

We now see that we have two methods by which we can control the reflective light images entering the camera to be recorded on the film plane. The film plane is located at the back portion of the camera behind the lens, where the unexposed film travels from the film cassette to the take-up spool as the film is advanced between exposures. The *focal plane* is where the reflective light of our subject is focused by the lens aperture on the light-sensitive film.

Depth of Field

The correct combination of shutter speed and aperture opening (f-stop) also influences that portion of your photographic documentation that is in focus. The area of your photograph from the foreground to background, which appears in sharpest focus, is the *depth of field*, which is important when composing your photograph. If a series of overall crime scene photographs is needed for orientation purposes, then a greater depth of field is desired. This is achieved with a lens of a shorter focal length.

Lenses are often described in terms of their focal length (usually measured in millimeters). Focal length is the minimum distance between the center of the lens and the film when focused on infinity. Many adjustable lenses are on the market, with focal lengths ranging from 8 mm (wide angle) to over 600 mm (telephoto). However, for our purposes of accuracy and documentation, it is generally accepted that the minimum wide-angle lens focal length is 28 mm. With this short focal length, we can accomplish satisfactory overall documentation of most crime scenes. When focusing for depth of field, remember that the area in focus is not equally distributed between the foreground and the background of our scene. The rule of thumb is to focus about 1/3 of the distance into the scene — then the depth of field will be distributed approximately 1/3 in front of the point in focus and 3/4 beyond (Figure 1.6).

Still another factor that will affect the depth of field is the distance of the point of focus from the camera lens. For example, imagine a crime scene within a room measuring 14 × 26 ft. The victim's body is on the floor 15 ft into the room from the doorway where you are taking your photograph. Also in the room is the weapon — a knife — which is on a coffee table located about 5 ft into the room from the doorway. To achieve an acceptable photographic documentation that includes both the weapon and body in sharp focus, the best point of focus would be the body. Using a smaller

Figure 1.6 Note the depth of field in the top photograph is limited to the foreground and area of the gun. However, the depth of field in the bottom photograph is inclusive of the foreground, gun, and front of the truck.

focal length wide-angle lens (28 mm) and focusing on a point (the body) 15 ft into the crime scene will give the best depth of field for the photograph. Therefore, working with these three factors — a shorter focal length lens, a smaller aperture opening (f-stop), and greater distance to the point of focus (subject) — will give you maximum depth of field (Figure 1.7).

Figure 1.7 This photographic documentation illustrates the difference in depth of field. The top photograph area of focus is limited to the center of the photograph. The bottom photograph has a maximum depth of field achieved by using a 28 mm wide-angle lens focused on a point approximately 15 feet into the crime scene, with an aperture setting (f-stop) of f-16 and shutter speed of 1/250 of a second.

Most lenses have a depth-of-field scale between the aperture (f-stop) ring and the distance (focusing) ring. This will help you choose the most suitable combination of aperture opening and distance to subject to achieve the desired photographic documentation (Figure 1.8).

Figure 1.8 The depth of field is found on most lenses between the aperture *f*-stop ring and the distance (focusing) ring.

One more thing to consider for depth of field, particularly with indoor or nighttime photography, is auxiliary lighting (flood lamp, electronic flash, etc.) Most cameras have a predetermined shutter speed synchronized with the electronic flash, usually 1/60 or 1/125 of a second. This will limit your selection of aperture settings (f-stop) and camera-to-subject distance for maximum depth of field.

Film

To complete our photographic documentation, we need a light-sensitive medium called *film* to record our "writing with light." Film is produced in many ranges and varieties for a multitude of uses. The variety of films, their speeds, and their applications will be discussed at length in subsequent chapters. Basically, the *film speed* is a measure of its sensitivity to light. In the past, film was rated by a standardized number, its American Standards Association (ASA) rating or the European equivalent, Deutsche Industrie Norm (DIN). The faster the film, the higher the ASA/DIN. In 1979, these ratings were replaced by the International Standards Organization (ISO) number.

Black-and-white films are divided into four basic groups: slow film (ISO 25/15-50/80), medium film (ISO 100/21-200/24), fast film (ISO 400/27-500/28), and super fast film (ISO 800/30-3200/36).

Color films come in two basic types: color negative and color reversal. Color negative film is the most popular; it produces a negative which is used to make a print. Color reversal film (also known as slide film) produces a transparent positive, which allows the most accurate color reproduction. It is not the intention of this author to slight instant cameras or films. Since some of the instant films have been adapted to other cameras with the use of special film backs, they have their place in the field of forensic photography. Additional information on their application will be given in Chapter 2.

Summary

For those of you who have a moderate to extensive background in photography, this chapter may have been repetitive, however, repetition does aid learning. A word to the beginner: I hope this chapter has stimulated your interest sufficiently for you to pick up the instruction manual that came with your camera and *read it*! Regardless of your expertise, it is imperative that you become familiar with features, operation, and capabilities of your photographic equipment. Now that we know what photography is, we can move on to the techniques employed in forensic photography.

Suggested Reading

New York State Office of Fire Prevention and Control, *Fire Investigative Photography* (course manual), Montour Falls, NY, New York State Academy of Fire Science, 1984.

Still Photography for Fire/Crime Scenes

2

Let us assume that you have been given the responsibility for photographically documenting the fire scene. You now have the chance to be the "hero" or the "goat" in future investigations. If your photographic efforts are satisfactory, you could be the hero. If not, you could be the one blamed for failure of the investigation.

Photographing a fire scene is like falling off the top of a ladder: you get one chance to grab the top rung. Likewise, you get one chance to photograph a fire scene correctly, so you had better have your act together, know what you are doing, and have faith in yourself and your equipment.

This chapter is not a basic or advanced course in photography or equipment operation. Official fire/crime scene photography should be done only by someone with a minimum of basic and preferably, advanced training. Therefore, at the risk of stepping on a few toes, I will assume the reader has received at least basic photographic training in one form or another.

As with the chapter on video, this chapter's theme will be practical application information based on years of personal experience by the author. Some — if not all — of the information will help to make fire/crime scene photography easier, more accurate, and more useful to the investigation and all concerned.

It is difficult, if not impossible, to write separate chapters on fire/crime scene still photography and video without being redundant; so many things pertain to both. It is suggested that you read both chapters regardless of your job responsibility. Information in both chapters can be applied to either method of photographic documentation.

Why Take Photos?

Still photography is one of four accepted principal means of providing courtroom participants with visual evidence of what took place or existed at a fire/crime scene. Sketches, movies, video, and still photos all complement and support one another in the preservation of evidence. Some individuals more readily comprehend one method than they do others. Keep in mind that it is usually not possible to return the jury to the scene; therefore, you must bring the scene to the courtroom. Use all the methods available to accomplish this.

Through the life of a fire investigation and court case, photos are used by investigators, fire officers, prosecutors, defense attorneys, witnesses, and others to accomplish the following:

1. Assist in mental reconstruction of the structure.
2. Clarify and aid interviews.
3. Identify witnesses.
4. Identify suspects.
5. Prove suspect's presence at scene.
6. Documentation of prefire condition of structure.
7. Prove in court that there was a fire and the amount of damage that resulted.

Photos are also indispensable aids in authenticating notes, report writing, and refreshing memory. You cannot use a videotape to illustrate your narrative report unless you convert your videotape to still photos.

Because a fire scene begins to change and deteriorate the very moment that first smoldering ember or ignition occurs, photography in one form or another is the only way to preserve or freeze a fire scene in time. Evidence must be documented in place prior to removal by investigators or alteration/destruction by firefighters, other personnel, or the fire's progression.

Comparison of Equipment

What we will compare here is not one brand against the other, but rather five different types of equipment. As a fire scene photographer, you may elect to use one or more types to accomplish your goal and responsibilities. Each has its own features, results, advantages, and disadvantages.

Whatever type or types of equipment you decide upon, keep the following facts in mind. First, satisfactory results can be obtained without using the most expensive equipment available. Second, the fire scene environment will subject a camera, lens, and flash equipment to some of the worst possible conditions. Everything your manual says not to do may occur over a period of time. The fire scene destroys photographic equipment regardless of brand name or cost.

Figure 2.1a shows a convenient arrangement of equipment that is very useful for fire/crime scene still photography. This arrangement is compact

Figure 2.1a Example of equipment arrangement suitable for fire/crime scene still photography.

Figure 2.1b Today's cameras have built-in light meters, but it is a good practice to have a backup hand-held meter for critical light situations.

Figure 2.1c This is an example of a set of close-up lens rings for macro photography.

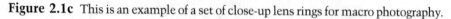

and self-contained, and it solves most of the problems associated with this type of photography. Figures 2.1b and 2.1c are close-up shots of the light meter and lens rings shown in Figure 2.1a.

The 35 mm single-lens reflex (SLR) body is equipped with a 35 to 135 mm f-35 zoom lens having macro capability. The adjustable auto flash has a maximum range of 70 feet. The flash is mounted on the camera, connected by way of a three-foot flash sync-cord, and is removable for use in side lighting. Immediately under the camera body is a motor drive that has the maximum capability of five frames per second. Below the motor drive is a rechargeable battery pack capable of providing thousands of flashes per charge and regenerating the flash in a fraction of a second. A self-contained monitor constantly informs you of the condition of the battery.

The extent to which you indulge yourself is limited only by time, money, and your photographic capabilities. To assist you in selection of the type of equipment, the following sections provide a comparison of the advantages and disadvantages of six types of still cameras.

Press Cameras

Although this type of camera is probably the most desirable for fire scene use, few agencies still use it. In terms of quality, it produces better photographs because of its larger negative. However, the quality factor is not enough to offset the disadvantages.

Press cameras use various sizes of sheet film or film packs that must be constantly removed and reloaded. Because of the larger format, the camera, associated equipment, accessories, and film developing are larger, heavier, more expensive, and inconvenient.

Snapshot, 110 Format Cameras

At the opposite end of the scale from the press type is the snapshot or pocket camera, which is usually the least expensive format available. Size and weight are minimal. Most of these cameras take size 110 roll or cartridge film and have a built-in electronic flash. The more expensive models have both normal and telephoto nonadjustable lens settings. Focus and f-stop are fixed, requiring no adjustment.

Although this type of equipment takes satisfactory snapshots, it is not recommended for fire scene usage. The major disadvantages are the nonadjustable focus and f-stop, limited film speed choices, and fixed flash position and power.

Snapshot, 35 mm Format Cameras

A more sophisticated snapshot format uses 35 mm film. Although the size and weight are somewhat more than the 110 format's, it is still small enough to conveniently fit into a pocket. Its focus and f-stops are fixed, but it may be capable of handling more than one speed of film. Some makes and models have built-in protective lens covers and dual-lens systems providing wide-angle and limited telephoto capabilities.

There are limitations to what can be accomplished with this equipment because of the fixed settings and limited range of the flash. Its big advantage is the 35 mm format, which produces better-quality print enlargements. Another very important feature to consider is its compatibility in film size with other 35 mm equipment. The snapshot-type 35 mm format pocket camera is very useful as a backup to your first-line equipment. One of these units loaded with short (6 to 10 exposures) rolls of black-and-white film is excellent for providing your own public relations photos to the media.

Twin-Lens Reflex

Some of the most expensive cameras on the market are the twin-lens reflex type. If being used for run-of-the-mill, everyday photos or in the studio, this is probably a very satisfactory piece of equipment. The problem arises with the parallax, or the difference between what you see through the viewer and what the camera sees through the lens. Distant scenes are not much of a problem, but when taking close-up shots one can miss all or part of the main subject of the photo. The photographer must be aware of parallax and constantly compensate. It is better to see exactly what the camera sees.

Single-Lens Reflex, 35 mm

The most suitable equipment for fire scene photography is the 35 mm single-lens reflex camera. Development of this format over the years has resulted in the most versatile system on the market. Its size and weight are intermediate, yet it is compact and quite rugged. Prices range to remain within most budgets. The features on various makes and models, as well as lenses, flash attachments, and other associated equipment, are virtually endless.

Films available include black-and-white, color, both positive (slides) and negatives (prints) in either indoor (tungsten) or outdoor (daylight), slide duplicating, infrared, and recording. Speeds of various films extend from 50 ASA or less to 25,000 ASA or more.

The versatility permits you to custom design and purchase a reasonably priced equipment package from the large assortment of makes and models available on the market. Whatever your requirements and demands, they can most frequently be met using the 35 mm single-lens reflex format.

Instant Print

One more type of equipment should be given consideration for fire scene photography. The instant print or Polaroid format has its place, not as first-line equipment, but rather as backup or insurance equipment. The reason you might want to use it is the feature that makes this equipment unique: it allows you to see the finished print within a few seconds. Taking a few instant photos of important scenes already photographed by your first-line equipment ensures that you will have a record in case of film, unknown equipment malfunction, or operator or processing problems. Always use the instant print format as a positive backup to your first-line equipment whenever you work at a fatal fire, due to the uniqueness of the situation.

Recommended Equipment Features

Some of the equipment features discussed herein will make your job as fire scene photographer easier and more successful and will produce higher-quality results. You will certainly survive if your equipment lacks some of the following features, but if you intend to replace existing equipment or purchase your first equipment, consider all of them when choosing your make and model.

Fully Automatic, Semiautomatic, or Manual Operation

Certain cameras (smart cameras) have so many automatic features that you as a photographer hardly have to think or make decisions at all. You are basically a camera operator. Others have one or two automatic features, and then there are the fully manual (dumb) cameras, which require you to make all of the decisions. It should not be said that a "smart" camera can be operated satisfactorily by a "dumb" photographer, but it does require a "smart" photographer to operate a "dumb" camera.

If you have an automatic camera, during your fire scene photo activities there will be times when it will be necessary or highly desirable to override one or more of the automatic features. For example, rising smoke or steam may cause a camera with autofocus to focus on the vapor cloud rather than the wall you wish to photograph in the distance. Personnel walking between you and the subject will change the focus. Under such circumstances, it would be advantageous to be able to override the autofocus with a manual setting operation. If you "go auto," be able to "go manual" when needed.

Whether you decide on fully automatic, semiautomatic, or manual operation, one of the major reasons for your choice should be how much faith you have in your operation of that particular method.

Camera Body

When purchasing a camera for fire/crime scene work, you may want to save money and not buy a body with a normal lens attached — buy only the body. You buy a separate combination macro/normal/wide angle/telephoto lens, which completes the camera and lens requirement.

The functional features contained in most makes and models of camera bodies are so similar and standardized that going into details or listing them at this time would only take up space. Regardless of the total features, make sure the camera body you choose does have the following, which will be useful — if not necessary — to your fire/crime scene photography.

1. FP and X sockets for flash bulb and electronic flash plus hot shoe flash synchronization.
2. Self-timer providing delays for shutter release.
3. Through-the-lens exposure metering with pointer needle or colored LED read-out dots denoting over-, normal, or underexposure.
4. Automatic winder and/or motor drive connection.
5. ASA 32 to 1600 film speeds.
6. Shutter speed from 1 second to 1/1000 second and B.
7. Cable release capability.

Electronic Flash

The very nature of fire scene photography requires flash more powerful than the run-of-the-mill snapshot flash. Small, less powerful units may provide satisfactory photos under most conditions a large percentage of the time, but you want satisfactory photos under all conditions all of the time. Remember, many of your photos will be of black on black. This condition absorbs light like a sponge absorbs water. Another reason you need a power flash is the distance that must be illuminated when taking nighttime exterior shots of buildings and lines of spectators. An illuminating range of 50 to 70 feet would be the minimum acceptable distance capability. To power such flash through hundreds of photos properly between charges and to rid yourself of the continuous problems of replacing dead batteries, be sure your flash is powered by or can be converted to a power pack. When properly maintained and charged, such a power pack will power your flash through most investigations with many flashes to spare.

It should be mentioned that among the many features contained in most flash units, it is important that your unit have a removable light sensor module, extension cord, or both. This is very useful when taking close-ups or char patterns or in other situations when it is desirable to remove the flash unit from the camera hot shoe for side lighting.

The flash unit must have features that permit you to automatically control and adjust the light output to best suit the conditions of each individual photo. A manual override capability should exist for special occasions. When evaluating various makes and models for intended purchases, the following list of features and capabilities will be helpful in selecting a flash unit that will meet your needs:

1. Open flash button — used for manually test firing the flash and for forming the capacitor.
2. Battery compartment — self contained power unit and/or connection for remote power pack.
3. Illuminated calculator dial — flash exposure determination guide.
4. Calculator dial light button — illuminates calculator dial under dim lighting conditions.
5. ASA/DIN indicator — programs the calculator dial to appropriate speed of film being used in the camera.
6. Zoom flash head — regulates spread of light to be compatible with close-up, normal, and zoom lens coverage areas.
7. Bounce flash head — adjusts to provide reflected lighting to subject.
8. Sufficient light indicator — tests and verifies for proper exposure settings prior to taking photo.
9. On/off switch — energizes or de-energizes the unit.
10. Ready light — indicates when capacitor is energized and ready to fire.
11. Lockable mounting foot — provides attachment to camera and flash/camera synchronization circuit.

12. Shutter cord connections — flash connection for cameras without hot shoe connection capability.
13. AC adapter connection — permits use of AC power from standard household 110v outlets via an AC adapter.
14. Power setting adjustment — allows fill-in flash control and reduces light output.
15. Distance scale and f-stop dial — used to determine proper auto mode for flash and f-stop setting for camera.
16. Auto mode selector and indicator — permits setting flash for manual or various automatic operations.
17. Removable adjustable sensor — measures light and automatically programs flash unit for correct amount of illumination for best exposure.

Sensor Cord

A very useful accessory item for fire scene photography is a 2- or 3-foot long sensor cord. This cord allows the flash to be removed from the camera hot shoe connection and be located several feet off to the side for cross lighting. If your flash has a removable sensor, it is removed from the flash unit and mounted on the hot shoe end of the sensor cord. This permits the sensor to measure the light at the camera rather than several feet away at the flash unit location.

Remote Auxiliary Flash

Another flash accessory that can be helpful in achieving quality photographs is the remote flash trigger. This light-sensitive triggering device makes it possible to fire a remote flash unit in synchronization with the primary flash on your camera without the need for connecting wires. Each remote triggering device requires a self-contained battery-powered flash unit to be attached. A low- or medium-priced flash is satisfactory but should have an illumination range of at least 30 feet.

At first, this equipment may seem exotic and unnecessary. However, once you have recognized its capabilities, you will find more and more occasions for its use. For example, if you have ever taken flash photos in a cellar, you have undoubtedly been plagued with support-post shadows obscuring portions of the background. Strategic placement of remote flash can eliminate such problems.

Illuminating the entire length and height of a building, a long hall, or an expansive area such as an auditorium is impossible without manually "painting with light" using slave flash units or large generator-powered floodlights. Painting with light will work but is very time consuming. This will be discussed in detail under Photography Tips. Disregarding the labor and inconvenience involved with large floodlights, the price difference between a floodlight system and remote slave flash will easily justify having two or three complete remote flash units.

Macro, Wide Angle, Normal, and Telephoto Lens

The most expensive and useless step you could take in obtaining equipment would be to buy a macro lens, a wide angle lens, a normal lens, and a telephoto lens. You may not want to buy these as separate pieces for a few reasons. The first reason is that you will tire of changing lenses after a couple of fires. You will put the normal lens on the camera, leave the others in the equipment case, and be satisfied with whatever photos you get. Second, it is not advisable to remove a lens (in order to change it) and expose the interior of the camera to the fire scene environment. Third, unless you elect to carry a fairly heavy, large camera bag with you, you will not have your other lenses when you need them.

The best and most convenient solution to the multiple-lens problem for the least money is to have one lens that contains a macro feature plus a range covering wide angle, normal, and telephoto. Such a lens will give you the capability of photographing all the elements of a fire scene, ranging from extreme forensic close-ups of tool marks and beaded wire to long-distance shots of spectators and burn patterns several stories up. A 35 to 105 mm, 29 to 70 mm, or 28 to 200 mm lens with range of f-3.6 to f-16 or f-22 makes an excellent all-around single lens unit. If a combination lens with an aperture larger than f-3.5 is obtainable and affordable, purchase it. If not, you may have to use faster film instead.

Cable Release

This item is a requirement for painting with light, time exposures, close-up macro-type photos, and any other photos where it is necessary to trip the shutter without causing the camera to move in the slightest. The steel cables vary from 12 to 40 inches in length. Air-pressure-operated shutter releases 33 feet long are available, but the 12 inch length is sufficient and easy to store. It is important that the cable have a time-exposure lock feature that, when activated, allows the shutter to remain open for as long as desired without effort on the part of the photographer. Air-pressure releases do not have this capability without continued pressure on the air bulb. For this reason, the steel cable release is recommended.

Automatic Winder/Motor Drive

Earlier in this section, under Camera Body, an automatic winder or motor drive was listed as a desired capability. Whether or not this accessory would be desirable depends on the type of fire scene photography you do. If you normally arrive on the scene hours or days after the fire, when the scene is cold, you have little or no use for capturing sequenced high-speed shots. However, if you are on the scene early during the action, one of these two items may be justified. The automatic winder permits you to take approximately two photos per second, whereas a motor drive will take approximately five photos per second. Actual rates may vary according to make and model. Use of a winder or motor drive does not interfere with the normal one-shot-at-a-time operation of your equipment.

Why would a fire scene photographer need to take five photos per second? Two major situations come to mind. It is advantageous to document building collapse, and if you can photograph this phenomenon in action, you have valuable photos. Another situation where sequential, high-speed photos are important is in the event of an explosion, BLEVE (boiling liquid evaporation explosions) or flash over. Normally, with one-shot-at-a-time camera operation, you would get one or possibly two photos in either of the above situations. You cannot be very successful with the one-shot capability. The problem is simple: if you see it and then attempt to take the picture, the event has already happened. With the capability of multiple shots per second, you begin firing at the beginning of the action, completely disregarding composition of the individual shots, and continue photographing until the event is terminated. Photographers using a motor drive capture those once-in-a-lifetime, prize-winning action photos.

Motor drives are more expensive than automatic winders, but the advantage of five frames per second versus two justifies the additional cost. Ten photos of a two-second wall collapse are better than four photos. There is only one drawback to having a motor drive hooked up to your camera: you must be careful to keep your finger off the trigger when not actually taking pictures. At five frames per second, you can accidentally run off half a roll of film before you hear the buzzing sound that indicates you have used the last exposure.

While an automatic winder or motor drive may be very convenient, do not sacrifice quality features or capability in your camera, camera lens, and/or flash unit in order to purchase one. It is not worth the price of putting up with inferior basic equipment.

Tripod

A tripod is one piece of equipment that is often considered unnecessary. However, to obtain quality, properly lighted, in-focus pictures of the subject, a tripod is essential. Do not attempt to take macro or close-up photos without one.

Still photography does not require as sophisticated a tripod as does video. A simple, lightweight tripod is all that is required. However, if you can afford only one tripod and will be using it for both still photography and video, you must purchase the more expensive fluid-head video tripod.

Equipment Case

Now that you have invested money in some or all of the aforementioned equipment, you must protect it against damage from heat, cold, moisture, dirt, and shock. Quality counts when it comes to selecting a protective equipment case. As you are well aware, a large percentage of the dramatic fire action takes place in the early stages of a fire. It is essential that you carry the equipment with you for quick response. Do not store it in the station house.

The equipment case should be the last item purchased. Prior to purchase, lay out all of your photographic equipment as you wish to have it arranged inside the case. This should include the primary camera body, lens, flash, cable release, sync cord, batteries, chargers, extra film, and protective camera cover. Measure the area needed, check the dimensions of cases available from different suppliers, and obtain one big enough to carry at least your primary equipment. Your secondary or backup equipment (camera, flash, remote flashes, etc.) can be housed in a second case if necessary.

Protective Filter

The hostile environment of the fire scene demands protection for your expensive camera lens. An inexpensive ultraviolet or haze filter placed over your lens will accomplish this. Because this filter does not affect your photos in any adverse way, the filter should remain on your lens at all times.

Chargers

The type of charger or chargers needed will depend on the type of power system recommended by the unit's manufacturer or converted to by you. These vary from a simple unit for AA batteries to nickel-cadmium (nicad) battery pack rechargers and more involved chargers for the lead-acid or gel type battery. Use the charger recommended by the manufacturer for each particular piece of equipment, even if it means buying another charging unit. Identify each charger with its related equipment with permanent labels or color coding. Over the years, you will become the proud owner of a vast number of look-alike chargers, and your memory will fail as to which charger goes with which equipment.

Film and Electronic Flash Batteries

If you were to ask a group of photographers which is the best film and battery system to use, you should not be surprised to receive many different answers. Seldom do photographers agree on the same items.

There is a great variety of films and batteries on the market today. In fact, the selection is so great, the average person can go bankrupt or crazy trying to make a decision. You can avoid a seemingly overwhelming problem from the beginning by analyzing your needs. The real challenge is to make the right decision the first time. It is extremely expensive and somewhat embarrassing, for instance, to set up your operation for black-and-white prints and then, a few investigations later, realize what you really want is color slides.

Black-and-White or Color Film

Before you take your first photo or even load the camera, a decision must be made as to the film you will be using. The agency you work for may already have a policy regarding film brand and type. This should not limit your thinking or restrict your choice. At first, ignore what is currently being used and do your own analysis. You may decide on something different, and if so, you had better have your facts together and be ready to sell your idea to those in command.

The first thing to consider is whether to shoot a color or black-and-white. This decision is easy — shoot color. Remember that a fire scene can be mostly black on black, especially at night. The limited color that does exist should be brought out and documented as the eye would see it. With rare exceptions, human beings see only in shades of black, white, and gray. The color of smoke and flames can sometimes be important to an investigation. If for some reason an occasional black-and white print is needed, it can be made from a color negative or slide, but short of computer colorization, you cannot make color from black-and-white.

Print or Slide Film

Now that the decision has been made to use color film, what end product do you want — prints, slides, or both? For this decision you must research the needs and requirements based on internal agency procedures, your job responsibilities, and uses to be made of your material. Here are a few things to consider:

1. Will you need only prints to support a narrative report?
2. Will your material be used for classroom training or public relations purposes requiring slides for projection?
3. Do the judge and district attorney prefer projecting slides or reviewing enlarged prints in the courtroom?
4. Do you provide material to the media? If so, what are their requirements?

5. What is your agency using now? If it is not what you decide is best, is management usually agreeable and flexible when it comes to change?
6. How do costs compare?
7. Can or will you be doing your own darkroom processing?

When you have completed your study, select the most versatile film in order to satisfy all of the present needs as well as anticipated future requirements. If you frequently require prints, use a print film and have the occasional slides made as second-generation copies. Conversely, if you primarily use slides, shoot slide film and have the prints made as second generations.

Instant Print or Slide Film

Previously in this chapter, it was stated that the use of instant print/slide cameras has a place as backup or insurance for your investigations. The use of such cameras will require using the film designed for this specific equipment. Your only decision is whether to use black-and-white or color film. It is advisable to use color in this instance also.

Fast or Slow Film

The vast variety of film with various film speeds on the market today provides a choice to fit all needs. Each type of film is manufactured for certain circumstances. The conditions under which you are photographing, the type or condition of the subject, your camera lens, and the intended final use of your photographic efforts all play a part in your choice of film speed. As a fire photographer, you will be taking photos under every condition imaginable and the results may be used for slides, 3-by-5 inch prints, or poster-size enlargements. Slow speed film (ASA 64) produces better enlargements but may be too slow for fire scene work. Fast film (ASA 1000) has more grain that may show up when enlarged, but that may be better for such work.

You may not want to use more than one type and speed of film. When film speed varies, so must the camera settings. Failure to readjust the settings could result in over- or underexposed photos or none at all. Settle on an intermediate film speed, somewhere between ASA 100 and ASA 400. The ASA 100 or ASA 200 films should cover your needs and provide satisfactory end products. Refer to the Photography Tips section later in this chapter for film tricks.

Electronic Flash Batteries/Power Systems

The type of camera and flash you choose for fire scene photography will determine what batteries or battery system you need. The smaller, simpler cameras with built-in nonadjustable flash may require only a couple of AA 1.5v batteries, either regular or rechargeable. If you use the regular batteries, you will find yourself doing three things: running out of power, particularly during a photo session; throwing away good batteries out of fear of running out of power; or purchasing batteries that go dead on the shelf. If you opt for recharge-ables and still run out of power on the scene, you can always get a "jump" or quick charge at the nearest AC outlet, recharging enough to complete the session. Nonrechargeable batteries are the least desirable source of power.

You may recall that in the earlier discussion of flash units it was recom-mended that you choose from the most powerful units — those with a range of 50 to 70 feet and more. These units are like the big luxury automobiles: they do the job, but you have to provide more fuel. This means more power used per flash.

The ideal power supply for your electronic flash will have at least the following special features:

1. Compatibility with your flash unit.
2. Power supply must be rechargeable, preferably without the "memory" effect associated with nicads. (See "Film and Batteries" later in this chapter under Postphotographing Procedures.)
3. Power reserve to supply hundreds of flashes required during an inves-tigation without interruption for recharging.
4. Fast recycle capability between flashes.
5. Capability to sustain a full charge during lengthy periods of nonuse.
6. Minimum size and weight.
7. If of the acid variety, be sure it is a type that will not leak or spill.
8. AC adapter for recharging.
9. Power outlet connections for more than one flash unit.

In addition to the above specifications, buy a system that indicates the status of the battery and conditions of the charge. You, as a photographer, must be relieved of the worry about power failure. If your system does not have such status indicators built in, get an inexpensive, hand-held meter for checking your batteries on a regular basis.

Will the original expense for such a deluxe, sophisticated system be greater than nonrechargeable throw-away batteries or more simple systems? Yes, it certainly will be. Like anything else, however, you get what you pay for and overall, such a system is less expensive in the long run and even on a per-photo basis. Small lead-acid or gel-type power packs are available that have all the desired features and capabilities. These provide excellent service for years. Prorated over its life span of many years, this type of power system will provide peace of mind and will be cheaper in the long run. Do not settle for less.

Training

Through necessity, photographic equipment has been developed to the point where anyone who can turn a knob or push a button can take a picture. This does not make everyone a professional photographer; nor does it make everyone capable of being a fire/crime scene still photographer. If you have any expectations of doing this as a hobby, a sideline, or a profession, realize that extensive training is required. Basic, advanced, specialized, and continuous refresher courses should be taken.

It is not necessary to be a professional, licensed photographer in order to have your photographic material introduced as evidence and accepted by the courts. However, as an investigative function, photography is a serious business. The results of your efforts may be responsible for a guilty person being convicted of a crime and an innocent person going free. Your efforts may also be responsible for a guilty person going free and an innocent person going to jail. This fact alone should prompt you to seek extensive training in this field.

Every organization's annual budget should contain a suitable request for training finances. Excellent basic, advanced, and general courses are provided by local schools, colleges, universities, continuous education programs, photography clubs, equipment manufacturers, dealers, and private individuals. More advanced, specialized fire/crime scene photography training is available through equipment manufacturers, state and national fire and law enforcement academies, the Bureau of Alcohol, Tobacco and Firearms, the Federal Bureau of Investigation, and others. Charges range from nominal fees for tuition, room, and board, to no cost at all to the participant. Last but not least, expertise can be obtained from others in the same field. Just be careful not to pick up their faults and errors in the process. Make certain your teacher's work is accurate and of consistently good quality. Both the teacher and his work should be recognized and accepted by his peers. Education in one form or another is out there. It is also necessary.

Safety

The subject of fire/crime scene safety will be covered extensively in Chapter 3. However, if you do not do video work, you might not read that section. The subject is important enough to be repeated here, as it also pertains to still photography. It makes little difference whether you fall through a burned-out floor with a still camera or a video camera — the bottom line is that you have fallen through the floor.

Equipment-Related Safety for Photographer

The first step is to read and understand the safety instructions contained in the manuals provided with the equipment. There is very little chance of being injured by a still camera unless you start trying to do your own internal repair work. Even the hot shoe remains "off" unless a shoe-mounted flash unit is attached. The small silver oxide batteries used to power the camera's internal circuits should never be disposed of where they might end up in a fire, because they may explode.

The flash unit can be a potential hazard if misused or not maintained properly. Be sure all power cords and plugs are in good condition and are recommended by the manufacturer.

When cleaning your equipment after a fire, be sure it is de-energized. Examine it thoroughly for any damage or wear it may have sustained. Smoke, water, high humidity, heat, and cold are all part of the fire scene environment; they are also the destroyers of photographic equipment, so protect your equipment at all times.

At some time in your career, your camera and/or flash will be dropped or damaged or receive a hard bump. It is advisable not to use it until it is examined by a qualified service person. This is especially important if the equipment happens to become immersed in water, because soaking received from fire streams may also present an electrical shock hazard.

Last, remember that the flash generates considerable heat during operation, so exercise caution when handling during or immediately after usage. Always let the flash unit cool before storing it away in a confined case.

Personal Safety

Fire scene photography can be a hazardous occupation. Slippery or iced-over floors, roofs, and ladders are an invitation to disaster. Unseen holes and weak spots in floors and stairs lay in wait. Many times you will be working in the dark with only a small hand light for illumination. The potential to trip over debris or receive injury from protruding nails, broken glass, and torn metal is high.

Your personal safety can also be in jeopardy while doing the exterior and spectator photos. The risk is higher during the hectic, early stages of a fire because of vehicle movements and suppression activities. Explosions and structure collapse are possible at any time. Do not get yourself into a situation inviting possible entrapment — always have more than one way out.

When dealing with hazardous material and highly explosive situations, make use of the telephoto capability of your equipment. Unless ordered and properly equipped to do otherwise, stay back and upwind.

Rural areas present opportunities for personal injury or embarrassment not usually encountered in the urban environment. One area of possible problems is dealing with animals, especially farm livestock.

Hazards more prevalent in rural areas are the ever-lurking dug wells, cesspools, and septic tanks located close to the structure. These often have shallow coverings that have been there for years and may have deteriorated with time. In summary, be alert and careful. Wear personal protective gear such as a hard hat, gloves, boots, coveralls, or bunker gear. If you are injured because you lack these items, your insurance coverage may become nonexistent.

Equipment Precautions and Protection

Camera, Flash, and Associated Equipment

Although not as fragile as video equipment, your still photography equipment must be handled, maintained, and stored properly. If not, it has a sinister way of letting you down when you need it most. Preventative maintenance is much cheaper than repair or replacement. The list below should be a basic guide, to which you should add your own precautions to fit your particular situations.

1. Learn to operate and maintain all equipment correctly by studying the manufacturer's manuals.
2. Handle the camera and flash units in a protective manner to prevent bumping and dropping.
3. Never hand-carry the camera by a camera strap that allows the unit to swing or rotate.
4. Limit exposure to sudden changes in temperature, which cause condensation in or on the equipment.
5. Restrict exposure to heat or cold exceeding that recommended by the equipment and film manufacturer.
6. Use only power cords and power sources compatible with manufacturer's recommendations.
7. Do not use mounts or tripods that are unstable.
8. A haze filter and lens cap must be used to protect the lens.
9. Use a plastic bag or other suitable equipment cover when working around fire streams and in a structure with draining water.

10. Provide a hard, protective case for storage and transportation.
11. When cleaning the lens and viewer, use the manufacturer-recommended cleaners and procedures.
12. Keep your fingers off the lens glass and the contact surfaces of batteries.
13. Use care to prevent any dust, foreign objects, liquid, or film chips from entering the camera.
14. Unless you are a qualified, factory-trained repair person, do not attempt disassembly, service, or repair of the equipment.
15. Have all service done by qualified personnel and use only authorized parts and accessories.
16. Never leave the camera case open at the scene with its interior exposed to water, for fear of humidity.
17. To prevent accidental dumping, always close and latch the camera storage case.

Film

Regardless of your other equipment, if your film is not good, your efforts will be for nothing. You will not know this until it is too late. Film must be properly cared for at all times. Follow the manufacturer's instructions for various types of film. Keep it cool, dry, and clean, and develop it as soon as possible after exposing.

Batteries

The batteries required in a manual camera may be needed only for operation of the exposure meter. Assuming that the operational function is turned off when not in use, these small batteries can last for years with normal use and care. This is good with regard to service, but it can lull you into a state of complacency; your batteries could die without any warning. Automatic cameras require more batteries than manual cameras, due to their many powered functions and features. The batteries in automatic cameras are also subjected to more power drainage. For these reasons, you must maintain more control over your batteries and their condition.

Regardless of the type of camera used, you must control your batteries or your batteries will control you. There is only one way to be sure of eliminating or at least greatly reducing the chance of battery failure, and that is to replace batteries at specific intervals. This should be done regardless of their present apparent condition. Do not trust old batteries. Dispose of the used batteries immediately so that the old do not become mixed in with the new. The worst thing you can do is to keep the old batteries in your camera case to use in case of an emergency. Nine out of ten times you will have a "double emergency" because the salvaged batteries will be dead as well.

S/N	PURC DATE	2/5 8G	6/20 BG	7/5 DR	9/14 TP	1/8 BG	1/29 DR	1/30 TP							
01	2/5/89	1000 1630		0920 1750			0230 1020								
02	6/20/89		2350 0540		1132 1920		0230 923								
03□	1/8/90					0900 1500	0230 1020								
04□	1/30/90							0745 1300							
05□															
06□															
07□															
08□															
09□															
10□															
11□															
12□															
13□															
14□															
15□															
16□															
17□															
18□															
19□															
20□															
21□															
22□															
23□															
24□															
25□															
26□															
27□															
□															

Figure 2.2 Section of typical log sheet from battery charging manual.

One simple and accurate way to know the age of each individual battery, schedule and control replacement, properly recharge, and justify purchasing new batteries is to identify each battery and maintain a battery charging manual and log book. The log sheet should have a place for the battery identifier, purchase date, and, if rechargeable, the date charged and the time charging began and ended. Figure 2.2 is a sample of such a log sheet.

The second part of your charging manual and log book should contain simplified step-by-step charging instructions for each type of rechargeable battery used. This may include still photography, video, vapor detectors, hand lights, and any other battery-powered equipment. Figure 2.3 shows typical pages of charging instructions from such a manual.

Public Relations

Why has the subject of public relations been stressed twice, in both the still photography and the video chapters? The reason is that good public relations are important to both media. Each photographer must foster his own relations with those individuals in related fields. Whereas the video cameraperson must cultivate the local TV station personnel, the still photographer needs to be on the good side of the press photographers and other newspaper personnel.

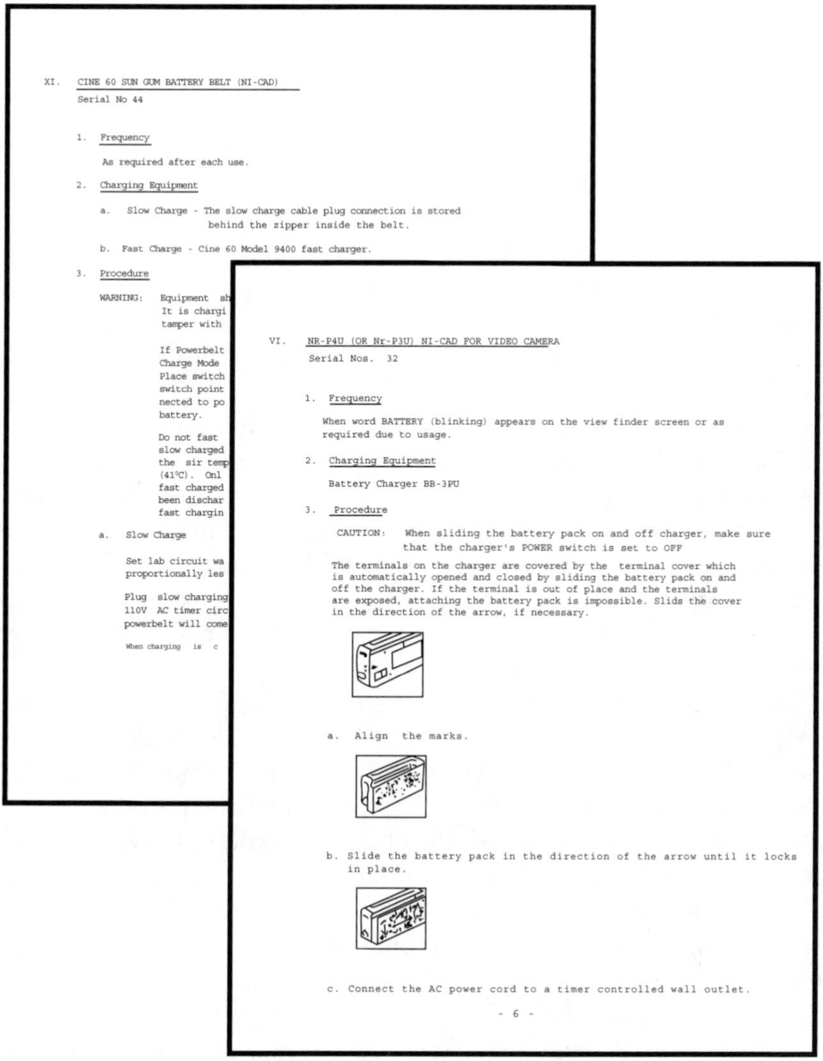

XI. CINE 60 SUN GUM BATTERY BELT (NI-CAD)
Serial No 44

1. Frequency

As required after each use.

2. Charging Equipment

a. Slow Charge - The slow charge cable plug connection is stored behind the zipper inside the belt.

b. Fast Charge - Cine 60 Model 9400 fast charger.

3. Procedure

WARNING: Equipment sh
It is chargi
tamper with

If Powerbelt
Charge Mode
Place switch
switch point
nected to po
battery.

Do not fast
slow charged
the sir temp
(41°C). Onl
fast charged
been dischar
fast chargin

a. Slow Charge

Set lab circuit wa
proportionally les

Plug slow charging
110V AC timer circ
powerbelt will come

When charging is c

VI. NR-P4U (OR Nr-P3U) NI-CAD FOR VIDEO CAMERA
Serial Nos. 32

1. Frequency

When word BATTERY (blinking) appears on the view finder screen or as required due to usage.

2. Charging Equipment

Battery Charger BB-3PU

3. Procedure

CAUTION: When sliding the battery pack on and off charger, make sure that the charger's POWER switch is set to OFF

The terminals on the charger are covered by the terminal cover which is automatically opened and closed by sliding the battery pack on and off the charger. If the terminal is out of place and the terminals are exposed, attaching the battery pack is impossible. Slids the cover in the direction of the arrow, if necessary.

a. Align the marks.

b. Slide the battery pack in the direction of the arrow until it locks in place.

c. Connect the AC power cord to a timer controlled wall outlet.

- 6 -

Figure 2.3 Sample pages from battery charging manual providing instructions for various types of batteries.

Many fire departments have their own photographers, who are some of the first people on the scene and have access where no one else is permitted.

In a relatively short time, the rise in the number of home video cameras and amateur operators has developed a source of material for the video professionals. Think how long still photography has been on the market and imagine how many amateurs are out there, snapping still photos of nearly every fire. Many of these are taken before the arrival of any official photographers, news media, or apparatus. If the proper public relations approach is used and credit given, very few amateurs will deny you access to their material. The same applies to professionals, unless their job restricts such releases. The amateur may be satisfied with a byline, an enlargement of some prints, or possibly just the processing of the film. The professional will probably charge a fee.

A case comes to mind wherein a four-family apartment house burned to the ground one night in less than an hour during a blizzard in February. The daughter of the fire discoverer snapped a photo of the burning structure with her small disk camera. Through proper public relations, the fire investigators found out about the photo, secured the negative, and had enlarged prints made. The information provided by that one photo pinpointed the origin of the total-burn fire. The total cost of that investigation solution and public relations effort was two 8 × 10 glossy prints: one for the amateur photographer and one for the display in a photographic mural.

Public relations is usually a case of one hand washing the other. The best way to get good public relations going between yourself and other agency people is to make the first move. Do not wait to ask them for something; you may not get it. Instead, when the opportunity arises, offer your assistance to them, in the form of services or material. If they accept your offer, they are in your debt. When the situation is right, you can collect the debt with no trouble or hard feelings.

Some newspapers have a limited staff of reporters and photographers, especially in small towns. They welcome being provided with a half dozen photos taken on a short (8 to 12 exposure) roll of black-and-white film. Give them a standard form with basic information pertaining to the fire. They will process the film and publish the photos, and you will have cultivated a great working relationship. Keep an inexpensive camera loaded with short rolls of black-and-white film just for this reason.

You must be sure not to compromise your investigation by divulging confidential information or photos. Many of the details on this subject in the video chapter are also applicable to still photography.

When cultivating public relations, you always think about agencies such as fire departments, law enforcement, television, radio, and newspapers. There are several other agencies and individuals with which it would be advantageous to have a good rapport. Photographic documentation of injuries and on-scene medical activities are accomplished much more easily if you are known by the individuals and they understand your mission. This applies to all members of the medical profession, from first responders and emergency medical technicians (EMTs) to the hospital nurses and doctors. In fact, good PR may be the only way such photos can be obtained.

Two other agencies or individuals must be included in your PR efforts. The first is the coroner. Whenever a fire fatality occurs, the fire scene photographer has a responsibility to document all aspects of this event. The coroner is usually in charge and may or may not be doing his own photography. It is essential that you and the coroner have a work-with-but-don't-interfere type of relationship, which should be established well in advance of the actual need. The second agency or individual that is sometimes overlooked in a PR plan is the pathologist, medical examiner or other individual responsible for performing an autopsy. When there is a fatality, your responsibilities as a fire/crime scene photographer do not end at the property line or loading of the body — they extend into the examination room and to the autopsy of the body. In this room, the medical examiner or pathologist is in charge and, as with the coroner, a work-with-but-don't-interfere relationship must exist. Take only those photos necessary and leave. It is extremely important that good public relations be established between the autopsy personnel and photographer prior to need.

Before closing this section on public relations, consider the following. When you experience an equipment malfunction, it is not practical to wait weeks or months for service. Select an authorized repair service (local or otherwise), explain the urgency of your work to the individual in charge, and make arrangements for service faster than the normal turn-around time. Get something in writing, if possible. Make arrangements in advance of actual need and update the agreement regularly in case of personnel changes.

Standard Operating Photo Procedure

General

You arrive on the scene of a structure fire. There are flames coming out of windows on the west side. You take photos of the front of the house and the west side, because that is where the action is. (Who knows, maybe you can get one of your pictures in the paper.) Eventually, the building collapses into the cellar. After doing a little personal PR with the firefighters and on-scene law enforcement, you leave the scene satisfied with photos of the front and west side.

A few hours, days, or weeks later, a witness comes forward and relates seeing a man with a plastic container stand on a wooden box under a window, break the glass and, while climbing through the window, appear to cut his arm. After attempting to wipe something off the window sill, he disappears into the house. A few minutes later, the individual exits via the same window, and in less than five minutes, all the rooms on the west side of the structure are fully involved with fire. You shot your photos of the west side of the house, therefore you did a good job. Right? Wrong! The witness saw the alleged fire setter break the window and enter the structure on the *east* side of the house. You did not photograph the east side for two reasons:

(1) nothing exciting was happening on the east side, and (2) it is not your standard procedure to photograph all sides of a structure through the use of overall and close-up shots. Neither are you required to photograph all windows and doors whether open or closed, broken or not. Imagine how much more valuable the witness's statement would be, though, if you had photographed an overall view showing the broken window with the box underneath. What about a close-up showing the broken glass with no smoke stain but having blood on it as well as on the window sill? Such documentation would be doubly important if, for some reason, the fire cause had been determined to be accidental.

There are two routes you can travel with fire/crime scene photography but only one logical choice. First, you can operate under the false pretense that you know everything, will remember to do everything, and can slip through an incident without taking all those "unnecessary" photos. Why bother to record photo data at all? If this is your attitude and modus operandi, let someone else to the job because you will be a detriment rather than an asset to your organization. The second route is the only choice you have — be thorough, standardize, and do the job for which you are responsible. Someone's future or even life may depend on the photos you do or do not take.

The photos taken of any incident should fall into two categories — those required according to your standard operating procedure and those required to document the particular unique aspects of that individual incident. Once you identify the basic photographic requirements and apply them to every incident, many of your scene documentation problems are over. It becomes second nature to do them, and there is less chance of an important photo not being taken. If a standard operating procedure is adopted, properly documented in writing, and used at all fire scenes, no one can find fault with your actions in any individual investigation.

Fire scene photography procedures vary in as many ways as there are fire photographers or departments. For this reason, you may add to, subtract from, or merely adjust this information to fit an existing operating procedure. If you have no procedure, this information can assist in generating one. The more experience you acquire, the more you will realize that each incident is unique in many ways. Regardless of this fact, certain steps or actions must be established as standard operating procedure. These standard actions must be accomplished at each incident. With the exception of life-threatening situations, there should be no variance in this rule.

Required Photos

The suggestions listed in Table 2.1 can be applied, with certain modifications, to virtually any type of fire/crime scene, whether large or small, vehicle or

Table 2.1   Existing Structure Fire/Crime Scene Standard Operating Procedure Photo Requirement

Category	Photos To Be Taken
1. Incident identifier	a. Close-up of 3 × 5 card with incident data for film identification
2. Incident location	a. Street name, structure number, rural mailbox number, and name. Include structure and identifier in an overall photo
3. Exterior	a. Straight-on 90 degree shot of all four elevations
	b. 45-degree off-the-corner shots showing two adjoining elevations at each of four corners
	c. Close-ups of all doors, windows, and any other means of entry or egress
	d. Close-ups of both inside and outside of accesses having forced entry signs
	e. Macros of forced entry signs on both outside and inside of forced access
	f. Documentation of condition of roof taken from elevated position. Four sides and/or corners if possible
	g. V patterns at doors, windows, and other openings
	h. Melt patterns of vinyl siding, window frames, doors, and soffits
	i. Suspicious tracks, containers, or other items unnatural to the scene
	j. Nearby livestock, pets, vehicles, and related housing
	k. Conditions indicating missing livestock, pets, vehicles, and related housing
	l. Scene from witness's viewpoint
4. Exposures	a. Sides exposed to the fire and 45-degree corner shots at each end
	b. Interior of exposures if exteriors damaged
5. Spectators	a. Document onlookers and vehicles, especially recognized suspects and persons who stand out because of their actions and/or inappropriate attire
6. Apparatus	a. Overall shots showing emergency vehicles, equipment, and manpower
7. Suppression	a. General views showing firefighting efforts including hand lines, snorkles, laddering, rescue, overhaul, ventilation, medical, injuries, and deaths
8. Fire progression	a. Repeat Steps 3a, b, f, g, and h and entire categories 4-7 periodically until fire is extinguished
9. Utilities (general)	a. Electrical: on or off, entrance, meters, fuses, circuit breakers, wiring, outlets, switches, evidence of tampering or repair, etc.
	b. Gas (city or propane): on or off, valves, piping, connections, evidence of tampering or repair, etc.
	c. Water (city or well): on or off, valves, meters, pumps, piping, connections, evidence of tampering or repair, etc.
10. Utilities (detailed)	a. All utility services located at or near the area of origin should receive detailed photographic documentation from point of origin to entry into the structure

Table 2.1   Existing Structure Fire/Crime Scene Standard Operating Procedure Photo Requirement (*continued*)

Category	Photos To Be Taken
11. Interior	a. All rooms, halls, stairways, closets, cabinets, storage areas, attics, and cellars
	b. Include walls, ceilings, and floors
	c. Furnishings and contents including location and arrangement
12. Extinguishment systems (general)	a. All types: on or off, valves, meters, gauges, piping, pumps, pressure systems, connections, and evidence of tampering or repair
13. Extinguishment systems (detailed)	a. All extinguishment systems located at or near the area of origin should receive additional detailed photographic documentation from point of origin to entry into the structure
14. Fire/heat flow indicators	a. Heat, smoke, burn, and char patterns throughout structure, from least affected area to area or point of origin
	b. Include walls, ceilings, and floors
	c. Directional pointers to area of origin caused by softening or melting of light bulbs, glass, plastic, candles, toys, etc.
	d. Rounding of edges of furnishings and structural members
	e. Tapering of structural members
	f. Point(s) of lowest burn
	g. V patterns
	h. Clocks
15. Heat sources (general)	a. Overall location and close-up of all heat sources throughout structure. Must confirm or eliminate all possible causes of fire
16. Fuel sources	a. All flammable items and materials contributing to growth and extension of fire: gas lines, paint, thinners, furnishings, foam, propane/acetylene/oxygen tanks, etc.
17. Area of origin	a. Before, during, and after excavation and reconstruction of area of origin, such as a particular room or dimensional radii from suspected point of origin
	b. Detail photos of burn patterns, char depth, damage, and destruction
	c. Location of heat sources in area
	d. All exterior sides of heat sources and general views of interiors
	e. Detail interior and exterior close-up/macro views of isolated damage areas of heat sources
	f. Nameplates and make, model, and serial number designations
	g. Installation, operation, and maintenance instruction plates
18. Point of origin	a. Record evacuation and reconstruction of point of origin
	b. Repeat Steps 17b, c above
	c. Show proximity of heat source(s) to combustibles/flammables
	d. Repeat Steps 17d-g above
19. Evidence	a. Each item of evidence taken: one alone *in situ* and one with identifier and scale
	b. Each control sample for evidence item taken: one alone *in situ* and one with identifier and scale
	c. General overall of area with identifiers marking locations of evidence taken
	d. Same overall of area in Step 19c but without evidence location identifier

Table 2.1 Existing Structure Fire/Crime Scene Standard Operating Procedure Photo Requirement (*continued*)

Category	Photos To Be Taken
20. Scene irregularities	a. Anything that is out of place or foreign to the area in which found
	b. Any artificial means used to increase the rate of fire spread as opposed to those conditions that would normally be responsible
	c. All indicators of possible arson (refer to Table 2.5)
21. Controlled substances, hazardous materials, explosives, arms and ammunition	a. Document item and location usually under direction of law enforcement in authority
	b. Container designation and make, model, and serial numbers
22. Fatality	a. Location of body(s) with respect to one another and surroundings immediately upon discovery
	b. Position and condition of unexcavated body
	c. Excavation of debris from and around body
	d. Position and condition of excavated body
	e. Obvious wounds and injuries
	f. Underside surface of body
	g. Surface body laid upon
	h. Weapons or personal items
	i. Recommendations of coroner
23. Autopsy	a. Condition of body exterior including lividity, soot, skin, hair, and extremities
	b. Wounds and injuries
	c. Condition of respiratory organs affected by heat, smoke, toxic fumes, or flames
	d. Condition of respiratory organ not affected by heat, smoke, toxic fumes, or flames
	e. Condition of organs indicating cause of death
	f. Recommendations of medical examiner
24. Forensic	a. Usually taken by a lab technician under controlled conditions using special equipment rather than the fire/crime scene photographer

structure. To simplify matters, the term "structure" will be used to denote the item involved. An all-encompassing standard operating procedure must be written from the assumption that you arrive early in the fire, that the fire is in process, and that the structure is still standing. A total-burn situation requires a somewhat different approach and will be discussed later. Table 2.1 is a general outline for establishing or revising such a procedure. The sequence is based on a typical 7-room house and may be changed to fit a particular incident.

Table 2.1 should impress upon you the need to take many photos. A lackadaisical attitude and unstandardized approach toward fire/crime scene photography will surely come back to haunt you at some future date. Don't press your luck — film is cheap compared with blowing an investigation.

Photo Records

When you are photographing several different fire scenes in a short period of time, taking a considerable number of photos at each incident and having the processing delayed for various reasons, several things have a tendency to happen. Assuming each roll was labeled for the particular incident, another identification problem still remains. You must be able to accurately explain why each particular photo was taken, its orientation to the overall scene, and what it depicts. At the time the photo was taken, only the photographer has the answers to these questions. A few hours later, even he may not remember 100% accurately.

Sooner or later, whether you like it or not, you must document in writing the backup information and date concerning each individual photo. Only one logical time exists to do this and that is immediately — as soon as each individual photo is taken and all aspects are fresh in your mind. It makes little difference at the time the photo is taken, whether the information is recorded on tape or handwritten on a form. Eventually it will have to be put on paper. The choice is yours. Figure 2.4 shows a record form used successfully by the author and various investigative agencies.

Structure Total-Burn Photography

At some time in your career as a fire scene photographer you will be faced with photographically documenting many total destruction fires, sometimes referred to as a "black hole" or "black spot" fires. Often the scene is neither black nor a hole. Structures without cellars or below grade levels do not leave a hole, and ashes are often gray or white, not black. The term used here will be total burn.

How total is a total burn? It is a structure fire in which no structure remains and all combustibles have been altered or consumed. All the normal indicators are gone — the walls with helpful V patterns, roofs with burn-through holes, floors with distinctive pour patterns, and so on, are not there for your viewing. If your duties are fire photography only or if you are a fire investigator taking your own photos, total burns have a tendency to separate the men from the boys. Although they are not much different from other assignments, they usually take more time and more physical and mental work. Figure 2.5 shows typical total-burn remains. Earlier in this chapter, Table 2.1 presented a suggested standard operating photo procedure for non-total burns, in which the structure is still standing. The scenario we will

PHOTO RECORD

Photographer: _____ No. Rolls _____ Incident No: _____
Camera: _____ Film: _____ ASA: __
Lens: _____ Flash:
Slides Processed by: _____ Date: _____ Process: _____
Prints Processed by: _____ Date: _____ Process: _____

NO.	FL	SUBJECT AND REMARKS
1		
2		
3		
4		
5		
6		
7		
8		
9		
0		
1		
2		
3		
4		
5		
6		
7		
8		
9		
0		
1		
2		
3		
4		
5		
6		
7		
8		
9		
0		
1		
2		
3		
4		
5		
6		
7		
8		
9		
0		

Sheet ___ of ___

Signature: _____ Date: _____

Figure 2.4 Form for documenting photo ID number, orientation, subject, and reason for taking.

assume here is that the structure is entirely consumed prior to arrival of the fire scene photographer.

Total burns, having different circumstances from non-total burns, require different actions on the part of the scene photographer. You will utilize some of the steps already given in Table 2.1, but obviously not all of them. You will have to add another systematic approach to photograph total

Figure 2.5 Typical total burn.

burns: this approach is called "scrounging." *Webster's Seventh New Collegiate Dictionary* defines *scrounge* and *scrounging* as "to collect by or as if by foraging; the acquisition of goods or services other than by direct purchase." Theft, usually referred to as "permanent borrowing," is neither suggested nor recommended.

Photographic documentation of the nonexistent structure is probably the second most important and helpful aspect of total burn investigations. Somewhere, there exist many or all of the photos needed for documentation of the structure's exterior, interior, and contents as they were prior to the fire. Table 2.2 details the photos required to document a total burn. Included are those portions of Table 2.1 applicable to total burns with the addition of those photos possibly obtainable by scrounging.

Photographic Scrounging

As stated previously, many of the photos needed for documentation of the exterior, interior, and contents of a total burn structure already exist. They are out there somewhere. You must locate and obtain copies in one form or another. A photocopy is far better than nothing at all. At no other time are your public relations skills needed more than now. Let us look into the various means of obtaining this material.

Two important sources for photos and film are the press and TV news media. Because of their deadlines, they must be contacted immediately.

Table 2.2   Total Burn Fire/Crime Scene Standard Operating Procedure Photo Requirements

Category	Photos To Be Taken
1. Incident identifier	a. Close-up of 3 × 5 card with incident data for film identification
2. Incident location	a. Street name, structure number, rural mailbox number, and name. Include structure and identifier in an overall photo
3. Exterior	a. Straight-on 90 degree shot of all four elevations
	b. 45-degree off-the-corner shots showing two adjoining elevations at each of four corners

Note: Obtain additional photos as described in Photographic Scrounging section

Note: In incidents where portions of the structure have been preserved because of outward collapse, the following photos should be taken:

	c. Close-ups of all doors, windows, or other means of entry or egress
	d. Close-ups of both inside and outside of accesses having forced entry signs
	e. Macros of forced entry signs on both outside and inside of forced access
	f. Documentation of condition of metal roofing taken from elevated position. Four sides and/or corners if possible
	g. V patterns at doors, windows, and other openings
	h. Melt patterns of vinyl siding, window frames, doors, and soffits
	i. Suspicious tracks, containers, or other items unnatural to the scene
	j. Nearby livestock, pets, vehicles, and related housing
	k. Conditions indicating missing livestock, pets, vehicles, and related housing
	l. Scene from witness's viewpoint
4. Exposures	

Note: Burn patterns, heat, and smoke damage on close exposures tend to reflect what was affecting the total burn structure

	a. Sides exposed to the fire and 45-degree corner shots at each end
	b. Interior of exposures if exteriors damaged. Document structure and contents
5. Spectators	a. Document onlookers and vehicles, especially recognized suspects and persons who stand out because of their actions and/or inappropriate attire
6. Apparatus	a. Overall shots showing emergency vehicles, equipment, and manpower. May consist of only wetdown or standby operations
7. Suppression	a. General views showing firefighting efforts including hand lines, snorkles, laddering, rescue, over-haul, ventilation, medical, injuries, deaths, etc. May consist of only wet-down or standby operations
8. Utilities (general)	

Note: Present location of some utility equipment maybe outside and/or inside the foundation, depending on original location and direction of collapse

Table 2.2   Total Burn Fire/Crime Scene Standard Operating Procedure Photo Requirements (*continued*)

Category	Photos To Be Taken
	a. Electrical: on or off, entrance, meters, fuses, circuit breakers, wiring, outlets, switches, evidence of tampering or repair, etc.
	b. Gas (city or propane): on or off, valves, piping, connections, evidence of tampering or repair, etc.
	c. Water (city or well): on or off, valves, meters, pumps, piping, connections, evidence of tampering or repair, etc.
9. Utilities (detailed)	a. All utility services located at or near the area of origin should receive detailed photographic documentation from point of origin to entry into the structure
10. Interior	

Note: Obtain the following photos as described in Photographic Scrounging section

	a. All rooms, halls, stairways, closets, cabinets, storage areas, attics, and cellars
	b. Include walls, ceilings, and floors
	c. Furnishings and contents, including location and arrangement

Note: Categories 11-21 will generally be located in the debris within the confines of the foundation. Extensive and cautious excavation may be required

11. Extinguishment systems (general)	a. All types: on or off, valves, meters, gauges, piping, pumps, pressure systems, connections, and evidence of tampering or repair
12. Extinguishment systems (detailed)	a. All extinguishment systems located at or near the area of origin should receive additional detailed photographic documentation from point of origin to entry into the structure
13. Fire/heat flow indicators	

Note: Indicators in a total burn will usually be limited to noncombustibles. Combustible indicators are sometimes protected and preserved, and they provide valuable clues when found. Therefore, several combustible burn indicators are included below

	a. Deformation, melting, and heat and rust patterns on metal beams, posts, ceilings, and roofs
	b. Heat, smoke, burn, and char patterns throughout the foundation from least affected area to area or point of origin
	c. Include walls and floors
	d. Directional pointers caused by softening or melting of light bulbs, glass, plaster, candles, toys, etc.
	e. Rounding of edges of furnishings and structural members
	f. Tapering of structural members
	g. Point(s) of lowest burn
	h. V patterns
	i. Clocks
14. Heat sources (general)	a. Overall location and close-up of all heat sources throughout structure. Must confirm or eliminate all possible causes of fire
15. Fuel sources	a. All flammable items and materials contributing to growth and extension of fire: gas lines, paint, thinners, furnishings, foam, propane/acetylene/oxygen tanks, etc.

Table 2.2   Total Burn Fire/Crime Scene Standard Operating Procedure Photo Requirements (*continued*)

Category	Photos To Be Taken
16. Area of origin	a. Before, during, and after excavation and reconstruction of area of origin, such as a particular room or dimensional radii from suspected point of origin
	b. Detail photos of burn patterns, char depth, damage, and destruction
	c. Location of heat sources in area
	d. All exterior sides of heat sources and general views of interiors
	e. Detail interior and exterior close-up/macro views of isolated damage areas of heat sources
	f. Nameplates and make, model, and serial number designations
	g. Installation, operation, and maintenance instruction plates
17. Point of origin	a. Record evacuation and reconstruction of point of origin
	b. Repeat Steps 16b, c
	c. Show proximity of heat source(s) to combustibles/flammables
	d. Repeat Steps 16d-g above
18. Evidence	a. Each item of evidence taken: one alone *in situ* and one with identifier and scale
	b. Each control sample for evidence item taken: one alone *in situ* and one with identifier and scale
	c. General overall of area with identifiers marking locations of evidence taken
	d. Same overall of area in Step 18c above but without evidence location identifier
19. Scene irregularities	a. Anything that is out of place or foreign to the area in which it is found
	b. Any artificial means used to increase the rate of fire spread, as opposed to those conditions that would normally be responsible
	c. All indicators of possible arson (refer to Table 2.5)
20. Controlled substances, hazardous materials, explosives, arms and ammunition	a. Document item and location usually under direction of law enforcement in authority
	b. Container designation and make, model, and serial numbers
21. Overhead views	a. Entire foundation area: overall and sectional shots
	b. Entire area surrounding and adjacent to foundation area
	c. Close-ups of areas of interest
22. Fatality	a. Location of body(s) with respect to one another and surroundings immediately upon discovery
	b. Position and condition of unexcavated body
	c. Excavation of debris from and around body
	d. Position and condition of excavated body
	e. Obvious wounds and injuries
	f. Underside surface or body
	g. Surface body laid upon
	h. Weapons or personal items
	i. Recommendations of coroner

Table 2.2   Total Burn Fire/Crime Scene Standard Operating Procedure Photo Requirements (*continued*)

Category	Photos To Be Taken
23. Autopsy	a. Condition of body exterior including lividity, soot, skin, hair, and extremities b. Wounds and injuries c. Condition of respiratory organs affected by heat, smoke, toxic fumes, or flames d. Condition of respiratory organ not affected by heat, smoke, toxic fumes, or flames e. Condition of organs indicating cause of death f. Recommendations of medical examiner
24. Forensic	a. Usually taken by a lab technician under controlled conditions using special equipment, rather than the fire/crime scene photographer

Amateur photographers among the spectators are another source. They, however, have a tendency to disappear. Offer to process their film in order to get your prints. If an individual does not wish to release his film, identify the person and ask to see the prints immediately after processing. Keep checking back on their status.

All types of photographs and renderings are sought, and they are acceptable when investigating a total burn. These include color or black-and-white, prints or slides, instant or otherwise. Do not reject paintings and drawings — accept all offers. You can sort, pick, and chose later. The first photos of the fire that will be available will be the spectators' Polaroids and news media prints. Others will require time to process. Running ads in local newspapers requesting photos or film may procure results from previously unknown sources.

Table 2.3 lists some of the many sources of five different categories of photos and exposed film. Of the 20 sources, lists, assessors, builders, insurance adjustors or agents, mortgage holders, and real estate agencies may have photos of the structure because of their business connections. Children, freelance photographers, friends, neighbors, the owner or occupant of the structure, and relatives of owner and occupant are good sources of photos as well. Think of how many parties, barbecues, weddings, holidays, and family gatherings have been recorded on film and have the interior or exterior of the structure in the background. The remaining sources listed are more likely to supply valuable photos of the exterior during and after the fire.

Whether scrounged from other sources or taken by yourself, photos from elevated levels during and after the fire are especially valuable. Table 2.4 lists various types of elevated positions and sources of elevated platforms. Use caution with all elevated platforms because of possible instabilities.

Table 2.3   Sources of Photos and Exposed Film

Source	Fire			Structure	
	Before	During	After	Inside	Outside
Assessors	×				×
Amateur photographers		×	×		
Builders	×			×	×
Children	×	×	×	×	×
Fire department photographers		×	×	×	×
Fire investigators		×	×	×	×
Freelance photographers		×	×		×
Friends of owner/occupant	×			×	×
Insurance adjustors			×	×	×
Insurance agent	×		×	×	×
Mortgage holder	×			×	×
Neighbors	×	×	×	×	×
News media	×	×	×	×	×
Occupant	×		×	×	×
Owner	×		×	×	×
Passersby		×	×		×
Police photographer		×	×		×
Real estate agency	×			×	×
Relatives of owner/occupant	×			×	×
Requests in newspapers		×	×		×

Table 2.4   Elevated Platforms

Types

1. Hills or raised ground	5. Telephone poles
2. Upstairs windows	6. Trees
3. Second-floor porches	7. Ladders
4. Adjacent rooftops	

Sources

1. Gas and electric company	5. Aircraft
2. Phone company	6. Vehicle roofs
3. Fire department	7. Cable TV company
4. Tree trimmers	

On-Scene Arson/Crime Indicators

The fire scene photographer has a minimum of three responsibilities to document at any incident. The first of these is what happened — what burned or collapsed, who was injured or died, what is missing or damaged, and so on. The second responsibility is to document what did not happen — what did not burn or collapse, who was not injured or killed, what is not missing or damaged. The third and often overlooked responsibility is the documentation through photos of why the incident occurred, i.e., what caused the fire/explosion or other incident.

If you are a fire investigator doing your own photography, this should be routine procedure. However, if you are strictly a fire photographer with no investigative authority or responsibility, the following may open an entirely new field for you. This additional knowledge is sure to increase the need for and value of your photographic services.

Two Types of Photographers

There are two categories of fire-oriented professional photographers, just as there are two types of investigations. The first involves fire investigations to determine origin and cause, and the second, arson investigations concerning the possible commission of a crime. Likewise, there are fire photographers who photograph the fire and its destruction, and investigative photographers who also document the criminal or arson aspects. The latter responsibilities are handled by an official investigator versed in this particular field, not just anyone with a camera and a little knowledge.

Although it is not the intent here to suggest or imply that an unauthorized fire photographer should venture unofficially into the field of arson or investigative photography while on the scene, it is unavoidable that the fire photographer will be confronted with existing evidence of arson and other crimes. These bits of evidence may soon be consumed, disappear, or even be overlooked by others later in the investigation. For these reasons, it would be ironic for a fire photographer not to be aware of this and photograph the basic indicators of possible arson or other crimes associated with the incident. In fact, it is impossible to photograph the fire scene and not photograph the indicators. Therefore, in a sense, it is impossible for a basic fire photographer not to photograph items of investigative interest.

Possible Crime Indicators

As a fire photographer you can provide valuable photos to an official investigation as long as you do not get in the way, infringe on another agency's or individual's areas of responsibility, or contaminate or destroy the scene and evidence. To assist both fire photographers and investigative photographers, Table 2.5 lists some indicators of possible arson or other crimes that should be documented upon detection, regardless of your job responsibility.

Table 2.5   Possible Indicators of Arson or Other Crimes

Exterior

1. Vehicles and individuals leaving scene
2. Exterior doors removed or opened
3. Windows open or broken
4. Window shades down or windows covered
5. Signs of forcible entry, jimmy marks, locks removed from windows and/or doors
6. Holes cut in walls (prior to fire)
7. Separate and unconnected fires
8. Color of smoke and flame (see below)
9. Indications of accelerants
10. Incendiary devices
11. Trailers
12. Deliberately created short circuit (exterior meters, etc.)
13. Disconnected or loosened oil or gas lines
14. Footprints
15. Pets and items of monetary or sentimental value removed from premises
16. Blood stains or splatters

Interior

1. Separate and unconnected fires
2. Color of smoke and flame (see below)
3. Window shades down; secured or covered windows
4. Holes cut in walls, floor, or ceiling (prior to fire)
5. Indications of accelerants
6. Incendiary devices
7. Streamers
8. Trailers
9. Burn patterns on floor and/or rugs
10. Unexplained holes burned in floors
11. Burn patterns on bottoms of doors, shelves, etc.
12. Soot on mirrors, windows, etc. from accelerants
13. Interior doors removed or opened
14. Signs of forcible entry, jimmy marks, locks removed from windows or doors
15. Footprints
16. Deliberately created short circuit (fusebox, wiring, etc.)
17. Disconnected or loosened oil or gas lines
18. Inoperative sprinkler systems
19. Inoperative fire doors
20. Inoperative alarm systems
21. Pets or livestock removed from premises
22. Items of monetary or sentimental value removed from premises
23. Substitutions of contents (older, cheaper, less-valued items)
24. Blood stains or splatters

Table 2.5 Possible Indicators of Arson or Other Crimes (*continued*)

Smoke and Flame Color		
Smoke	Flame	Possible Combustible
White to gray	Yellow to white	Benzene
Gray to brown	Yellow to red	Wood, paper, cloth
Brown	Yellow	Cooking oil
Brownish black	Yellow to red	Lacquer thinner
Black to brown	Yellow to white	Turpentine
Brown to black	Straw to white	Naphtha
Black	Yellow to white	Lubricating oil, Gasoline
Black	Yellow	Kerosene
Black	Blue	Acetone

Scene Lighting

Nearly every fire scene you photograph, whether night or day, will require some kind of supplemental lighting. The very nature of the dark, light-absorbing, charred, and smoked surrounding requires more illumination. The amount of equipment you can obtain and the amount of money that can be spent on lighting is endless, from a single flash unit to portable lights to mobile truck generator units. This section will cover systems affordable to the average individual or agency that provide sufficient illumination to do the job well. Figures 2.6 through 2.10 compare photographic results obtained using various equipment and camera settings. All original photos were taken on Kodak Extrachrome 200 color slide film.

Painting with Light

Another useful method of illuminating large areas of a fire, crime, or accident scene at night without elaborate equipment is painting with light. This operation is best accomplished with a minimum of two people and the following equipment: camera with lens between 28 and 55 mm (preferably 35-mm SLR); a tripod; a locking shutter-release cable; a portable electronic flash with manual firing capability; film (ASA 400 is preferred, but others will work); a lens cap or other suitable light proof cover; and fully charged power source(s).

Select a placement for the camera in relation to the subject so that no strong lights are shining toward the lens. Streetlights, signs, and vehicles must be eliminated if at all possible. Set the loaded camera at eye level on a tripod. Prior to taking any photos, you must determine the area you wish to photograph and the number of individual flashes required to cover it.

First, determine the left and right extremities of the viewing area of the lens. This can be accomplished by having an assistant, holding a small lighted flashlight walk slowly outward, perpendicular to the object to be photographed. The photographer watches these proceedings through the camera viewer, and when the assistant steps outside the viewing area, the light can no longer be seen in the viewer. A marker of some sort should be placed an additional two to three feet beyond this point of disappearance. Perform this procedure for both left and right boundaries of the viewing area. Several boundary markers or the use of barrier tape may be necessary on each side if the area to be photographed is extensive. This will ensure that the flash operator or spectators do not venture into the viewing area and appear silhouetted in the photo.

If you are alone, the viewing area boundaries may still be determined. While observing through the camera viewer, shine a spotlight down either the left or right side of the viewing area. Move the light so that its center spot travels in and out of the viewing area. Note the points of disappearance and mark them as described previously.

Once you have established the area to be photographed, it is necessary to determine the number of flash firings required to illuminate the subject and surroundings. This will vary depending on whether the subject is light or dark, the texture of its surface, the distance between the subject and the camera, and the power capability of the flash. For example, if the area to be photographed is 100 linear feet and your flash properly illuminates a 25-linear-foot area, four separate flash firings will be required.

When you have determined the viewing area and the number of flash firings, you will be ready to begin painting with light. Proceed with the following steps: adjust the lens opening to f3.8 or larger; set the shutter speed indicator to B (bulb); attach a shutter-release cable to the shutter-release button; adjust the release cable to lock the shutter open; focus on the image at the halfway point into the field of view; cover the lens with a light-proof, loose-fitting cover, such as a cloth; advance the film one frame; set the portable flash to full power for maximum distance.

Always remember to point your portable flash away from the camera and toward the scene to be illuminated — never back toward the camera. When operating with two people, the person assigned to operate the camera always remains there to operate the equipment and to protect it from being knocked over in the dark.

Upon receiving a verbal "ready" signal from the person operating the portable flash, the camera operator will remove the lens cover carefully — so as not to move the camera — and verbally notify the flash operator. The first flash illumination will then be activated from above and behind the camera lens, toward the subject. After this happens the camera operator will

Figure 2.6a One flash on camera. Flash setting manual (full power). Shutter 1/60 sec. Aperture f3.2.

Figure 2.6b One flash on camera plus one additional slave flash. Flash setting manual. Shutter speed 1/60 sec. Aperture f3.2

Figure 2.6c Three 500-w floodlights. Shutter speed 1 sec. Aperture f3.2.

Figure 2.6d Three 500-w floodlights. Shutter speed 2 sec. Aperture f3.2.

Figure 2.6e Three 500-w flood lights. Shutter speed 4 sec. Aperture f3.2.

Figure 2.6f Three 500-w floodlights. Shutter speed 8 sec. Aperture f3.2.

Figure 2.7a One flash on camera. Flash setting manual (full power). Shutter speed 1/60 sec. Aperture f3.2.

Figure 2.7b One flash on camera plus one additional slave flash. Flash setting manual. Shutter speed 1/60 sec. Aperture f3.2.

Figure 2.7c One flash on camera. Flash setting manual. Shutter speed 1/60 sec. Aperture f5.6.

Figure 2.7d One flash on camera plus one additional slave flash. Flash setting manual. Shutter speed 1/60 sec. Aperture f5.6.

Figure 2.7e Two 500-w flood lights. Shutter speed 4 sec. Aperture f8.

Figure 2.7f Two 500-w flood lights. Shutter speed 16 sec. Aperture f8.

Figure 2.8a One flash on camera. Flash setting "auto" for 2 to 15 feet. Shutter speed 1/60 sec. Aperture f5.6 (*manufacturer's recommended setting).

Figure 2.8b One flash on camera. Flash setting "auto" for 2 to 15 feet. Shutter speed 1/60 sec. Aperture f8.

Figure 2.8c One flash on camera. Flash setting "auto" for 2 to 15 feet. Shutter speed 1/60 sec. Aperture f11*.

Figure 2.8d One 500-w photo studio light. Shutter speed 1/60 sec. Aperture f4.

Figure 2.8e One 500-w photo studio light. Shutter speed 1/30 sec. Aperture f6.

Figure 2.8f One 500-w photo studio light. Shutter speed 1/2 sec. Aperture f22.

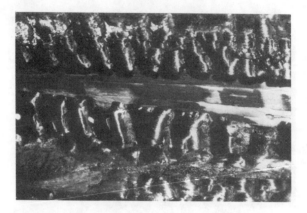

Figure 2.9a One flash on camera. Flash setting "auto" for 2 to 9 feet. Shutter speed 1/60 sec. Aperture f8 (*manufacturer's recommended setting).

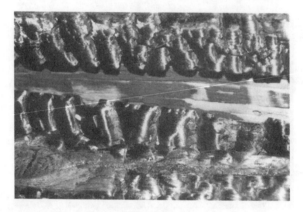

Figure 2.9b One flash camera. Flash setting "auto" for 2 to 9 feet. Shutter speed 1/60 sec. Aperture f11.

Figure 2.9c One flash on camera. Flash setting "auto" for 2 to 9 feet. Shutter speed 1/60 sec. Aperture f16*.

Figure 2.9d One flash on remote PC cord. Flash setting "auto" for 2 to 9 feet. Shutter speed 1/60 sec. Aperture f4.

Figure 2.9e One flash on remote PC cord. Flash setting "auto" for 2 to 9 feet. Shutter speed 1/60 sec. Aperture f5.6.

Figure 2.9f One flash on remote PC cord. Flash setting "auto" for 2 to 9 feet. Shutter speed 1/60 sec. Aperture f8.

Figure 2.10a One flash on camera. Flash setting "auto" for 2 to 12 feet. Shutter speed 1/60 sec. Aperture f8 (*manufacturer's recommended setting).

Figure 2.10b One flash on remote PC cord. Flash setting "auto" for 2 to 12 feet. Shutter speed 1/60 sec. Aperture f8.

Figure 2.10c One flash on camera. Flash setting "auto" for 2 to 12 feet. Shutter speed 1/60 sec. Aperture f11*.

Figure 2.10d One flash on remote PC cord. Flash setting "auto" for 2 to 12 feet. Shutter speed 1/60 sec. Aperture f11*.

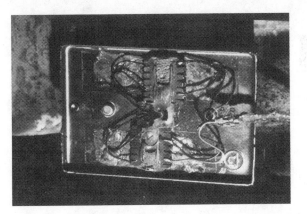

Figure 2.10e One flash on camera. Flash setting "auto" for 2 to 12 feet. Shutter speed 1/60 sec. Aperture f16.

Figure 2.10f One flash on remote PC cord. Flash setting "auto" for 2 to 12 feet. Shutter speed 1/60 sec. Aperture f16.

Figure 2.11 Structure illuminated by single flash on camera.

re-cover the lens. (If you are working alone, it is necessary for the lens cover to remain off until after the last flash illumination is made.) The flash operator repositions at intervals along the outer edges of both sides of the scene, using caution not to position his body between the area being illuminated and the camera lens. Such positioning will cause silhouettes of the flash operator to be photographed, as mentioned previously. At each new position the sequence of uncovering the lens, firing the flash toward the subject, and re-covering the lens is repeated.

Visible roof areas and foreground should also be illuminated as the flash operator advances. A sequence of firings out of sight behind the subject, directed toward the outer edges of the top and sides, will produce a distinctive outline of the subject. Upon completion of the last illumination, replace the lens cap and release the shutter cable lock, thereby closing the shutter. The painting-with-light procedure is now complete. Proper application of this process can produce exceptional photos; all it takes is practice.

Figure 2.11 shows a structure illuminated at a distance of 50 feet, with one flash positioned on the camera, flash setting manual, aperture f3.8, film speed 400.

Figure 2.12 was obtained by the painting-with-light process, with multiple flashes set at manual (full power), aperture f3.8, shutter on B, film speed 400.

Figure 2.13 is a diagram showing the sequence and flash positions used to produce Figure 2.12.

Figure 2.12 Example of multiflash painting-with-light technique.

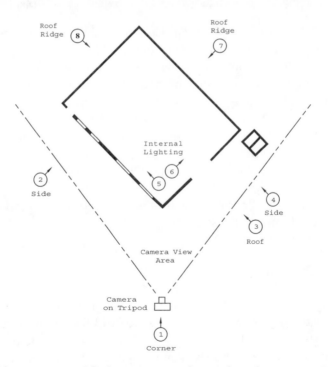

Figure 2.13 Sequence and flash positions used to produce the image on Figure 2.12.

Figure 2.14 Example of painting-with-light technique using a single portable floodlight (approximately 13 light passes averaging 20 seconds each).

Figure 2.14 illustrates what can be obtained in a dire emergency with very little equipment, in which a small area is painted with a single portable hand light. (Lights with hot-spot centers are not desirable.) Set up the camera as described previously for flash painting. Lock the shutter open, remove the lens cover, and illuminate the area by moving the single light back and forth over the area several times. After the desired number of passes are made, turn off the light and close the shutter. Advance the film, and repeat the process for several different frames, each time doubling the time required for each light pass. The results may be streaky and substandard, but they will be better than nothing.

Figure 2.15 is the result of a 10-minute exposure using only existing moonlight to illuminate the structure.

Photography Tips

Years of experience will teach you many tricks and assists you can apply to fire scene photography. The process can be speeded up by taking advantage of someone else's experience and hard knocks. The following are some photographic tips and so-called gems of wisdom that may be of some help. Many have been mentioned previously but are repeated here because of their importance.

Figure 2.15 Structure illuminated only by moonlight (10-minute exposure).

1. Know your capabilities and those of your equipment.
2. Learn how to use your equipment, and train continuously.
3. Handle, maintain, and store equipment properly.
4. Always use the same speed film.
5. After using the camera and flash, always check for the following:
   a. Is the camera reloaded with a new roll of the proper film?
   b. Is the film speed setting on the camera the same as the film's ASA rating?
   c. Is camera film advance working properly? (The rewind knob should turn when film is advanced.)
   d. Is the camera shutter speed set on the speed for flash synchronization (usually 1/60 sec.; indicated on camera as 60x)?
   e. Is the flash set for maximum distance or full power?
   f. Is the lens aperture set correctly for flash power setting?
   g. Are camera and flash batteries charged or replaced?
   h. Are all electrical systems turned off?
6. Critique your photos for possible improvements.
7. Carry your equipment in your vehicle at all times.
8. Use a tripod and cable shutter release for close-up/macro photos for proper focus.

9. Until you become extremely proficient, always take three photos. Bracket all shots one f-stop above and one f-stop below the camera meter indication.

10. When you reach the point where you believe you are extremely proficient, continue to bracket the difficult situations.

11. Attach a small AA or AAA flashlight to your camera to assist in focusing on an object in the dark.

12. Avoid using special-effect filters, with the exception of haze or Polaroid types.

13. Be consistent in what photos you take — that is, establish a standard operating procedure.

14. Use the smallest aperture opening (largest number) possible, thereby obtaining the greatest depth of field.

15. Use multiple flash, portable lights, or painting with light when photographing large areas at night.

16. Label each roll of film with incident information to prevent errors and mixing of incidents.

17. Internal or major maintenance/repair should be performed by the factory or authorized repair facility.

18. Carry a minimum of two extra rolls of film, besides one in the camera, and one complete set of fresh batteries.

19. Carry a plastic bag for camera and flash protection from dripping water, hose streams, and inclement weather.

20. When taking more than one photo of a subject, vary the angle of each view to provide different perspectives and to rule out possible photographic or processing abnormalities; items not appearing at one angle may in another.

21. At the fire scene, do not move or rearrange switches, dials, controls, or other evidence prior to photographing and approval by investigator in charge.

22. Do not scrimp on the number of photos taken. Shoot first and ask questions later.

23. Photographically document what is not there as well as what is there: a kitchen without a refrigerator or stove, a closet without clothes, and a gun cabinet without guns are a few examples.

24. Photograph all heat sources in a structure whether or not they are responsible for the fire, especially in the area of origin. Do not stop at the first one found — you must confirm or rule out all possible causes of the fire.

25. Take photos of ceilings with the back of the camera directly on the floor, trip with timer or long cable release.

26. Always use large-quantity rolls of film, such as 36 vs. 24 exposures, to:
    a. Encourage tendency to take more photos;
    b. Minimize exposure of camera interior to the fire scene environment via less frequent reloading;
    c. Make efficient use of processing time (same for long roll as for short roll); and
    d. Economize (less expense per negative)
27. Place a small, self-sticking label with incident identification on the outside of the film roll or canister, and transfer the label to the negative or slide strip after processing to identify the negatives.
28. Keep your camera loaded with a full roll of film at all times between incidents.
29. Do not photograph more than one incident on a roll of film — start photographing each incident on a new roll of film.
30. Autopsy photos must be made under the direction of the medical examiner or pathologist in charge. Tell that person what you need to photograph (i.e., contributors to and/or cause of death); he will advise you of when and what to photograph. Otherwise, keep out of the work area and restrict photo taking.
31. Until proven otherwise, consider all fire deaths to be homicide or suicide and conduct the photography accordingly.
32. Whenever the photo subject is of great importance to the outcome of the investigation, apply the three-shot rule: an overall shot showing the subject's location, a general shot of only the subject, and close-up or macro shot of a particular feature.
33. Mount the flash a few inches away from the camera lens to eliminate reflections and red-eye.
34. Charred and smoked surfaces require more light to be photographed properly. Open lens one f-stop more than meter indicates.
35. Charred surfaces should be cross-lighted to bring out depth of char.
36. When photographing evidence around a building's exterior, such as a gas can in the yard, always photograph the evidence object with the structure in the background. Both must be in focus.
37. When photographing a dark area next to a light area, such as the dark interior of a lighter-color car or the dark exterior of a house silhouetted against a bright sky, move in and take the exposure reading in the darker, shaded area, then step back and take the photo using that setting, in order to properly expose the darker, shaded areas.
38. Structural damage to the building (char, not smoke) is required to prove arson. Be sure to photograph charring.
39. Photograph undamaged as well as damaged areas.

40. As a backup to your photo record sheet, make a sketch of the scene showing the location of the photographer and the direction in which the photo was taken.

41. If the fire is incendiary, be sure to photograph all possible sources of heat in the area of origin that did not start the fire in addition to the cause of the fire.

42. Photograph evidence at the scene prior to its removal:
    a. From two different angles.
    b. To show relationship to surroundings.
    c. To include specific items of identification, such as nameplates, serial numbers and labels.
    d. Including one photo with a size-comparison object, such as a small scale, and one photo without the comparison object.

43. When excavating an area, regardless of size, photograph each layer as it is uncovered.

44. When it is necessary to position the flash close to the subject because of area restrictions or when doing close-up work:
    a. Cover the flash head with one or more layers of clean white cloth, and/or
    b. Use reflected light by bouncing it off a light-colored surface.

45. Eliminate harshly illuminated close-ups with hot spots by remaining a few feet away and zooming in on the subject. Set flash according to distance to subject.

46. When the scene illumination is not sufficient for the speed of film you have and no supplemental lighting is available, excellent photos can still be obtained by the following procedure:
    a. Conditions:
       1. You have only ASA 100 film with no way of obtaining faster film or larger aperture.
       2. You have no means of providing supplemental lighting.
       3. Scene illumination does not register sufficient on the light meter.
    b. Solution: "pushing" the film. (WARNING: NEVER ATTEMPT THE FOLLOWING WITH A ROLL OF FILM ALREADY PARTIALLY EXPOSED. AFTER TAKING REQUIRED PHOTOS, DO NOT FINISH ROLL WITH PHOTOS TAKEN AT ANY OTHER ASA FILM SPEED SETTING ON THE CAMERA.)
       1. Load the camera with a new, unexposed roll of film.
       2. Set the film speed indicator on the camera to ASA 400, 800, or 1200 — whatever is required to obtain a sufficient reading on the light meter.
       3. Set the aperture as indicated.
       4. Take all required photos.

5. Remove the rewound film and reset the camera to the film speed normally used.
6. Place a label on the film canister stating: "WARNING — SPECIAL PROCESSING REQUIRED — ASA 100 FILM SHOT AT ASA 800" (or whatever speed it was shot at).
7. Place the same warning statement on the outside of the processing submittal envelope.
8. Explain the situation to the processor in person if possible.

c. Processing:
1. The processor will compensate for the special situation involving this roll of film and provide quality prints or slides.

Post-Photographing Procedures

Upon completion of your assignment in the field, certain responsibilities must be taken care of before the job is done. Among these responsibilities are proper care of the equipment and film. These duties start immediately after you take your last photo and prior to leaving the scene.

Camera, Lens, and Flash

Never place wet or dirty equipment into its case or storage container. There are at least three major reasons for this. First, the storage case becomes contaminated with dirt and moisture, which will soil and contaminate your clean equipment in the future. Second, your good intentions to remove the dirty equipment and clean it at soon as you return to your quarters are not always followed through. The next time the case is opened, you have a piece of destroyed photographic equipment. The third reason is simple, and is also a valid reason for termination of your services. Failure to handle and maintain the equipment properly shows a lack of initiative and responsibility.

Manuals that come with the equipment when purchased provide details for cleaning and proper storage. Visually examine the equipment thoroughly for possible damage. Operate all controls to verify that no malfunctions exist. Visually check that the electronics are functioning properly. If any problems exist, substitute another piece and make arrangements for repair. Never leave inoperative equipment in the case, where it may mistakenly be taken to the next incident.

Experience has shown that many times, poor quality photos — or no photos at all — result from not complying with the simple advice given below. Photographic documentation of entire investigations has been ruined because no film was in the camera, or the film was over- or underexposed because the film and film speed setting were not compatible, or all flash exposures were half-frame because the flash and camera were not synchronized. This is embarrassing and costly, to say the least. Therefore, the last steps before closing the equipment case are to verify once again that (1) the camera is reloaded with a new roll of the proper film, (2) the film speed setting on the camera is the same as the film ASA rating, (3) the camera film advance is working properly (the rewind knob should turn when the film is advanced), (4) the camera shutter speed is set on the correct speed or flash synchronization (usually 1/60 sec.; indicated on the camera as 60x), (5) the flash is set for a maximum distance or full power, (6) the lens aperture is set correctly for flash power setting, (7) the camera and flash batteries are charged or replaced, and (8) all electrical systems are turned off.

Film and Batteries

Your film has been exposed and removed from the camera, and all rolls pertaining to a particular incident are ready for processing. This may be accomplished by you, your agency's photo department, or a commercial processor. Whichever action is taken, be sure to record it as part of the incident photo record (see Figure 2.4).

Batteries and power supplies should be recharged or replaced as the need arises according to type. Some require charging after use, whereas others, such as nicads, should be fully discharged in order to eliminate the "memory" charge and thereby take a full, long-lasting charge. Full discharge can be achieved by applying a resistance, such as a light bulb, across the battery contacts to drain energy from the battery.

Never store batteries in a discharged condition. Keep a record of the purchase date and recharging dates of each battery. This can be indicated on the battery itself or recorded elsewhere. Refer to the section on Equipment Precautions and Protection earlier in this chapter.

Replenish your supply of new film by replacing film used. Always carry extra film in reserve as a safety factor and for extended on-scene requirements. Keep individual rolls sealed in original package until actually needed. This keeps dirt and other contaminants from entering the roll and causing damage and transfer to camera interior.

If a tape recorder was used as a means of documenting on-scene information describing the photos as they were taken, replenish the supply of tapes and recorder batteries. The same applies to any other auxiliary equipment such as hand light batteries and extra bulbs.

Photo Record Report

In the section on Standard Operating Photo Procedure earlier in this chapter, the generation of a preliminary taped or handwritten on-scene photo record was discussed. This preliminary record must now be transformed into the final report, which will be part of the official investigation records. Prepare this report as soon as the slides or prints are received from the processor and events are fresh in your mind. Identify each photo in the preliminary report. Write your final photo report starting with the first photo taken, adding any vital information not documented in the preliminary report. Identify each photo with the corresponding record sheet number, the incident number, the date, and the photographer identifier. A copy of the final report (Figure 2.4) should be included with the prints, slides, and/or negatives when filed. More details on handling and filing this evidence will be covered in Chapter 9, Legal Aspects of Visual Evidence.

Summary

Remember the old adage, "A picture is worth a thousand words"? This is not always true — at least, not always in regard to fire scene photography. The photos you take must speak out, but unlike other fields of photography, they must not deviate from being fair and accurate representations of the scene at the time the event took place. People who can take everyday snapshots may not be as good as fire/crime scene photographers. In addition to knowing photography, you must be a thinker and a nit-picker, you must understand investigation procedures, and you must constantly think from the standpoint of the investigation. You must also be willing to give that extra bit of effort that is quite often required.

Suggested Reading

B+W Filterfabrik. *The B+W Program.* Wiesbaden, Germany: 1978.

Cougin, J. *Conklin Creative Filter System.* Paris: 1978.

Eastman Kodak, Consumer Markets Division. *Kodak Master Photoguide.* Rochester, NY: 1976.

Gordner, G., and Valentine, E. *Investigating Total Burns.* Owego, NY: Tioga County Fire Investigation Team, 1986.

Hoya Corporation. *HOYA HMC Filters.* Tokyo: 1975.

National Fire Academy. *Fire Arson Investigation Course Manual.* Emmitsburg, MD: Federal Emergency Management Agency, 1982.

New York State Academy of Fire Science. *Fire and Arson Investigation Course Manual.* Montour Falls, NY: New York State Office of Fire Prevention and Control, 1981.

New York State Academy of Fire Science. *Fire Investigative Photography Course Manual.* Montour Falls, NY: New York State Office of Fire Prevention and Control, 1983.

Vivitar, Ponder, and Best, Inc. *A Guide to Filters.* Santa Monica, CA: 1975.

Weber, D.L., Fazzini, E.P., and Regan, T.J. *Autopsy Pathology Procedure and Protocol.* Springfield, IL: Charles C. Thomas, 1973.

Videography for Fire/Crime Scenes

3

This chapter is not intended to provide technical electronic data regarding video equipment, which would entail writing a chapter on each brand available. It is not intended to be either a comprehensive training manual or a guide on how to produce an entertaining, amusing, edited video program. Quite the opposite. What you will be producing is a documentation of facts and events only.

Operational training for your particular equipment will be fully covered in the manuals you receive when you purchase it. The various makes and models operate in basically the same fashion, with only slight variations.

If you do not have a video electronic background, the greatest thing you can do for your equipment is *to do nothing*. Patronize a reputable dealer and service center for maintenance and repair. It will be cheaper in the long run.

This chapter may seem to contradict what you have heard or learned about taking video recordings. Instruction manuals and most courses place great emphasis on the special-effect capabilities of your equipment such as fade-in/fade-out, zooming, and filters. This chapter will explain why these entertaining recording habits should be broken.

The theme of this chapter will be information on practical applications based on the personal experience of the author. It is hoped that the information will help the reader to obtain better fire/crime scene video recordings for use as evidence with considerable savings in time, money, sweat, and tears.

Why Video?

Why video? That is a question you will be faced with over and over, especially if you are just considering getting into this field. The question will be asked by your superiors and associates; those with whom you work, and those responsible for providing the necessary dollars, unless they are already aware of the necessity and advantages of video. You must be ready to respond with a reasonable, justifiable answer.

The first answer to "Why use video?" is simply that it exists. It is an accepted media tool with a great capability to assist you in obtaining your investigation goal. If, because of restricted supervisory vision, tight budget funding, or some other reason, the departmental decision is to not have video capability, keep in mind that video can be used by anyone, including your opposition. I can think of no better way to influence a jury than to provide video that cannot be disputed by another video.

Every suspected or known fire/crime scene should be documented in three ways — by making sketches, by taking still photos, and by videotaping. Video should not replace the sketches and still photos but, rather, complement and support them.

Numerous reasons exist for video recording. Some will be based on your particular circumstances and needs. However, two basic reasons apply universally — to document and to visually prove an event.

The most basic and often overlooked reason is to visually prove that a fire or crime actually took place. Does this sound ridiculous? It shouldn't. I once spent three days at an arson trial wherein not one piece of photographic evidence was presented to the jury proving to them visually that a fire actually existed. This reflected lack of participation by fire investigators and lack of knowledge by the prosecution. The prosecution lost the case; would the prosecution have won if they had used video? We can only guess. Don't let such a situation occur — justify video to all concerned.

Additional reasons for using video are to document the extent of damages and extent of material not damaged, items of physical evidence present or absent at the scene, and injuries sustained and individuals with no injuries.

Such documentation is extremely useful not only during the investigation and trial, but also in the settlement of insurance claims. One-room fires have a tendency to be claimed as total burns. Insurance claims for inventories are rarely for less than the actual loss, and mysterious personal ailments and incapacities crop up between the time of occurrence and the court date. Without proof to the contrary, you may be in for a tough case and lose it in the end.

Usually it is not practical to physically transport the jury, judges, lawyers, witnesses, and other trial participants to and from the fire/crime scene. Often, by trial time, the scene has been contaminated or altered beyond usefulness. It may become completely destroyed or no longer exist. Because of these possibilities, probably the most important reason to videotape is that video, like no other media, has the ability to bring a fire or other crime scene right into the courtroom, to place it visually in front of all concerned. Video walks

Table 3.1 Video Format Descriptions

Name Format	Description
8 mm 8-mm tape cassette	Home-movie film size, ultra small and lightweight Lower quality and less capability than VHS
VHS ¹/₂" tape cassette	Most popular format
VHS-C ¹/₂" tape minicassette	More compact than VHS, lighter weight, but less recording time
S-VHS ¹/₂" tape cassette	Super VHS, better quality picture; special equipment needed to record and play
BETA ¹/₂" tape cassette	Sony format, not as popular as VHS
U ³/₄" tape cassette	Better quality picture than ¹/₂" VHS but more expensive; professional category
B 1" reel-to-reel	Used by professionals; expensive
C 1" reel-to-reel	Used by professionals; expensive
QUAD 2" reel-to-reel	Older professional format; very expensive

the judge and jury through the scene as it was at the time of the occurrence. With video, visual revisitations can be made as many times as required. The importance of these capabilities cannot be overemphasized.

If you cannot justify the use of video with any other reason, consider what it would mean during the course of your investigation to be able to review the tapes, thereby visually returning to the scene over and over, with no legal violations or restrictions. When reviewing video recordings, you will be amazed at what you see recorded on the tape that you, as the camera operator, were not aware was present during your recording activities.

Comparison of Equipment Categories

It would be impractical, as well as misleading, to select particular makes or models of video equipment and make comparisons and recommendations. By the time you read this, the data would be outdated because of progress and new developments. The intent of this section is to instruct you about the general categories of video equipment, taking into consideration your particular operations, requirements, and available finances.

Nine general equipment formats are currently available. Not all are suitable for fire/crime scene use for one or more reasons. Table 3.1 provides a brief description of each of the 9 formats.

After consideration of expenses, usability, and end quality, only 8-mm, VHS, and VHS-C are practical for all-around use in fire/crime scene documentation. Super VHS and BETA may be used but are not as adaptable as the first three. The remaining formats — ³/₄-U, B, C, and QUAD — are highly professional equipment such as that used by schools, industry, or television stations for broadcast and will not be covered. Their cost of purchase, operation, and maintenance is beyond the needs and capabilities of most fire and law enforcement agencies.

The first group, which shall be referred to as Category A, covers the so-called semiprofessional or heavy-duty VHS format, which usually entails more sophisticated electronics. The second group, Category B, is the home-movie or medium VHS equipment that is available to consumers. The third group, Category C, covers light equipment. Table 3.2 provides a general comparison of some features and specifications related to each category. Variations will occur among makes and models. Figure 3.1 provides a visual comparison of the three categories mentioned above.

Before making your final decision, obtain data and prices from reputable dealers selling each category. Compare and analyze what you get for the dollar. Then consider the pros and cons of each category: weight, size, power requirements, ease of operation, accessories, portability, and features. Can one person operate the equipment? Will it be practical in confined places and when climbing ladders? What is the quality of the tape produced? Is your equipment and end-product tape compatible with other agencies'? The list is endless. The best advice can come from individuals who have experienced this dilemma, have made the decisions, and are either satisfied or not. You will profit by their experience.

Once you purchase a particular category of equipment, accessories, and supplies, you are locked in; it is very expensive to change to another category later on. In general, the medium Category B VHS equipment should fill your crime-scene video needs with sufficient features at a reasonable, affordable price. In the final analysis, it is you who will have to make and justify the decision as to which category you should obtain.

Recommended Features

Most video camera/recorders on the market today have more features than you will ever require for fire/crime scene documentation. Prices for equipment vary depending on the features incorporated. The more features and capabilities, the higher the price. Be sure you get what you need but do not waste money on things you do not need. The best method for determining which make and model gives you the desired features for the least money is to make up a matrix table or chart listing the information by make and model. This permits a visual comparison and will assist in making a decision. Keep in mind that the more required features that are accomplished automatically, the less chance for error, and less the operator has to think about.

Table 3.2 Data Comparison of Typical Equipment Categories

Specifications and Features	Category A 1/2" VHS Format		Category B 1/2" VHS Format Camcorder	Category C 1/2" VHS Compact Camcorder[a]	Category C 8-mm Format Camcorder
	Camera	Recorder			
Price range[b]	$4000 or more for both		$900-$1700	$900-$1000	$850-$1100
Weight	8-9 lbs.	13 lbs.	5 lbs.	1 lbs., 5 oz.	2 lbs., 10 oz.
Dimensions	8"w × 10"h × 17"d	11"w × 4"h × 13"d	15"w × 8"h × 4"d	7-3/4"w × 2-5/8"h × 2-1/4"d	4-1/2"w × 5-1/4"h × 12-1/2"d
Power source	12 VDC	12 VDC	12 VDC	9.6 VDC	6 VDC
Power consumption	9 w	21 w[c]	11 w	11 w	6.5 w
Lens	10 : 1 zoom f 1.8		6 : 1 zoom f 1.2	6 : 1 zoom f 1.2	8 : 1 zoom f 1.4
	10.5 mm-105 mm auto/manual zoom/macro		8.5 mm-51 mm auto/manual zoom/macro	9 mm-54 mm auto/manual zoom/macro	8.5 mm-68 mm auto/manual zoom/macro
Filter diameter	77 mm		46 mm	49 mm	46 mm
Minimum light	30 lux		7 lux	7 lux	4 lux
Optimum light	1500 lux		1500 lux	300 lux	300 lux
Viewfinder	1-1/2" CRT/indicators		2/3" CRT/indicators	2/3" CRT/indicators	2/3" CRT/indicators
Operating temperature	32°F-104°F	32°F-104°F	32°F-104°F	32°F-104°F	32°F-104°F
Storage temperature	-4°F-140°F	-4°F-140°F			-4°F-140°F
Color bar generator	×		—	—	
Auto fade-in/out	×		×	—	×
Record view	×		×	×	×
Auto white balance	×		×	×	×
Manual white balance	×		—	×	×
Auto/manual focus	×		×	×	×

Table 3.2 Data Comparison of Typical Equipment Categories (*continued*)

Specifications and Features	Category A 1/2" VHS Format — Camera	Category A 1/2" VHS Format — Recorder	Category B 1/2" VHS Format Camcorder	Category C 1/2" VHS Compact Camcorder[a]	Category C 8-mm Format Camcorder
Iris control					
auto	×		×	×	×
manual	×		—	—	—
Power supply					
AC	×		×	×	×
DC	×		×	×	×
Battery pack DC	×		×	×	×
Character generator	×		—	—	—
EVF indicators[d]			—	×	×
Indoor/outdoor	×		×	—	×
Time/date	×		×	×	×
Recording	×		—	×	×
Insufficient light	×		×	×	—
Tape counter	×	×	×	×	×
Memory on	×		×	×	×
High-speed shutter	×		×	×	×
Battery strength	×		—	—	×
Mode checks	×		×	×	×
Tape warning	—		×	×	×
Battery warning	×		×	×	×
Dew warning	×		—	—	—
Iris setting	×		—	×	×
White balance	×		—	×	×

Table 3.2 Data Comparison of Typical Equipment Categories (*continued*)

Specifications and Features	Category A — 1/2" VHS Format — Camera	Category A — 1/2" VHS Format — Recorder	Category B — 1/2" VHS Format Camcorder	Category C — 1/2" VHS Compact Camcorder[a]	Category C — 8-mm Format Camcorder
Playback					
Still	×		×	×	×
Fast forward	×		×	×	×
Rewind	×		×	×	×
Video in/out	×	×	×	out only	×
Audio in/out	×	×	×	out only	×
Slow motion	×		×	×	×
Pause/stand by		×	×	×	×
TV recording		×	×	—	×
Audio racks		two	one	one	one
Gain select	×		—	—	—
Accessory shoe	×		×	—	×
Carrying handle	×		×	—	—
Earphone jack	×		×	—	×
Hand strap	×		×	×	×
Indoor/outdoor filter	×		—	—	—
Fade mode selector	×		—	—	—
Fade color selector	×		—	—	—
Camera on/off switch	×		×	×	×
Recorder on/off switch	×		—	—	—
Start/stop switch	×		×	×	×
Lens grip	×		—	—	—
Color balance	×		—	—	—

Table 3.2 Data Comparison of Typical Equipment Categories (*continued*)

Specifications and Features	Category A 1/2" VHS Format — Camera	Category A — Recorder	Category B 1/2" VHS Format Camcorder	Category C 1/2" VHS Compact Camcorder[a]	Category C 8-mm Format Camcorder
Eye cup	×		×	×	×
Tracking control	×		×	×	—
Remote control	×		×	×	×
Record/pause switch	×		×	×	×
AC adaptor	×		×	×	×
EVF vision adjustment[d]	×		×	×	×
Tally light	×		×	×	×
Clock battery warning	—		×	—	—
Built-in microphone	×		×	×	×
External mike jack	×		×	×	×
Stereo recording	×		—	—	—
2-camera sync.	×		—	—	—
Interchangeable lens	×		—	—	—
Audio dubbing	×		×	—	×
Video dubbing	×		×	—	×
Back lighting	—		×	×	×
Recording time (SP)	2 hrs.		2 hrs.	20 min.	2 hrs.

a Mini-cassette. Requires adapter to play in VHS VCR.
b Prices are estimates for camera/recorder only and are subject to change.
c With camera.
d EVF = electronic viewfinder.

Figure 3.1 Examples of typical video equipment described in Table 3.2.

Figure 3.2 Example of additional type of video equipment suitable for fire/crime scene documentation.

Based on past experience, the following features or functions are required or at least desirable for fire/crime scene documentation.

1. Power zoom and macro — allows distance and close-up work without need to physically change lens.
2. Automatic and manual focusing — situations arise where each method has its advantages and drawbacks.

3. Automatic white balance — provides quality tape through continuous, automatic adjustment for optimum color balance.
4. Automatic iris — maintains light level for proper picture brightness and contrast.
5. Playback — allows you to view the recorded tape through the camera's viewfinder. Fast forward, still, and rewind search features should be available in addition to playback.
6. Indicators in viewfinder — recording indicator, date/time clock, and battery strength indicator are the minimum requirements.
7. Three-way power — indoor AC adapter, outdoor battery pack, vehicle cigarette lighter, and car battery cord.
8. Light mounting — capability for on-camera light.

In addition to the aforementioned features, specifications should be carefully compared. Weight and dimensions are two major factors, because equipment seems to get heavier and larger the longer you use it on the scene.

Also, remember to consider the need for operational accessories such as battery pack belts, separate recorders, and lights. Is the equipment portable enough to allow one to travel through confined places and climb ladders? How does the power consumption compare? If your equipment is damaged, lost, or destroyed can you afford to replace it? Is it compatible with other equipment on the market? Is it a one-person operation or is it crew oriented? Here again, discussions with experienced people will be of great help in selecting your equipment. Check other agencies and see what they have and if they are satisfied. Take the time to investigate and evaluate. The final decision is yours and you must live with it, right or wrong.

Accessories and Ancillary Equipment

Years ago, Mr. Sears and Mr. Roebuck knew that the way to sell things was to publish a catalog and circulate it. The philosophy and procedure continue today, and the field of video is no exception. However, like some of the features and capabilities available on video equipment, many of the accessories and ancillary equipment are nice but not required for fire/crime scene work.

Your available budget will probably dictate whether an item is required or just desired. Your ability as a salesperson might swing the balance in your favor. The following list will help you arrive at a practical accessories list without breaking the budget, thereby making both the video operator and the supervisors happy.

1. Camera and recorder or camcorder — basic unit(s) necessary for obtaining the data and recording on tape.
2. Video cassette recorder (VCR) — table-mounted cassette player/recorder used in connection with a TV or monitor.
3. Monitor — regular TV set or one with limited features.
4. Combination telephoto/wide angle/macro lens — obtain as original equipment rather than using individual accessory lenses. It is not wise to expose the camera interior to contamination by removing and changing the lenses on scene.
5. Lens cap — protects the ultraviolet filter and may come as standard equipment.
6. Ultraviolet filter — protects camera lens when lens cap is not in use.
7. Extra batteries or power pack — necessary for backup while recharging used batteries and for covering long-term recording; also provides spares in the event of battery malfunctions.
8. Charging equipment — necessary for maintaining charged batteries.
9. Video tapes — buy enough to cover anticipated usage for a certain purchase period plus a percentage safety factor.
10. Light and associated power — minimum would be a compact camera-mounted light powered by a rechargeable battery pack also capable of providing supplementary or emergency power to camera.
11. Camera raincoat — whether custom made or a plastic bag, this protection is required.
12. Tripod — must be fluid-head type (still-camera tripod is not suitable for video panning). Necessary for close up work.
13. Cases — equipment being transported or stored needs protection from the elements and damage.
14. Carrying strap — has advantages and disadvantages. Try it, you can always remove it.
15. Cleaning maintenance kit — required for lens, filter, and exterior of equipment.
16. AC adapter — power source where 110 AC is available.
17. Car battery adapter — power source where vehicles available.

Tapes and Batteries

Purchasing new top-of-the-line equipment and accessories is one way to ensure satisfactory operation and good results. Regardless of the brand name or price paid, however, satisfactory results cannot be attained if a battery or tape malfunctions, which could damage the equipment in the process. Good batteries can be expensive — use what the manufacturer recommends or an approved substitute.

Tapes are so numerous and varied that selection can be confusing, especially for a beginner. Many companies offer comparison charts at little or no charge describing the particular features and advantages of each tape in their line. The information and assistance received is worth the effort to obtain it.

Use a good brand-name tape if you want to be assured of a good end product. Keep away from the cheapest lines to maintain quality and proper function. This is not to say that the highest quality, most expensive tape is necessary. At a fire/crime scene, you will not be documenting classical music or a Hollywood movie. Under most circumstances, a middle-range tape will be more economical and provide satisfactory results. As with any photographic film, the cost of tapes is minor considering the benefits you obtain from their use. The cameraperson should always have extra fully charged batteries and unused tapes. Don't make the mistake of having extras only in the supply room. Always keep a reserve supply with the equipment, ready for use.

Training

Knowledge required to operate most portable video equipment today has been simplified to three operations: loading the tape, pushing an on/off switch, and pushing a record button. Simplifying operation was necessary to make video acceptable to the amateur snapshot-oriented market. Simplicity is to your advantage, but don't let it lead you or your finance-providing superiors into complacency.

The many avenues for training in the field of video are restricted only by desire and money available. Formal schooling ranges from correspondence school to college-level and manufacturer-sponsored courses. Such courses are usually oriented toward commercial entertainment or production programming, but the basics they teach can be applied to crime scene taping. The more aspects you learn about, the better you will be in your particular field. Previous experience in the fields of still photography and/or movies would be a considerable advantage but is not a prerequisite to video camera operation. Take courses whenever possible. Put money in your budget for training and argue your case to get it.

If you are fortunate enough to have a friend or acquaintance knowledgeable in the field of video, obtain as much information from him as possible. Depending on the individual and your relationship, it may be possible to obtain a wealth of knowledge from one or two informal conversations.

Regardless of whether or not you receive any formal training, you should self-study in the form of reading. There is no excuse not to do this. Remember, you cannot operate a motor vehicle or firearm, or become a law enforcement officer, firefighter, or any other professional or specialist without training. Conversely, you should not be expected or required to produce acceptable documentary evidence video without training.

Safety

Video safety can be categorized in two ways: equipment safety and personal safety. No real division exists between the two because one can readily affect the other.

Equipment-Related Safety for the Operator

The first few pages of most equipment manuals will be devoted to safeguards. Read and heed the advice given for your particular equipment. The most likely way to receive an equipment-related injury is by an electrical malfunction caused by carelessness on the part of the operator. Although such situations are covered in the manuals, it is important to mention a couple of possibilities here.

Many times you will be operating equipment under adverse conditions, such as smoke, water, high humidity, or a combination of all three, and you should protect your equipment from these (refer to the section on Equipment Precautions and Protection later in this chapter). Be sure your power cords and power supplies are in good condition with no frayed cords or damaged plugs. Use only those plugs, power cords, and power sources recommended by the manufacturer. Never clean or attempt maintenance on an energized unit.

Operator-Related Safety

When operating a video camera, your vision is restricted and you become engrossed in what you are seeing in the viewfinder. This tends to make the camera operator unaware of existing, unsafe conditions. Probably the most physically hazardous situation for a camera person is a fire scene or other type of structure collapse. In such circumstances, it is imperative that you plan your route of movement ahead of time and keep an eye on it while you work. The two-open-eyes viewing method detailed in the section entitled General Shooting Tips should be normal procedure.

If you have an aversion to wearing a hard hat, change your mind. A hard hat and a pair of leather gloves will prevent a lot of injuries. If you have some difficulty wearing gloves and operating the equipment controls, alter the gloves

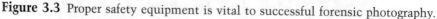

Figure 3.3 Proper safety equipment is vital to successful forensic photography.

as follows: remove the tips of the glove fingers back to the first joint for those fingers used to operate controls. The end can be removed entirely, or you may prefer to make only a slit halfway around the finger on the palm side. The tip of the finger can be extended out through the slit when needed to operate controls. At other times, it can remain protected and warm inside the glove.

Slippery or missing floors or roofs, ladders with or without ice, dangling wires, protruding nails, and sharp objects are only a few of the potential hazards, as shown in Figure 3.3. Be especially cautious of moving vehicles while doing exteriors. Despite your agency's safety policies, and especially during the early stages of an incident, many fire apparatus and police vehicles are backed up without guidance from an assistant capable of seeing behind him. Backup warning signals are lost in the excitement and other on-scene noises. Pick a safe location out of the traffic pattern before becoming engrossed with the viewfinder.

If you face a hazardous material or explosive situation, play it safe: stay back, use your telephoto lens, and live.

Equipment Precautions and Protection

Electronic Equipment

Always remember that video equipment is electronic and should be given the consideration and protection you would give any other expensive electronic hardware. Repair or replacement can be very expensive; it is cheaper to take steps to prevent damage. The following list contains a few precautions that will protect your electronic equipment from damage and misuse:

1. Read your manuals and learn proper operation.
2. To prevent electrical shock, do not expose your equipment to water or moisture, and do not energize it if it gets wet.
3. Avoid aiming the camera at the sun or other bright light or object. Permanent damage to the pick-up device can result.
4. Turn off all equipment when not in use.
5. To prevent condensation in or on the equipment, do not expose it to sudden variations in temperature.
6. Do not expose equipment to heat from direct, intense sunlight for long periods.
7. Provide proper protective cases for storage and transportation.
8. Use only recommended power sources and power cords.
9. Do not use unstable tripods or other mounts.
10. Avoid dropping, bumping, or other shock to equipment.
11. Protect the lens from damage by using a haze filter and lens cap.
12. Clean the lens using an optical lens cleaner and the recommended procedure.
13. Do not touch the surface of the lens with fingers.
14. When cleaning equipment, do not use abrasive or liquid detergents.
15. Do not allow any objects or liquids to enter the units.
16. Do not attempt to repair, disassemble, or service the equipment; have all service and repair handled by qualified service personnel.
17. Use only authorized parts and accessories.

Video Cassettes

Although video cassettes are not electronic equipment, they are made with precision and should be handled with care. Some precautions on use and storage are given below:

1. Protect cassettes from vibration, shock, and contamination.
2. Do not open or disassemble the cassette or insert anything inside.

3. Keep fingers off the tape.
4. Do not attempt to splice the tape.
5. Avoid storage in areas of dust, high humidity, or magnetism.
6. Protect cassettes from sources of heat and direct sunlight.
7. Store cassettes vertically in protective covers.

Battery Packs

For a battery pack to function properly and to extend its life span, the following precautionary steps should be taken:

1. Always keep batteries fully charged by using an approved charger.
2. Store in a cool, dry place.
3. Batteries should never be placed near or disposed of in a fire.
4. Do not use a battery pack under conditions where temperatures exceed its safety limits.
5. Do not use damaged, insufficiently charged, or worn-out battery packs.
6. Protect from dropping and strong jolts.
7. Protect from cold temperatures to prevent faster discharging.

In Chapter 2 of this book, Still Photography for Fire/Crime Scenes, the section on equipment precautions and protection presents many details regarding the need for a combination battery charging manual and log book. The same system should be adapted to video equipment batteries. Figure 2.3 shows samples of some of the charging instructions provided for various batteries.

Most of the aforementioned equipment precautions and protections can be accomplished by use of common sense and a little thought on the part of the operator. There are, however, two things to stress. The first is to have an equipment case for storage and transportation. This case should have a hard exterior, preferably metal, with a padded interior capable of providing protection from heat, cold, and shock. The second item is protection from water or moisture. This becomes a serious problem when it is necessary to use equipment during a storm or at a fire scene. There are at least two ways to reduce exposure. One way is to use a plastic "raincoat," which is available from commercial sources. Some raincoats cover only the camera and have a hole or clear plastic area for the lens, whereas others cover both the camera and the operator. A less expensive but readily available alternative is to use a plastic bag large enough to cover the camera. An opening is provided so that the lens barely protrudes, and a rubber band secures the plastic to the lens. A clear plastic bag is recommended, to allow the operator to see controls and indicator lights.

Public Relations

If you are a police officer making a video, you should be on good terms with fire fighters, news media, and other police agencies operating in the area. If you are a fire fighter you should be on good terms with all police agencies, news media, and other fire departments operating in the area. If you are a free-lance photographer, insurance investigator, or private investigator, you should have good public relations with everyone.

The reason for having good public relations and rapport among individuals and among agencies is that it leads to cooperation. Without cooperation, successful completion of your mission will be difficult to say the least, and it may even be impossible. Good public relations usually do not just happen, especially between rival individuals or agencies. A personal relationship must be cultivated between you, as an individual, and other people.

Personal experience has shown that poor public relations usually result from a defensive reaction on the part of the other individual, which arises from his lack of knowledge about who you are, what you are trying to do, and why you are trying to do it.

Have you ever experienced difficulty crossing a police line barrier tape or rope? The crime scene is not the time or place to introduce yourself to a member of another agency. Accomplish this on your own well in advance. Do whatever is required, ranging from merely a personal introduction and conversation with an individual to a full-blown seminar with representatives from all the agencies with whom you will associate. Remember that coffee and doughnuts are great ice breakers. After such a seminar, in which you modestly toot your own horn, you will be recognized when you appear on the scene. Who you are, what you are trying to do, and why you are doing it will not be questioned, and your mission will be accomplished to everyone's satisfaction.

You should always remember this important fact about public relations: it is a two-way street. If you expect to receive, you must be ready to give. Both parties have a job to do and an objective to reach, so cooperation must work in both directions.

One important matter should be stressed — make sure anything you give, whether it is verbal or actual material, will not compromise your case. For example, it would be understandable for a fire investigation video cameraman to request and obtain footage of the fire taken by the media prior to his arrival on the scene. That is cooperation on the part of the media. It would not be wise for the fire investigator on his own to provide the media with access to the contents of his investigation recording. That type of cooperation should not be expected by the media. Until such time as ruled otherwise, the investigator's recorded tape should be considered as evidence and treated as such.

Two Types of Videotaping

Before starting to videotape a scene, it is wise to decide the reason and end use of a particular tape. Are you documenting for department training or record purposes only? Is the tape intended to be evidence related to a case? The end use determines how you should take the video.

Nonevidential Tape

If your video is not to be used for evidence, how you record and what is recorded depends on what you want in the end. Conversations between individuals and comments in the background are rarely detrimental. In fact, they have been known to add a little color. Conversation or a running narrative is usually required for a meaningful tape. Alteration of the original recording through dubbing and editing is acceptable and usually required.

A nonevidential tape might be obtained by connecting the tripod-mounted camera to a reliable, long-term power source (such as a vehicle), orientating the camera to cover the desired area, turning it on, and letting it run continuously. Keep in mind that whatever happens or whatever is said goes on tape.

Evidential Tape

The recording of a tape that will be used as evidence should be handled differently from that of a nonevidential type. Keep in mind those well-known words, "what you say may be used against you." What you record on the tape — both visual and oral — is evidence and therefore open for examination by the opposition. If, in the documentation process, your microphone picks up conversation or comments inappropriate to your case, there is nothing you can do. Remember, this is an evidential tape and must not be edited or altered in any way. A smart opposition attorney is sure to pick up on any inappropriate conversation and use it against you. With the exception of situations where audio would have a positive bearing on the case, it is recommended that no audio be recorded on a fire/crime scene evidential tape. If you prefer to record audio, take precautions to advise all individuals in the vicinity that audio is being recorded.

Always retain the original tape. A high-quality, second-generation unedited or edited tape should be adequate for courtroom use. Never use a third- or fourth-generation copy in court. Not only will the quality suffer, but it opens the door for the evidence to be declared inadmissible. Make no copies of an evidential tape without official documented approval from all concerned. For protection against loss of damage from magnetic fields, heat, or moisture, several backup copies should be made as soon as possible.

Situations occur when it is advantageous or necessary to use an edited tape. When this happens, retain the original in its unchanged form for record purposes. Documentation of all editing activities is advisable.

Playing it Safe

How can you be sure whether your videotape of a fire/crime scene will be evidential or nonevidential? At the time you record the tape, there is no way to know positively. Any videotape made whose existence becomes known by either side may be commandeered as evidence. The best and safest way is to figure that any taping you do will be evidence at some time or another. Therefore, it is wise to treat all tapes as evidential in the beginning. You can always dub in background audio later if it is required for nonevidential use.

Once again, it must be stressed that you must use caution when making copies of evidential tapes for nonevidential use, especially if the investigation is still in progress or the case is still open. Two negative situations could result if you do not use caution. The first is that confidential evidence may become disclosed to the public,. Second, there is always the possibility that the tape could accidentally be erased. Before any copy is made, be sure to obtain written approval from the responsible authorities.

Taping Tips

Objective

Always keep in mind the five main objectives you must accomplish when taping a fire/crime scene. These objectives and end results are:

1. To provide an unbiased documentation of facts, conditions, and the sequence of events.
2. To provide visual proof that there was a fire or other crime.
3. To visually bring the crime scene into the courtroom.
4. To enable the jury, attorneys, judge, and witnesses to be visually transported back to and through the scene as it was at the time of the occurrence.
5. To refresh memory.

General Shooting Tips

Practice, critique your results, and practice some more. This should be your first priority when starting out or becoming familiar with new equipment. The fire/crime scene is not the place to practice and make mistakes. Operation of the equipment should become automatic and entail very little delay or effort on the part of the operator. Study the operating manual and practice until it becomes second nature.

One of the most important but greatly overlooked requirements is to have your equipment readily available. Carry it with you in your vehicle at all times. Precious time can be saved this way, especially in responding to an active fire situation. Video equipment stashed away in the photo department or storage closet is virtually useless.

Always use standard speed when recording. Do not try to extend the recording time on a tape by recording at extended speeds (EP, ELP, LP, etc.) because you lose quality. Also, some duplicating and playback cannot be accomplished at speeds other than standard speed.

Make it a general rule to take video at eye level as it would normally be seen by the individual viewing your tape on a monitor. Restrict the use of high, low, or angled shots to situations where they are the only way to show the subject. Even then, such use should not distort the facts. Until such time as you become proficient in the operation of your camera, try not to walk and videotape at the same time, especially when panning. All movements and vibrations are greatly accentuated through the camera. Whenever possible, brace yourself and the camera by leaning against a steady object or by standing in a stable position. Exaggerated motion will immediately place your recording in the amateur status. Your audience will lose interest in your product and doubt your capabilities.

Train yourself to monitor the recording indicator in the camera viewer. You may think you pushed the record button but did not. A lot of time can be spent viewing the scene but putting nothing on tape. Also, checking this indicator will assure you that you have ceased recording, thereby preventing undesired taping.

Whenever possible, preplan or do a dry run of your next sequence before actually recording. This can reduce problems caused by turning off the camera as you reposition yourself in order to video the entire scene. Some camera mechanisms will roll back each time the "off" switch is activated, so that when the camera is turned on and recording resumed, the last segment of the previous recording is wiped out. This roll-back situation can be solved two ways. Either record a couple of extra seconds that you can afford to lose at the end of each individual scene or use the "pause" switch instead of the "off" switch to stop the tape recording.

Train yourself to operate your camera with both eyes open. This is done by having one eye outside the camera viewer for normal visual observation of the area and the other eye observing through the camera viewer. This may be unnatural and difficult at first. However, one trip to the cellar through a hole in the floor that was not visible in the viewfinder will impress upon you the merit of the two-open-eyes system. The eye whose vision is not restricted by the rubber eyecup on the viewfinder will cue you into impending dangers, as well as your next objects or area to record without needing to stop or pause the camera. The left eye does the planning while the right eye monitors the recording, or vice versa.

Be consistent in your on-scene video operations. Use the same procedure for each occurrence. Do not provide an opportunity for someone to claim that you did something to hurt them that was not part of a normal investigative procedure. In other words, eliminate any possibility of a claim of discrimination. Videotape all incidents the same way each time.

Time and Date Indication

During the first three or four seconds of your recording of a fire/crime scene incident, the time and date should also be recorded. Usually this can be superimposed on the tape electronically. This superimposed information is distracting to a viewer and may cover vital pictorial information, however, so do not leave the time/date indicator on for the length of the tape. The exception to this rule would be situations in which it is essential to have sequenced timing of events being recorded. Even in such situations, it is usually sufficient to show occasional indications of time only for a moment or two every few minutes or at major scene changes.

If your equipment has a time and date generator and you wish to show that no portions of the finished tape have been edited in or out, let the generator run continuously. This works best in situations where the camera also runs continuously once it is turned on. If your equipment has an automatic, continuous running clock in the time/date generator, the clock will continue to advance whether recording or not. When resuming recording after a five-minute advance in time, it will appear the same as if you had edited out five minutes of the tape. Any variation in the recording of a continuously running time generation must be explainable if you are questioned.

Focusing

Focusing your picture should be done prior to recording, especially if you plan to use your zoom capability. Always focus the subject of the picture with the lens zoomed in as close as possible. Once you do this, your picture will always be in focus regardless of whether you are zooming toward or away from the subject. Circumstances will dictate whether you must use manual focus or automatic focus. If the situation is such that objects continuously pass between you and your subject, your camera will constantly attempt to focus on the temporary objects. As a result, your subject will go in and out of focus. Smoke or steam can also cause this to happen, especially at a fire scene. Under these conditions, especially if they last for a significant period of time, it is best to program your camera for manual operation.

Depth of Field

Depth of field is that area in your picture from the foreground to the background that is in focus. When using the telephoto feature of the lens, this portion of your picture will be relatively small. Increasing the in-focus area or depth of field can be accomplished by zooming toward wide angle. The wider the angle, the more the depth of field and, therefore, the more of the picture that will be in focus.

Panning

The capability of panning or pivotal movement of the camera is one of the features movies have over still photography. Today video has the same advantages. However, a good thing also has its down side. Most people new to video, as well as some with more experience, overdo panning both in frequency and speed. The best way to pan is with the use of a tripod. However, in most cases, at least your preliminary recording will be made without one.

Whenever possible, rehearse the pan before recording. Make sure you can cover the desired scene comfortably without moving your feet. Pivot at the waist and keep the camera perpendicular. Pan the scene twice: first from right to left (or vice versa) and, after a hesitation, back again over the same area. The double panning does several things for your audience. The first panning pass will orient the audience. The second pass allows more detailed observations. Items and details missed the first time are seen on the second presentation. Requests for rewind and playback will be greatly reduced. Using this simple procedure presents your evidence twice. Always keep the following very important advice in mind: when rehearsing your pan, visualize how slowly you should pivot to allow your future viewers time to observe and comprehend. When you actually record, pan at least half as fast as you did in the dry run. If this still results in too fast a pan on your finished tape, remember to slow down your pan even more the next time you record another incident.

Zooming

After high-speed panning, zooming is probably the most overused feature of your equipment. Limit actual zooming in and out when recording. The effect obtained is not a natural visual phenomenon; it is a visual enhancement. A zoom lens is very useful in its capability to combine telephoto, wide angle, and possible macro features in one unit. It is recommended that the zooming motion be done before actually recording to compose the shot.

For every rule there are exceptions, though. Exception to the no-zoom rule would be when it is desirable to show a wide, overall relationship among two or more items followed by zooming in for close-ups to impart clarity to and identification of the individual items. As with panning, visualize how slowly you should zoom and then go half that speed. Erratic, high-speed zooming can leave viewers gripping their chairs.

Fade-In/Fade-Out

If your camera has this feature, it is recommended that you ignore it. Remember, you are not making the tape for entertainment, so don't get fancy. Fade-in/fade out becomes monotonous and your viewers lose interest. Also, a dark screen or monitor is a waste of court time.

Close-Up/Macro

Doing professional macro close-up work successfully requires the use of a tripod. Although it can be accomplished without one, it is not recommended. Using a tripod ensures that the subject is steady and in focus when being viewed.

Lighting

Scene lighting will be required so frequently that some form of lighting equipment will be a necessary part of your gear. Even during daylight hours, dark rooms, cellars, and the black-on-black of fire scenes require supplementary illumination. Do not request that lighting be provided by or depend on other agencies on the scene. Illuminating your scene is not their responsibility.

The scope of lighting equipment is limited only by your individual desires, capabilities, and available finances. Transportation and handling of heavy-duty, portable-generator-powered lighting would not be practical if your video operation consists of one. individual. Generator noise in the background of your tapes should also be considered. Such lighting is only semiportable, given that it is limited to the length of the power cords.

Lighting systems have improved to the point where small, lightweight, completely portable, camera-mounted units are sufficient for most requirements. Some units have batteries enclosed within the light itself, similar to a flashlight. Others have a separate shoulder-bag battery pack connected by a power cord. This type of battery pack can also be utilized to power the camera. Although less bulky and lighter weight, most lights with self contained batteries do not provide as brilliant illumination for as long as a light powered by a battery pack. The light and its power source should be capable of providing the required illumination for at least 20 to 30 minutes.

If you choose a camera-mounted light, be sure it has the capability of hand-held, off-camera operation. Side lighting (holding the illuminating source to the side) will greatly enhance the images of char patterns, tracks, and signs of forcible entry, to name a few. Off-camera side lighting or bouncing may also be necessary to prevent reflections back to the camera when confronted with a lightly reflective surface such as glass or when shooting outside during a rain or snow storm.

Backlight

Although acceptable video can be made without the use of the back-light function, having this capability will greatly enhance a large percentage of your taping when you cannot keep the sun behind you. Whenever the illumination coming toward the camera from behind the subject is brighter than the subject itself, activation of the backlight function will automatically compensate for the varying contract in light and prevent the subject from being silhouetted. Exteriors of structures with bright sky, sun, or snow in the background, objects in windows or doorways, and fire char patterns are types of situations requiring use of backlight. Activation of the backlight should be done prior to start of actual recording of the tape in order to avoid the annoying apparent flare of light on the subject that occurs when the difference in contrast is rectified.

Filters

When taping fire/crime scenes, do not use special filters such as starburst, multi-image, or varicolor to obtain entertaining, dynamic effects to jazz up your video. Use of a polarized filter may be acceptable to eliminate surface reflections produced by water or glass, thereby allowing the camera to see below or behind the surface. Noting the fact that a polarized filter was used, and taping the scene from the same spot and angle both with and without the filter, is recommended. The use of an inexpensive ultraviolet (UV) or haze filter should not be objectionable and could save considerable money by protecting the lens from dirt and scratches.

Sneaky Tactics

When photographing people, such as spectators at a fire/crime scene, the one thing you do not want to do is attract attention. To be less conspicuous, cover the small blinking red recording indicator light, which is on the front of most cameras, with a small piece of plastic electrical tape. With the light hidden, the fact that you are recording is no longer evident, and spectators are not attracted by your activity by the blinking light. People shying away or posed, grinning photos are virtually eliminated.

A video camera being held at eye level is assumed by most people to be in operation. A camera held under the arm, at waist level, or even lower is assumed not to be in operation. This is not always true, but as a gatherer of information, you can use these assumptions to your advantage. Place your camera in one of these unorthodox positions. Adjust the viewfinder upward so you can glance down into it occasionally. Turn the camera on, and tape some people; note how much more relaxed, normal acting, and especially free speaking they are.

Embarrassing Situations

Sometimes your sneaky tactics work so well they create embarrassing situations for you and your colleagues. Make certain that on-scene personnel are aware you are recording audio as well as video; then you have at least done your part to eliminate or at least reduce the occurrence of obscene or inappropriate conversation and gestures. Remember, you should not edit evidence tapes for courtroom use. A fire or police officer making an inappropriate comment or gesture on camera can be embarrassing in court and hazardous to his career. Also, the camera operator must be extremely cautious of any words or noises he makes.

Shooting Sequence

The sequence for taking fire/crime scene video is essentially the same as for still photography. However, there is no hard and fast rule that can be adhered to 100% every time. You must use your own discretion and make immediate decisions as opportunities present themselves. Better to be out of procedural sequence at one point than to miss the happening altogether.

The following is a generalized ideal-situation sequence that may be varied according to your agency-established procedure or the circumstances surrounding the particular incident. First, videotape the spectators and emergency equipment on the scene — both have a tendency to change or leave completely. Show the time and date on the tape to establish presence of individuals, suspects, and emergency equipment. If you have a chance, return later and redo these two subjects (especially the spectators) for possible on-scene documentation of suspects. Establish a record of the location of the incident by videotaping the incident subjects and address on the mailbox or other address locators. Circle the exterior of the structure or vehicle, recording its condition and any related evidence, such as broken or open windows and doors, forced entry, tracks, and containers. Upon entering the structure, videotape from the least burned to the most burned area. The latter is usually the area of fire origin. Upon completion of the generalized documentation, work with the fire and/or police investigators by taping what they want documented.

Reusing Tapes

Nonevidential tape can be used over and over with few or no problems. Evidential tapes should be retained for the same length of time as any other evidence pertaining to the case. Always keep in mind that a case may be reopened in the distant future — saving the cost of one tape is not worth losing a case in court.

Postrecording Procedures

The actions you take immediately upon completion of your video assignment may very well determine the success of this and future arrangements.

Identification

You may add identifiers to the end of the tape electronically if your equipment has built-in titling capability. If your equipment is less expensive without the feature, print the identifiers on a card and videotape the card for the length of time required to read it slowly. The ideal place for identifiers is at the beginning of the tape. However, many times all the identifiers are not known prior to starting your taping. If some identifiers are known, start the tape with at least the time, date and location. The information should be repeated at the end, with the addition of remaining identifiers, such as complaint number and the name of the cameraperson. The dual insertion of identifiers defines an official beginning and end of the recording.

Review of Recorded Material

Before leaving the scene, always play back and review what you have taped. Never assume that what you see through the camera viewfinder is on tape. There are times when distractions, excitement, and pressure will lead even the trained professional to forget to watch for the record indicator in the camera viewfinder. Although the scene is portrayed in the viewfinder, "record" may not be activated — and nothing is being recorded on tape. Reviewing the tape before leaving the scene allows you to notice such errors and permits reshooting the missing information.

It is best to have specifically approved adapters capable of plugging into both an AC and a vehicle 12 VDC power source in order to save the camera's batteries during review. This is desired for two reasons. First, a long recording session may have drained your batteries so that review is not possible. Second, current drain resulting from review of the recording may result in insufficient power supply to retape the scene. Review can be accomplished on scene one of two ways. You can use a small DC-powered monitor obtaining its power from a vehicle or you can observe through the camera viewfinder. The length of time the recorded portion of the tape runs should be noted for inclusion on the cassette label.

Erasure Prevention

Assuming that all taping is completed satisfactorily, identifiers have been added, and the reviewer verified these conditions, your next step is to protect what you have. You must prevent the recorded material from being erased or recorded over. Immediately upon removal of the cassette from the camera, break off the tabs on the cassette case. Do not put off this simple action of insurance until later. If, at some future time, you want to add to the recording or reuse the tape, this can be accomplished by covering the removed tab hole with tape.

Label Recorded Tape

The tape cassette you now have is no longer only a videotape, it is a piece of evidence and should be treated the same as any other evidence.

As soon as you have broken off the cassette tabs, immediately affix an evidence label to the cassette. The label should be filled out with all pertinent information, including name of subject, date taken, case or complaint number, name of cameraperson, tape __ of __ (if more than one), brief description of tape contents, and number of hours and minutes recorded. The tape should now be submitted to evidence control according to your particular agency's procedure.

Battery/Tape Removal

Do not leave batteries or tapes in the camera for extended periods when not in use. Regardless of how well batteries are constructed and the assurances given by the manufacturer, the risk of corrosion and swelling is there. Don't risk it. Some spring-type electrical contacts have a tendency to set if compressed for an extended period. Eventually, this can result in poor electrical contact and equipment malfunction. Removal of batteries also eliminates the chance of leaving camera on and draining the battery.

The same applies to tape cassettes. Remove them to prevent wear on mechanical connections. Getting into the habit of removing cassettes may prevent evidential tapes from being taped over, erased, or remaining in the camera rather than being properly placed into the evidence locker.

Maintenance and Supplies

Service and repairs should be accomplished by qualified service personnel. As stated previously, nothing can be more destructive to the equipment than an individual with a little knowledge and a big screwdriver. However, this section pertains to the everyday post-use maintenance and care that should be provided by the operator or individual in charge of equipment. The following subjects may be the most important to the success of your next assignment.

Prior to putting the equipment away, be sure all items used are clean and dry. Commercial lens-cleaning kits are available and recommended for this particular use. Q-tips, soft bristle brushes, and air blowers are useful for exterior cleaning. Leave internal cleaning to the professional. Do not use liquids or abrasives. For manufacturers' recommendations, refer to your equipment manual.

Your battery supply should be a minimum of two sets. This enables replacing the batteries last used with a set that is fully charged. Never assume the replacement batteries are fully charged. Check them to be sure. The batteries used last should be placed on charge at this time. This ensures longer battery life and guarantees a reserve supply of power on hand. Never store batteries in a discharged condition. Keep a record of the purchase date and recharging dates of each battery. This can be indicated on the battery itself or recorded elsewhere.

Replenish your supply of new tapes by replacing those used. Always carry extra tapes in reserve as a safety factor and for extended on-scene requirements. Keep individual tapes sealed in their original package until actually needed. This keeps dirt and other contamination from entering the cassette, transferring and causing damage to the camera interior. An unopened tape is a guarantee that the tape has not been used previously.

High-Speed Video

The field of high-speed video is a highly specialized field requiring sophisticated equipment, training, and knowledge. High-speed capability is not usually associated with run-of-the-mill on-scene video documentation, but rather, it is more applicable to the laboratory and forensic science. The average cameraperson has neither the background training nor the equipment available to handle this technique. Those interested in high-speed video should refer to Chapter 8, Evidence Documentation, for details on this subject.

Courtroom Video

This entire chapter pertains mainly to on-site video activities and related information. Your video responsibilities are not restricted to, nor do they end with, the on-site activities. Before you record your first inch of tape, you must know what the court and the law allow and will accept. Details of evidence preparation, courtroom requirements, applicable laws, and opinions cannot be covered here in the length and depth necessary. Refer to Chapter 9, Legal Aspects of Visual Evidence, for specific information on courtroom requirements and procedures.

It is very important that you know your final objective before you begin. All of the on-scene efforts and hours spent in training sessions and the dollars consumed in both categories will be for naught if your end product is not acceptable in court. The subject of tangible evidence is extensive in scope. Read up on the subject of video evidence requirements, handling, and preparation for trial. After you have obtained some overall background knowledge, talk to the local district attorney, trial lawyers, and judges for their general opinions, likes, and dislikes. This is an effort that need be expended only once, unless there are extensive personnel changes in the local court system or you relocate.

Summary

Ten or more years ago, if you mentioned using videotape at a fire/crime scene or in the courtroom, most people would shudder and turn pale. The process had to be argued and proven. Today it is an accepted means of documentation and an extremely valuable investigative tool. Not only is it accepted, it is necessary. There are no justifiable grounds for not capitalizing on video. As with any other capability, there is the initial financial outlay for equipment and training. Crime also costs money. Which is cheaper in the long run?

In this chapter, the theme has been to provide information and advice not found elsewhere except through years of experience and expensive, time-consuming trial and error. You may not agree with all its contents and may object to some. As a result, you may develop your own philosophy, policies, procedures, and use of video for fire/crime scene investigations. If this happens, my efforts have been successful.

Suggested Reading

New York State Academy of Fire Science. *Fire Service Video Production Course Manual.* Montour Falls, NY: New York State Office of Fire Prevention and Control, 1988.

JVC Video Equipment Instruction Manual. Elmwood Park, NJ: JVC Company of America, 1982.

Panasonic Video Equipment Instruction Manual. Secaucus, NJ: Panasonic Company, 1988.

Motor Vehicle Accident Scene

4

Many two-vehicle accidents are not photographed, and as a result it may be difficult to determine which driver was at fault.

Motor vehicle accidents usually occur on public highways. This alone can be an obstacle to the proper documentation of the precollision, accident, and postincident events. Whether the accident involves simple (noncriminal) property damage, a potential felony, or fatalities, the objective is to get the scene documented and cleared as soon as possible. Although serious personal injury and fatal accidents are for the most part adequately recorded with photography/video, all too often accidents of lesser consequences are neglected. Many single-vehicle accidents with stationary objects (trees, utility poles, guardrails, etc.) are frequently not photographed. We encounter such cases when called upon by insurance companies to investigate product failures or manufacturers' defects alleged to be responsible for the accident.

Forensic photography, as a means of recording valuable information about an accident, is in every sense "worth a thousand words." Photographs are a permanent record of your observations, as well as an aid to recalling pertinent facts at a later date. Often when reviewing photographs, the investigator will note new information previously missed, even at the time of the scene investigation. Photographs are an essential aid to scene sketching and measurements but are not to be used in lieu of these critical methods of scene documentation. A reprint of a certain photograph can be marked with notes, arrows, and even dimensions to highlight specific observations. Although such a photograph may not be admissible as evidence in certain legal proceedings, it can be as useful as any notes you have prepared.

Sources of Accident Scene Photographs

Besides the law enforcement investigating officer, there are a number of other resources for accident scene photographs. Some departments have special divisions, often referred to as Accident Investigation Units (AIUs), for documenting and reconstructing the more serious motor vehicle accidents.

They are trained in special techniques of photographic documentation. Other departments rely on the detective or criminal investigation division, particularly in those incidents involving fatalities or pending criminal charges.

Freelance photographers usually monitor police, fire, and rescue radio transmissions on a scanner monitor. Their photos, which frequently show rescue activities and crowds of curiosity seekers, may be useful in identifying potential witnesses or verifying damage caused by rescue workers as opposed to that caused by the accident. Newspaper and television photographers tend to emphasize the human interest aspects of the accident. Again, they frequently document "people events," which may include potential witnesses. Professional photographers may be retained by law enforcement agencies, insurance companies, and attorneys. Their photographs are often the exclusive property of the party who retains the services. To obtain copies would, at the very least, require a formal, written request and probably a fee.

Insurance appraisers, adjusters, and investigators may all be working on the same case, but for specific reasons, each may take his or her own photographs. Appraisers and adjusters are generally concerned with establishing a dollar figure for the loss (property and bodily injury). The insurance investigator, however, is interested in documenting cause and responsibility.

Amateur photographers may be passers-by, those who live in close proximity to the accident scene, or members of the fire/rescue department. Although their photographs or videos may not be technically accurate, they are often the first photographic documentation made, even before law enforcement personnel arrive.

Legal Constraints

Because most motor vehicle accidents occur on public streets and highways, taking photographs at the scene is not prohibited. As long as photographers do not interfere with the emergency personnel in the performance of their duties or create a risk to the safety of others, they will not be prohibited from the accident scene regardless of their status.

However, those photographers outside the field of law enforcement or their agents may be requested to surrender their film to the police officer in charge of the investigation. Generally this is done with the understanding that the police agency will incur the expense of processing the film and return the negatives or videotape after copies have been made.

If you are not affiliated with the law enforcement agency having jurisdiction, particularly on limited access highways such as toll roads and interstate highways, you should be aware that you are prohibited from taking photographs. The section of the vehicle and traffic law differs from state to state, but generally it is unlawful to stop on a limited access highway for other than emergency situations. An example of this was vividly etched in my memory back in 1985 on the New Jersey Turnpike between Exits 6 and 7. My associate and I were retained by an insurance company approximately two weeks after an accident. We were conducting a follow-up investigation of a fatal accident between a seven-passenger van (carrying nine members of a single family) and a tractor trailer. The van cut in front of the tractor-trailer in an attempt to pull into a rest area. Unfortunately, when the vehicles collided, the van was struck in the left rear quarter panel at the gas filler-pipe location. The van ended up on its top in the ditch spilling gasoline into the passenger compartment. It ignited almost immediately, resulting in the fiery death of eight of the nine members of the family. The only survivor was an eight-year-old girl who was thrown free of the vehicle.

During an inspection of the accident scene, we were detained by members of the New Jersey State Police. We were advised of the section of law we were violating in reference to unauthorized stopping for purposes of taking photographs. They impounded our film and cameras, and we were escorted to headquarters to meet with the supervisor. As it turned out, they returned our cameras and film and even provided us with copies of their original photographs taken the night of the accident. A lesson well learned: call first — cooperation goes a long way in this business.

If for some reason the vehicle(s) you are assigned to document have been moved to private property, you have two options for obtaining your photographic objectives. The preferred option is to ask the property owner for permission. If this is not feasible, you may use a telephoto/zoom lens and take your photographs from a public access (street, sidewalk, parking lot, etc.).

Additional Circumstances Encountered

Because law enforcement personnel are frequently the first on scene, they must assess severity of injuries and protect life and property from further harm before concerning themselves with what photographs to take. The next problem may be keeping curiosity seekers and other motorists clear of the immediate scene, as they only obscure attempts to document positions of vehicles in relation to one another and reference points (trees, buildings, highway markers and signs, etc.). Curiosity seekers and other motorists, especially on nonlimited-access highways, many times disturb vital evidence at the scene. Because of the geography of the scene and surrounding area, there may be problems with proper or adequate overall scene documentation.

One of the worst accident scenes in my experience was a 14-vehicle, chain-reaction pileup on a New Jersey expressway near one of the Hudson River Bridge crossings. This scenario involved a fiery, fatal collision approximately three-quarters of the way behind the initial accident scene. The roadway was divided

Figure 4.1 The use of lacquer paint to mark vehicle positions on the roadway helps to facilitate removal of the vehicles sooner to alleviate traffic congestion as well as allowing the investigator to return at a later date to complete all aspects of documentation.

and consisted of both local and express lanes. The overall accident scene was located between exits, and it extended over a quarter mile. Compounding the problems of photographic documentation were the two most frequent detrimental factors, weather and darkness. The time of the accident was approximately 11:00 p.m. and it was raining heavily.

Encountering these and other problems does not mean you should not attempt to get preliminary photographs. This may be the only opportunity to obtain a true and accurate representation of the circumstances and evidence. Once the vehicles or bodies are moved, their locations and positions must be reconstructed. As few as four to six photographs of the overall scene and the relationship of the vehicle(s) to reference points will suffice for the initial documentation. Then, mark vehicle positions on the roadway in order to facilitate removing the vehicles and allow traffic flow to be restored as soon as possible. One of my associates uses spraly lacquer paint to mark vehicle positions on the roadway so he can return as many times as necessary to complete all aspects of documentation (Figure 4.1). Location marks are identified by numbers or letters and are sprayed on the road with waterproof lacquer paint and photographed. The back sides of the photographs are marked with the photographer's name, the date, and the time the photographs were taken. The photographer should be prepared to testify in court as to where he was standing in relation to the vehicle, including distance.

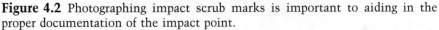

Figure 4.2 Photographing impact scrub marks is important to aiding in the proper documentation of the impact point.

Photographs of impact scrubs (tire markings on the roadway that occur at the point of impact) can be very effective in determining the impact point. Police officers and any other investigators must be qualified to define these scrubs (Figure 4.2).

Any photographs take by investigators should be compared with those taken by police photographers. Useful evidence may have been removed between the times the two sets of photographs were taken. Photographs of damage inside the vehicle, when compared with injuries sustained by the occupants, may show evidence that front-seat occupants were not wearing seat belts (see Figure 7.1, Chapter 7). Very seldom will an occupant of a vehicle admit that he was not wearing a seat belt.

Photographs of the crash sustained by vehicles taken at a level above the vehicles would be of assistance in determining the angle of impact, especially in head-on collisions (Figure 4.3).

Evidence indicating the point of impact which may be destroyed or altered, such as glass fragments and undercarriage dirt, must be photographed as soon as possible. Delay in photographic documentation of this critical evidence and others such as road surface condition (ice, snow, loose gravel), detached vehicle parts, and bloodstains, could mean it is lost forever.

Figure 4.3 Photographing the crush/impact sustained by a vehicle from above assists in determining the angle of impact.

The accident scene sometimes requires return visits to complete documentation, as happens often because of darkness or inclement weather conditions. Delay in completing photographic documentation may be desirable because daylight or improved weather conditions may facilitate better photographs. Not only can you permanently record evidence and contributing factors (e.g., obstructed views), you may discover evidence of situations obscured by the lack of adequate lighting. Tire marks, property damage, or gouges in highway surface may have been missed. It is particularly important to closely examine the vehicle(s) under better lighting conditions. The importance of documenting and interpreting latent physical evidence on the vehicles, road surface, guardrails, utility poles, and so forth cannot be ignored. The technical aspects of forensic photography will be dictated by the unique conditions of every accident, but most importantly, photographs should always be taken.

Equipment

In previous chapters I discussed the variety of cameras, accessories, and film, and their general application. Here I will be more specific regarding the best all-around combination of equipment, film, and technique.

The 35 mm camera and film is the most flexible and convenient for our purposes, especially if it has interchangeable lenses. The most convenient and versatile lens is a variable zoom with 28 to 35 mm wide angle up to 80 to 125 mm telephoto. Another useful lens capability is a close-up macro function. This multifunctional lens enables you to complete all photographic documentation, often during less-than-optimum conditions, without a variety of cumbersome changes.

Auxiliary lighting is a must in accident scene documentation. Obviously, many scenes do not afford the luxury of ideal lighting conditions because accidents frequently occur at night or during inclement weather. The electronic flash compatible with your camera, together with a flash cord and slave unit, facilitates removal of the flash unit from your camera for special lighting techniques to be discussed later in this chapter. Although a tripod may be somewhat inconvenient and time consuming in application, it is necessary for low-light scene documentation.

The choice of film (color or black-and-white) is commonly based on department policy and photography budget. However, keep in mind that color film produces the most true and accurate representation of the scene. The subject matter of the accident scene, whether at night or in daytime, is for the most part stationary, so your film selection can be limited to ISO 100 to 400. However, if a nighttime or subdued-light accident scene requires photographic documentation of visibility, use IS 64.

Filters are used to modify the effects of colored subjects and color of the light source. In photographic documentation of night visibility with color film designed for daylight use (IS 64), use a Number 80 A (light blue) filter to reduce the yellow tint caused by tungsten light sources, such as motor vehicle headlights.

If black-and-white film is used to document blood stains, use a Tri-X Pan film with a Kodak Wratten Filter Number 25 (red) to make bloodstains appear lighter on dark backgrounds. Use a Kodak Wratten Filter Number 47 (blue) to darken bloodstains on a light background.

One last thing — keep spare batteries handy and your equipment dry! Anyone who has taken photographs in the rain or snow will confirm that you do it only once. Preventative measures can be as inexpensive as a big, brightly colored umbrella (for visibility) or a plastic sandwich bag. Waterproof bags are commercially available for underwater photography, which I have used on rainy occasions with good success.

Photographic Documentation of the Scene

The ultimate reconstruction of the events leading up to an accident is accomplished by a systematic series of photographs. Initial photographs will depict the scene from the direction of all vehicles and/or pedestrians involved.

Figure 4.4 Overall accident scene shot from the farthest distance of approximately one block.

Usually the first photographs will be taken from a distance of 100 feet, and close in on the vehicle/pedestrians involved. Be sure to include reference points and all details relevant to the cause and responsibility for the accident. Some investigators prefer to document the scene in reverse order, commencing with closest photos first and working back to the overall scene photographs. Remember, these photographs are for orientation purposes in conjunction with measurements and a sketch, not in lieu of them (Figures 4.4 to 4.7). When composing the overall accident scene photograph, a wide angle lens of 28 mm or 35 mm will be useful. You get more area coverage, particularly at night when flash lighting drops off quickly. The wide-angle lens allows you to get closer and take advantage of your light source. Additional problems and their solutions regarding night scene photography will be addressed later in this chapter. A second series of photographs depicting the scene after the vehicles and/or bodies have been removed should be taken from the viewpoint of the vehicle operator. In other words, position the camera at the eye levels of the drivers relative to their positions on the highway at the time of the accident (Figure 4.8). This practice also applies to pedestrian position and perception (Figure 4.9). The purpose of this technique is to accurately document obstructed views of intersections or of traffic control devices (stop, yield, speed or road character signs, etc.). If there are witnesses, whether pedestrians or other motorists, be sure to get photographs from their perspectives as well. Before moving on to close-up photographic documentation of

Figure 4.5 Another view of the accident scene as the vehicle approached the intersection where the accident occurred.

Figure 4.6 View of the accident scene showing the skid marks in relation to the intersection.

Figure 4.7 A close up of the skid marks on the roadway from the closest perspective.

Figure 4.8 Among the series of photographs documenting an accident scene should be one taken from the drivers' perspective (eye level), relative to their position on the highway at the time of the accident. This technique can be accomplished in one of two ways. First, using an identical size vehicle, take a photograph from the measured eye level of the driver viewing through the windshield. The second method is to mount the camera on a tripod at the measured height of the driver's eye level in the vehicle.

Figure 4.9 Photographic documentation should include all witnesses' perspectives regardless of their position. This practice applies to pedestrians, and the same techniques should be used as described previously with drivers' positions.

the vehicles and pedestrians, be sure to photograph the vehicles and a fixed reference from four angle views: north, south, east, and west.

Documenting the Vehicles

At the risk of sounding repetitive, be sure to take close-up photographs of *all* four sides of each vehicle, including photographs of the front and rear license plates (Figures 4.10 to 4.13). It is also recommended that two additional perspectives be included, one at an overall 90-degree angle from above the vehicle, and one of the undercarriage. This may require assistance of a service garage to lift the vehicle for your inspection and photographic documentation. Be sure to use fill-in flash to record detail (Figures 4.14a and b). Close-ups of the impact damage to all vehicles, as well as physical evidence such as paint transfer, scrapes, broken glass, and bloodstains, should be documented both as found and with a scale of reference. The tires should be photographed so that tread pattern and wear will be accented. This is easily accomplished with cross-lighting by using a flash extension cord to hold the flash unit off the camera at a 45-degree angle to the tire tread (Figure 4.15). Equally important is the condition of vehicle lamps (headlamps, turn signals, side marker lamps, and taillight assemblies), comparison of pedals with imprints of driver's footwear, latent fingerprints, and equipment failure

Figures 4.10a through 4.10d illustrate the proper documentation of all four sides of a vehicle.

Figure 4.10b

Figure 4.10c

Figure 4.10d

Figures 4.11a through 4.11i document the reconstruction of the relations of vehicular damage to injuries sustained by passenger in the right rear seat.

Figure 4.11b

Figure 4.11c

Figure 4.11d

Figure 4.11e

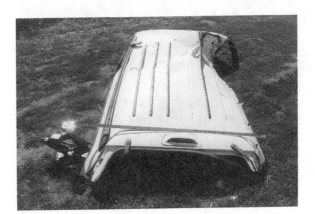

Figure 4.11f

Figure 4.11g

Figure 4.11h

Figure 4.11i

Figure 4.12 This photograph shows the laboratory setup for close-up documentation of the ignition lock assembly from a burned vehicle.

Figure 4.13 Photograph taken with the setup shown in Figure 4.12.

Figure 4.14a This photograph of impact damage lacks detail of the physical evidence.

Figure 4.14b This photograph shows that "fill in flash" lighting helps to bring out the detail of impact damage, as compared to Figure 4.14a.

Figure 4.15 The technique of "cross lighting" is very simple and effective in documenting tire tread, wear, defects, and the distinct patterns.

(brakes, exhaust system, fuel system, doors, safety restraint equipment, etc.). The majority of this detailed forensic documentation can and should be obtained under ideal conditions. Photographic documentation is time consuming and cannot be rushed, so removing the vehicles to an impound or salvage yard is recommended. There, the forensic photographer can document the evidence through techniques such as macrophotography and microphotography. The latter would require removing a part from the vehicle for further microscopic examination in the laboratory of items such as lamp filaments or paint chips (Figure 4.16). It would be good practice to photograph the removal of the part from the vehicle.

Remember, automobile accidents create distorting damage to the vehicles, which casts contrasting lights and shadows. Fill-in flash is very useful in documenting the details of impact point and other damage. It is also useful for documenting the subjects of interest in the engine, trunk, and passenger compartments. Occasionally, impact damage will prohibit access to the passenger compartment because of jammed doors. In this case, interior photographs can be taken through the window glass. To avoid flash reflection, hold the flash slightly above and away from the camera. Place the camera lens and flash against the glass, which is nothing more than a clear filter (Figure 4.17).

Figure 4.16 Some photographic documentation of physical evidence is best accomplished in the laboratory setting, as shown in this example of a lamp filament.

Figure 4.17 To avoid flash reflection, the technique illustrated works very well in documenting the interior of a vehicle where access is limited.

Figure 4.18 This photograph shows distortion (shortening) of the skid mark lengths due to use of a telephoto lens.

Documenting Post-Accident Artifacts

After the preliminary overall, scene, vehicle, and victim photographs are completed and traffic is restored, it is time to focus on the physical evidence. Reconstructing depends on documenting, preserving, and evaluating the results of the accident. Artifacts like skid marks, ruts or tracks in mud and snow, scrub marks on curbs, gouges in pavement, guardrails, utility poles, and trees, as well as detached vehicle parts, are critical objects of evidence.

Perspective plays an important role when documenting skid marks, ruts, and furrows of any significant length because they can easily be distorted. If a telephoto lens is used from a distance, they will appear short (Figure 4.18), whereas a wide-angle lens from a close range tends to lengthen them (Figure 4.19). A suitable solution would be to use a normal lens (45 mm to 55 mm) from two positions (Figures 4.20 and 4.21). First, photograph skid marks head-on to document directionality, and second, from the side to show overall length. An elevated vantage point will permit the best overall perspective. Use of available embankments, overpasses, buildings, or modified vehicles (truck or roof of vehicle) will serve the purpose. When photographing lengthy tire marks, the greater the depth of field, the sharper the overall focus (see Chapter 1, Principles of Photography). Under near-ideal conditions (bright, natural daylight), an aperture setting of f32 will produce the

Figure 4.19 Distortion of skid mark length will also occur if a wide angle lens is used from close range; skid marks will appear longer.

Figure 4.20 A normal lens (45 mm to 55 mm) shows a more accurate perspective of the skid mark length.

Figure 4.21 Photographing skid marks from the side with a normal lens also produces a more accurate perspective of the overall length.

best results. Close-up photographs showing isolated areas of tire marks such as feathering, yaw marks, gouges, or collision scrubs are important to show unique detail. These should be photographed both as found and with a scale of reference. Also, when several marks are to be documented at a scene, be sure to identify them with a series of either letters or numbers (Figure 4.22).

Comparison Photography

As in many other investigations, the importance of photographically documenting a match between a mark and the object that created it is critical forensic scene reconstruction. Macrophotography is often used to preserve and compare matching of an object with its imprint. This also applies to the transfer of latent evidence from one object to another. Often paint chips are transferred between vehicles as well as to a victim's clothing. This author and an associate were involved in two interesting fatal hit-and-run accidents. The first occurred in upstate New York. A pedestrian who was walking along the shoulder of the road was struck from behind by a vehicle, which fled the scene. The victim was wearing a full-length herringbone overcoat. The suspect vehicle (a four-wheel-drive pick-up truck) returned to the scene, and law enforcement officials, who were still investigating the accident, noted

Figure 4.22 If the accident scene requires documentation of several items of evidence, some of which may be too small, the use of markers helps to orient them in a single photograph.

unusual damage to its right rear quarter panel. Upon inquiry, the nervous operator changed his story several times, prompting the officers to detain him and ultimately charge him with driving while intoxicated and leaving the scene of an accident. His vehicle was impounded, and we were asked to examine the vehicle damage and the victim's clothing for any evidence of positive comparison. We found a definite match between the victim's overcoat pattern and a mirror-image impact print in the paint on the right rear quarter panel of the vehicle.

The second was a Long Island case involving a young intoxicated man who was struck and killed while attempting to cross a divided highway. The driver of the vehicle that was the last to strike him was the only one to stop. He stated he thought he saw a pile of rags in the road, and when he hit it, he realized it was something more serious. Examination of the victim's clothing revealed a small piece of turn-signal lens embedded in the weave of the red sweater he had tied around his waist. Macrophotography was used to document the part number, which identified it as the right front turn-signal lens from a General Motors vehicle (Figure 4.23).

The victims of motor vehicle accidents, whether driver, passenger, or pedestrian, should be photographed. If they are deceased, use the same procedures as for any assault of homicide case, and photograph them at the scene before moving the bodies. If they are injured, try to get photographs at the scene, but do not interfere with emergency medical attention. Photographic

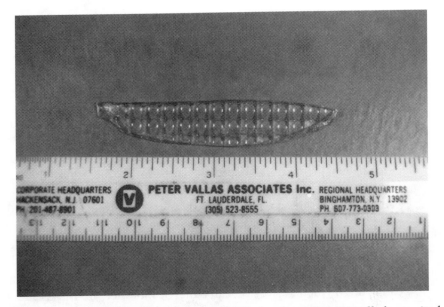

Figure 4.23 Another method of photographic documentation usually best suited to the laboratory is microphotography, shown here in the documentation of a part number on a turn signal lens from a motor vehicle/pedestrian fatal accident.

documentation of bruises to the skin surface and injuries can be accomplished at the hospital after the victim is stabilized. Be sure to confiscate the victim's clothing for more detailed microscopic examination and photography. Later, if the suspect vehicle is located, valuable artifactual evidence found on the victim and clothing may be compared and photographically preserved.

Some important comparisons are (1) impact damage on the vehicle showing a fabric pattern matching the victim's clothing; (2) vehicle lights and glass damage matching fragments recovered at the scene or embedded in victim's body surface or clothing; (3) damaged ornaments, molding, door handles, steering wheel, and so forth matching bodily injuries/bruises; (4) latent fingerprints on vehicle matching the victim's (driver, passenger, or pedestrian); (5) blood, tissue, hairs, and fibers from victim matching imprint on body damage of the other vehicle, the victim, or victim's clothing; and (7) brake and accelerator pedal matching imprint on sole of shoe.

Problem Situations

There are times when inclement weather makes it necessary to use alternative lighting techniques. Reflection can be reduced on rain, snow, sleet, and fog by holding the flash unit above and slightly away from the camera. Sometimes a yellow filter on the light source may help.

Night and dusk also create challenging photographic situations. The extreme contrast of light and shade created at sunset may require you to photograph the scene both with natural light and an auxiliary flash.

Documenting overall accident scenes at night is best accomplished in two ways:

1. *Painting with light* requires use of multiple manual flashes. It is a useful technique to illuminate an accident scene. The procedure is the same as would be employed to illuminate a large fire or crime scene area. Refer to Chapter 2 for detailed explanation on the application of painting with light.
2. *Flash slave exposures* use multiple flash units. The camera's shutter and flash are synchronized to flash at the same moment. This requires several flash units equipped with photoelectric slaves, which respond to the flash unit on the camera. This procedure will result in all flash units simultaneously illuminating the accident scene. The flash units controlled by the slave devices can either be mounted on tripods along the accident scene or assistants can hold them. This equipment can also be used in the painting-with-light technique.

Photographic Documentation of Night Visibility

The amount and type of available light are important when documenting motor vehicle accidents at night. It is essential that forensic photographic documentation also include a record of the actual light level and its source at the time of the accident. What would be normally visible to a motorist or pedestrian could be substantially less than that revealed by our photographic record of the scene aided by flash techniques. Therefore, night visibility photography should be as close as possible to what the driver, passenger, pedestrian, or other witnesses could see. Additionally, the source of light, (street lights, vehicle lighting equipment, store front windows, and advertising lights) must be documented. Do not forget the natural light from the stars and moon.

Variables to Consider

Weather conditions, the person's age, and whether he wears corrective lenses must be considered when using the following technique for night visibility photography. Generally, it takes 15 minutes or more for a person's vision to fully adjust to the darkness.

Some of the night or low-light accident scenes that will require this technique are those involving:

1. motor vehicle and pedestrian
2. motor vehicle and motorcycle, ATV, or snowmobile
3. motor vehicle and bicycle
4. trains, railroad crossings, and vehicles or pedestrians
5. highway construction areas
6. traffic detours, barricades, or signs
7. motor vehicle and stray animals
8. boating and other aquatic accidents

An important requirement in the reconstruction of these and other night vision scenarios is that everything be staged as accurately as possible — from using the same type of vehicles to using similar clothing (at least in color) worn by pedestrians. It is also important to conduct your reconstruction as close as possible to the same time of the night under similar weather conditions. On one occasion I used night vision photography to document an accident involving an off-road motorcycle and motor vehicle. The accident occurred when the automobile was entering an unlit parking lot and the motorcycle was proceeding through the parking lot without lights. The only available light was from the automobile's headlamps, an adjoining convenience store's lighting, one street light, and the moon. With the aid of my son (who was the same age and physical stature as the motorcyclist) wearing similar dark clothing, an identical vehicle, and an associate to aid in observations, several photographs were taken during the simulation to determine at which point the motorcyclist was first observed. To make our reconstruction more credible, we used reference targets at various points approaching the point of impact. These targets were constructed of sturdy illustration board, gray in color (approximately 18% gray scale), measuring 12 inches square with black, 6-inch-high numerals. Three reference photographs were made, starting from the farthest distance, with the vehicle slowly approaching the point of impact. One photograph was taken from a distance at which the motorcyclist was not visible. The second photograph documents the point where the motorcyclist was barely noticeable, and the third, where he was clearly visible (Figures 4.24 to 4.27).

Procedure, Equipment, and Viewing

Because this technique requires exposures of several seconds, it is necessary to use a tripod or other method of keeping the camera stationary. For best results, use IS/ASA 64 or 100 color film exposed at f4 for 4 seconds. Also, an 80A (light blue) lens filter is necessary to reduce the yellow tint to photographs created by tungsten lighting (headlights, etc.). Remember to bracket your shots at each setup; one at the suggested setting (f4), one at the next smaller aperture (f2.8), and the third at double the aperture (f8).

Figure 4.24 This night scene reconstruction of a passenger vehicle and motor-cycle accident shows that the motorcycle is not visible from the driver's perspective in the automobile.

Figure 4.25 This photograph is taken from a distance where the motorcycle is first noticeable to the driver of the automobile.

Figure 4.26 At this point the motorcycle is clearly visible to the operator of the automobile.

Figure 4.27 A final overall photograph is taken to show the distance between the "targets" used in marking the distances between the various points depicted in the previous photographs.

Finally, the recommended viewing distance for prints is approximately 15 inches, hand-held at eye level. Slides (color transparencies) should be viewed from about eight feet (projected image size is five feet diagonal).

Photographic Mapping

One other important photographic technique used by accident reconstructionists is perspective grid mapping, also referred to as *photogrammetry*. Representing the accurate size and shape of accident scene evidence can be very complicated. The correct size requires many measurements, but often the shape is inaccurate. On the other hand, photographs document the shape but not the size, even with scales of reference such as a ruler or tape measure.

The perspective grid technique is particularly suited for documenting both size and shape. It will give the investigator a very good base for a rectangular scale map of the overall scene. A target of known dimensions (two feet square) made of heavy illustration board placed on a flat surface in the scene photograph can save time recording dimensions. It is not essential, however, that the grid be two feet square; any square or rectangle of known dimensions will suffice.

The technique does have its limitations. It works best for accuracy on relatively flat surfaces. When composing your photographs of the overall scene or portions thereof, take one photograph without the grid target to avoid objections that something of importance may have been covered. The second photograph is then taken with the grid target's bottom edge positioned near the lower edge of the field of view in your camera. The mapping process is much easier from this position. Crime or accident scenes with drastic variation in topography (sharp inclines or declines) will be more difficult to accurately reconstruct. In these situations, the higher the camera's elevation, the more accurate the grid mapping will be.

Another limitation of this technique is the maximum distance of the camera of about 40 feet. If the items of importance being documented extend beyond the 40-foot limit, take additional overlapping photographs with the grid target. It is recommended that one edge of the grid target be parallel to the edge of the roadway or a lane stripe and the bottom edge of the grid target be parallel to the lower edge of the camera viewfinder. The focal length of the camera lens does not affect the accuracy of the photo perspective grid. It is recommended, however, that either a normal (45 to 55 mm) or wide angle (28 to 35 mm) lens be used.

Summary

By using the techniques and equipment described in this chapter to produce color photographs or slides, the investigator will best accomplish the desired end result of true and accurate representation of the facts.

Suggested Reading

Duckworth, J.E. *Forensic Photography.* Springfield, IL: Charles C. Thomas, 1983.

Samsone, S.J. *Modern Photography for Police and Firemen.* Cincinnati, OH: W.H. Anderson Co., 1971.

Siljander, R.P. *Applied Police and Fire Photography.* Springfield, IL: Charles C. Thomas, 1976.

Aerial and Underwater Photography

5

Aerial and underwater photography — the high and low of fire and crime scene photography — will be covered in general. Each subject could be a book in itself, depending on the scope of coverage of the various subcategories within each individual field. This chapter is intended to show how each field applies to and can be helpful in fire, crime, and accident investigation.

If you are not already involved in aerial or underwater photography, perhaps you should consider expanding your personal and departmental expertise along these lines. Even if the decision is to hire these types of services, it is still good business to be familiar with the necessary requirements and expected results.

Many publications are available that explain, in great technical detail, the scope of aerial and underwater photography. Specialized cameras, lenses, and accessories are available for both fields. This chapter is restricted to basic crime scene investigation aspects. Photo requirements for high-altitude flying and deep-sea diving are not within the scope of the average investigator's expertise or duty.

Aerial Photography

Aerial photography has many applications for fire, crime, and accident scene investigations. Many property owners have aerial photos of their property that were taken at some time prior to a fire, explosion, or other destructive occurrence. These are of utmost importance in reconstructing the scene. Details not able to be seen, or that go unnoticed at ground level can be observed and photographed from an elevated platform. Aerial photography is the ultimate elevated platform.

Structural collapse patterns are much more evident from above. Whether the area involves one building or many city blocks, total destruction and the fire path can be documented in a single photo. The same applies to brush and forest fires, many of which are the result of arson. Scattering of debris resulting from explosion shock wave and aircraft impact is best documented overall by using aerial photos. Aerial documentation of motor vehicle accidents involving single as well as multiple vehicles is becoming more commonplace.

The ability of an aerial photograph to show the relationships between objects that are great distances apart or not visible to one another at ground level is of utmost importance in accident or crime investigations. In some instances, it is the only way to graphically document certain evidence.

Equipment

There is no limit to the amount you could spend, but as with any field of endeavor, available money can have a great bearing on equipment purchase. Depending on the scope of your department's aerial photo requirements, you may not be required to purchase any additional equipment. That which you already have and use for everyday investigations may be sufficient (refer to Chapters 2 and 3 on still photography and videography).

If your organization's activities require aerial and/or underwater photos on a continual basis and funding is available, more sophisticated equipment and training may be obtained. Although the material contained herein would still apply, this chapter is intended to guide those investigative photographers who may occasionally be required to provide such services with limited equipment and expense.

Camera and Lens

In 1947, I took aerial photos of a disastrous flood by sticking my head and a 35 mm Argus C3 out of the canopy window of a low-wing Aerocoupe (which had to be rolled on its side to get the wing out of the photo). The camera lens was a 50 mm f3.5. Its fastest shutter speed was 1/300 second and focusing was through a coupled split-imaged range finder. The light meter was hand held. As crude as the method may have been, the black-and-white prints were good enough for newspaper publication and, eventually, purchase by the Federal Government Flood Control Agency (Figures 5.1 through 5.3 and 5.8 through 5.10).

While it need not be elaborate and high-tech, the equipment should have adjustable lens shutter speeds from 1/100 second up to at least 1/1000 second. High shutter speed capability is recommended to prevent blurring from aircraft motion and vibration.

Two camera formats suitable for aerial as well as everyday fire/crime scene photography are the 2 × 2³/₄ inch format (6 × 7 cm) and 35 mm. The 6 × 7 format will provide slightly better print quality because of its larger negative, but the equipment is larger and more expensive to purchase and operate. The 35 mm format has proven its capability in the field of aerial photography, as it has in nearly all fields. An automatic focus camera relieves the operator

Figure 5.1 Aerial photo taken in 1947 with 35 mm Argus C3 camera.

of the task of manually focusing on each take. Autofocusing problems have been known to occur during the early morning and late evening because of low light level. This can be eliminated by scheduling your flight time for hours of better lighting.

A recommended 35 mm lens would have an aperture setting capability of f 2.8 or f 3.5. A good lens choice would be a 28 to 210 mm or 35 to 200 mm f3.5 zoom lens. A 70 to 210 mm lens has been proven to be satisfactory. The wide angle gives plenty of area coverage at low altitude. The zoom capability permits zeroing in on the pertinent area from a higher altitude. This eliminates or reduces the necessity of additional flyovers at different altitudes. The minimum altitude restrictions for fixed-wing aircraft necessitate having telephoto or zoom lens capability. It is not advisable to use telephoto lenses longer than 400 mm for hand-held cameras because of the effects of aircraft vibration. In such situations, gyrostabilization of the camera or the entire aircraft is necessary. If you have a relatively fast zoom lens for your regular photographic work, it will probably serve the purpose.

In order to obtain the best quality aerial video, it is recommended to use a commercial grade broadcast camera. Refer to Chapter 3 on videography for more details.

Filters

One of the similarities between aerial and underwater photography is that the medium through which you are photographing (air or water) is full of obstructions between the camera and the subject. Aerial photography must contend not only with water vapor droplets but also with smoke, dust, and a multitude of pollutants suspended in the air. All tend to obscure the transmission of light waves and true color. Rain tends to produce a gray tone, smoke and water vapor produce a blue tint, and various types of smog can cause your photos to have a green or yellowish cast.

The farther away your subject is, or the more oblique its angle, the more light is scattered and the more muted the colors will be. This is the aerial perspective, and it can also be experienced taking ground level landscape photos involving considerable distance. Atmospheric haze, which increases with altitude and horizontal distance, tends to scatter ultraviolet radiation. Films are more sensitive to ultraviolet light than are your eyes, and films will record more haze than you observe. Filters cannot remove the obstructions in the air, but they can reduce the resulting haze effects. Filters will not penetrate heavy mist or fog, and for safety sake, you should not be flying under those conditions.

Black-and-White Filters.   There are at least 3 filters for use with black-and-white film that reduce the haze problem by filtering out the ultraviolet. These are yellow (No. 8), deep yellow (No. 15), and red (No. 25).

Color Filters.   When using daylight transparencies (slides), a Skylight filter (No. 1A) can be used to eliminate ultraviolet light and to reduce the blue cast of haze. If you are shooting color negative film (prints), the Skylight filter has no advantage except as a lens protector. In this situation, blueness can be reduced by the developer during processing. An ultraviolet (UV) filter reduces the effects of ultraviolet and scattered light where haze is not wanted.

Polarized Filters.   A polarized filter may be helpful in reducing haze, glare, and reflected light when photographing near or over a water surface. These filters may be used in combination with other filters and are suitable for use with black-and-white or color film.

Conversion Filters.   Conversion filters are designed to enable you to use artificial-light film for daylight photos or daylight-balanced film with artificial lighting. These filters change the existing light source color quality to match the light for which the film was designed. A No. 85B filter is required when exposing tungsten-type films in daylight. Type A films require a No. 85 filter. Some aerial photographers contend that the use of artificial-light film in daylight with conversion filters assists in the elimination of the haze effect.

Cameras with through-the-lens (TTL) exposure reading automatically compensate for any light absorbed by the filters. If your equipment is not of this type, you must manually adjust for this lost light. Refer to manufacturer's data supplied with each particular filter.

Film

It is difficult to discuss film and refrain from using names of various manufacturers. Each photographer has a brand with which he has been successful in the past and undoubtedly will select this for aerial work. There are special films designed for high-altitude aerial photography. Since most crime scene investigative aerial photography is relatively low altitude, conventional films are suitable. The following information will be general in nature and applicable to any brand you desire to use.

Your choice of black-and-white, color slide, or color print film will depend on the end result desired. This decision-making process is discussed in detail in Chapter 2, Still Photography for Fire/Crime Scenes, and is applicable to aerial photography as well. Whatever your personal decision, it is suggested that the film be color with a minimum ASA 400 rating. If you plan to greatly enlarge the prints, a slightly slower and fine grain film (ASA 200) may be more suitable. Always keep in mind that the faster film allows faster shutter speeds, thereby helping to solve the aircraft vibration problem. The resulting fast-film grain may not be as bad as the slow-film blur that would result from vibration. Faster film is an advantage when using autofocus cameras in low-light situations.

Accessories

Aerial photography does not require a lot of accessories or gadgets beyond the camera, lens, filters, and film already mentioned. An exception would be the capability for automatic film advance. This could be a feature of the camera itself or an automatic winder/motor drive attachment. There should never be extra lenses, cameras, meters, and so forth loose in the aircraft. In most situations, there will not be room or a need for a camera and equipment storage case. If you must carry on accessory items, confine them to a small shoulder bag or belt pouch. Try to limit accessories to filters and film.

Choosing the Aircraft

There are two major types of aircraft you may use for typical aerial photo requirements. Although low-level aerial photos have been taken using kites, radio-controlled model aircraft, and hot-air and gas-filled balloons, this chapter will evaluate only fixed-wing and rotary-wing aircraft. Each has its advantages and disadvantages. Availability of a particular aircraft type may also have a bearing on which you use.

Regardless of type, the aircraft must have a window, hatch, or door that can be opened during the flight or removed in advance — complete removal may invoke a safety restriction on the top airspeed allowed for the aircraft. The plastic windows in small aircrafts are rarely devoid of scratches, nicks, dirt, and discoloration. Window curvature, reflections, and vibration will distort and blur your photos. For these reasons, never photograph through the curved windshield or bubble.

Fixed-Wing Aircraft

If a fixed-wing aircraft is chosen, a high wing is preferred to a low wing because of the necessity to roll a low wing nearly 90 degrees to get the wing clear of the photo area. Figures 5.2 and 5.3 clearly show the problem of a low wing protruding into the photo.

Fixed-wing aircraft are restricted by the Federal Aviation Administration (FAA) to a minimum altitude of 1000 feet in populated areas and usually 500 feet elsewhere. Be sure to check local regulations. Forward airspeed and area required for maneuvering for additional flyovers must also be taken into consideration. Fixed-wing aircraft are more suitable for panoramic aerial views than for a small specific area. Figures 5.4 and 5.5 are examples of aerial photos taken from fixed-wing aircraft.

Rotary-Wing Aircraft

Rotary wing aircraft, better known as helicopters or simply "choppers," have certain advantages over their fixed-wing cousins. Even though its charter cost per hour may be three times the cost for fixed-wing aircraft, a helicopter may be the best choice when you taken into consideration its advantages. The capability to virtually hover over your target or move left, right, forward, and backward gives the photographer complete control over positioning the camera in relation to the subject.

The absence of a fixed-wing and its related struts provides an unobstructed view below. Also, helicopters are not hampered by the 1000-foot minimum altitude restriction. As long as the down draft does not start kicking up dust, you can hover and photograph as low as you want, safety and surroundings permitting. (Figures 5.6 and 5.7 were taken from a helicopter.)

Helicopters with four rotor blades provide a smoother ride than do those with two rotor blades. The more blades, the less vertical vibration is produced. A turbo-powered aircraft also has less vibration than one powered by a piston engine. These two vibration-reducing qualities are especially important when taking video. The use of a two-blade helicopter may be suitable for still photos but is not recommended for videography.

Safety and Choosing Aircraft Charter Service

As a photographer, you have very little control regarding safety in flight except related to your own actions and equipment. Flight safety and condition of

Figure 5.2 Problem of low wing intrusion into photo area during level flight.

Figure 5.3 Problem of low wing intrusion into photo area while in roll-up attitude.

the aircraft are the responsibility of the pilot and the charter service. There are some steps you can and should take to ensure your safety and the quality of your photos.

Prior to actual need, make a survey of the various charter services available in your area. It is important to know the exact location where aircraft

Figure 5.4 Typical photo obtained from fixed-wing aircraft.

Figure 5.5 Typical photo obtained from fixed-wing aircraft.

Figure 5.6 Typical photo obtained from rotary-wing aircraft.

Figure 5.7 Typical photo obtained from rotary-wing aircraft.

are based in relation to a scene to be documented. Try to use the charter service closest to the scene to reduce flight time and overall expense. Check into their backgrounds, histories, safety records, and maintenance policies and procedures. Talk with both ground and flight personnel. Observe the condition of the facilities and aircraft. Shop around. The lowest price should not be the sole determining factor.

When talking to the service personnel, explain your requirements and what you expect from them. Are they agreeable to your requests? Do they have past experience with aerial still photography and videography? Ask the pilot for background information. Most pilots are not versed in aerial photography requirements. Much time and expense can be wasted if the pilot does not understand how to position the aircraft for the best possible shot. In essence, the pilot should be flying the camera. He must be familiar with what you want and make the aircraft work for you (see Figure 5.8).

Does the particular service have aircraft suitable for the purpose? Although it may seem like a waste of time and an imposition on the charter service, it is highly recommended that you should rehearse with the available aircraft. Sit in the aircraft with your equipment. Maneuver your camera as you would during flight. Check for maneuvering clearance and clear field of view with the window, hatch, and door open, as well as completely removed. Note the advantages and disadvantages of each aircraft. Record the individual aircraft's identification number so that when the time comes to actually charter one, you can request the best suited craft.

When the time comes for flight, the pilot must make the required on-ground, preflight inspection of the aircraft and its functions. If no such inspection is made, the pilot is in violation of FAA regulations and you have a right to cancel the charter. At all times while in flight, use the seat belt and/or any other personal restraint devices provided in the aircraft. Do not exit the aircraft while in flight to get a better view. Standing on the landing skid or using struts is for stuntmen, not investigators.

In the case of a helicopter, experienced pilots advise against hovering at low altitudes for several reasons. The main reason is the inability or difficulty of making a safe landing in the event of engine failure. There is also the tendency for unclean air to enter the rotor system thereby affecting the lift and stability. Vibration is more severe when hovering as well. A slow (20 to 30 mph) forward speed while circling over the scene is preferred to a stationary hover. A virtual hover can be obtained safely by taking advantage of a headwind. For instance, a 30 mph headwind reduces a 30 mph indicating air speed to 0 mph ground speed. As far as the ground is concerned, you are hovering. As far as the aircraft and its functioning, you are flying along in a safe mode.

Figure 5.8 Professional fixed wing aircraft and pilot.

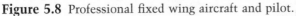

A recommended safety accessory is a strap or harness that secures the portable hand-held camera and keeps it from falling from the aircraft during flight. In addition to the expense of equipment loss, there is danger of possible damage to your aircraft, and property damages that occur on the ground where your equipment impacts.

One last item under the subject of in-flight safety. Many years ago when flying along a creek a few feet above water to photograph a bridge, I delayed in taking the photo and did not signal the pilot until the bridge span filled the camera viewer. Fortunately, the pilot made the decision to pull up without my signal. Remember, objects are closer to you than they appear to be in the camera viewer. Fill the print by enlarging in the darkroom, not while in flight.

Weather and Atmospheric Conditions

Whether you fly or not depends on the weather and the decision of your pilot. There should never be photographic flights during bad weather. If a charter offers to fly under such conditions, take your business elsewhere. If the service is careless regarding flight safety, you can bet your life (literally) that it is careless elsewhere in their operations.

The clearer the weather, the better the opportunity for good aerial photos. (See Figures 5.9 and 5.10.) High clouds are not a problem. It is the fog, mist,

Figure 5.9 The clearer the weather, the better the opportunity for good aerial photos.

Figure 5.10 Aerial view from helicopter shown in Figure 5.9.

or haze below you that hinders photography. Days with air movement are usually better than those with stale, stationary air. Air may be less polluted and clearer immediately after a rain shower, but temperature inversions and smog alerts are not conducive to good visibility.

Depending on the type of activity in the area to be photographed, certain times of day are better suited than others. Peak vehicle traffic periods contribute more haze, as do the smoke and other emissions from local industries. Wind direction may assist or hinder your operations by clearing or contaminating the area. A bright day with a high overcast above your flight level can provide excellent photos.

Aircraft Positioning

Proper positioning of the aircraft with relation to the sun and your subject can make the difference between success and failure of your mission. To obtain the high-quality photos, always position yourself and the aircraft so the sun is at your back. This reduces the problems of haze and light reflection. As explained previously, pilot experience and knowledge of your positioning requirements will have a great affect on your work. A video monitor is sometimes used to assist the pilot in seeing exactly what the videographer is viewing through the camera lens.

Shutter Speeds and F-Stops

Shutter speed settings above 1000 feet altitude should be at least 1/250 second, with 1/500 second preferred as minimum. Make it a rule to use the fastest shutter speed possible under the existing conditions, regardless of altitude.

F-stop settings for altitudes up to 2000 feet are the same as for taking photos on the ground. A through-the-lens meter will provide accurate data. If you need to photograph at a higher altitude, up to 4000 feet, remember that bracketing all shots is cheap insurance toward obtaining satisfactory results. Film is cheap, charters are not.

Shadows and Time of Day

Shadows play an important part in your aerial photos. Without some shadows, there is no contrast, form, or height to objects and structures. Some shadow lines help to give three dimensions to your otherwise flat photos. However, excessive shadows that overlap adjacent structures and areas may defeat the purpose of your photo.

The best shadow time for documenting work generally varies with the subject and the results desired. When photographing at an oblique angle or vertically below 1000 feet altitude, the best results are obtained before midmorning (10:00 a.m.) and after midafternoon (2:00 p.m.). If little or no shadow is desired, shoot around midday (noon). Times vary with your latitude and time of year. Photographing into canyons, deep mining pits, mountain valleys, and so forth may be hampered by unwanted shadows at all times except at or near high noon, especially if the depression is oriented north-south.

One shadow you do not want to appear in your photos is that produced by your aircraft. This problem usually is not associated with fixed-wing aircraft because of the minimum altitude flight requirement. A low-hovering helicopter could, under the right situation, cast a shadow or partial outline over part of the photo subject. Reposition the aircraft at a higher altitude and make use of the telephoto lens. Quite often a slight horizontal change in aircraft position with relation to the sun is sufficient to move the shadow out of camera view.

Hiring Aerial Photographic Services

Few fire/crime scene investigators are professional aerial photographers, and sometimes these photographs are not only desirable but necessary. Therefore, they become a case necessity and possibly a job responsibility. One way or another, these photos must be obtained. If you have claustrophobia or a fear or flying, explain this to your superiors and hire another photographer. If hiring is the only alternative, what you want in the photos must be made known to the hired photographer. This can be difficult if not impossible to accomplish accurately. The individuals hired should be briefed prior to flying and the areas of interest to be covered in the aerial photos should be explained both verbally and visually. Detailed instructions as to type and quantity of photos as well as sketches and/or maps with compass orientations should be provided. All efforts should be made to obtain satisfactory photos of the subject on the first attempt; in fact, consider it mandatory. Rates are usually hourly from the time the photographer enters the plane until he exits. Costs vary with type of aircraft, your location, and how busy the flying service is.

Summary

The following tips are usually necessary to obtain quality aerial photos.

1. Survey your charter service options.
2. Dress for conditions at higher altitudes with open aircraft.
3. Load camera with the maximum number of frames possible to eliminate the need to reload in flight.
4. Take photos through an opening, not through window material.
5. Focus the camera at infinity.
6. Use the fastest shutter speed possible.
7. Use a fast film and a fast lens.
8. Make use of appropriate filters, weather, time of day, and position of aircraft to reduce effects of haze.
9. When photographing, never allow the camera to come into contact with any part of the aircraft.

10. Do not brace your body, head, arms, or hands against the aircraft to steady the camera.
11. If possible, shoot the photo in the direction the aircraft is traveling in order to reduce the possibility of blurring.
12. Consider safety at all times.
13. If you are not capable of taking aerial photos, hire the required services.

Underwater Photography

In 1856, William Thompson produced what has been credited as the first underwater photo taken with a camera. The apparatus was crude and filled with water, but a discernible image of the river bottom was obtained. The idea lay dormant for about 36 years. It was not until 1892 that a zoologist named Louis Boutan began to develop underwater photography as a method of documentation for his lectures and studies. His efforts included the development of various underwater cameras, photographic plates, underwater flashbulbs, and submersible floodlights. For his efforts, Boutan is recognized as the father of underwater photography.

The first underwater color photograph was taken approximately 30 years later in the 1920s by W. Longley. It took 30 more years and the invention of the Aqualung by Emil Gagnan and Jacques-Yves Cousteau to make diving accessible to the general public.

As stated in the beginning of this chapter, our interests and the material contained herein will focus on and be limited to relatively shallow water and documentary type of photography. Deep dives are usually not required by crime scene investigators documenting the location of weapons, stolen property, or bodies.

Prerequisites for Underwater Photography

Aerial photography does not require that you operate the aircraft. This is accomplished through the skills of your pilot and capability of the aircraft. Underwater photography is different in this respect. With the exception of very shallow water photography accomplished either by wading or from an overhead bridge span, the participant must be a competent swimmer and underwater diver as well as a photographer.

Whenever you enter into a different environment for which your body was not designed, there are hazards, risks, and restrictions involved. You must be both physically and mentally capable of venturing into and working within this medium. It is of utmost importance that you be familiar with the difficulties to be encountered and how to solve them. Enter a certified school and

Figure 5.11 Comparison of unpolarized (left) and polarized (right) photos of a weapon in shallow water.

learn correctly from the best instructors available. The same applies to your diving equipment and its maintenance. You should never stake your life on second-best information or second-hand equipment.

Categories of Underwater Photography

There are four methods of taking photos of underwater objects that a crime scene investigator may use. Two take place above the water's surface and two below. The equipment used for your regular investigative photography work can be used for the above-surface methods. The below-surface methods require specialized items.

Polarizing Filter

If you need to photograph an object submerged at shallow depth in relatively clear water, this can be accomplished using a polarizing filter. This filter eliminates the reflections of the water's surface, allowing the camera to see beneath it. This method is used when wading or from an elevation such as a bridge. Figure 5.11 shows the advantage of using polarized filter.

Viewing Box

Very few agencies have a glass-bottom boat at their disposal, but a glass-bottom box or tank may be useful and can be inexpensively made. The depth obtained by the enclosed camera is restricted by the height of the box and the depth into which you can wade. A black cover over the open end of the box or a polarizing filter will be necessary to eliminate reflections on the inside surface of the glass bottom.

Snorkel

A snorkel, which consists of a short breathing tube and mouthpiece, allows you to swim with your face just below the water's surface and still breathe surface air. With a snorkel and face mask, you can view the underwater scene below. Diving deeper below the surface is possible, but necessitates holding your breath.

Shallow dives (6-8 feet) permit use of rather inexpensive, flexible, water-tight housings for camera protection. Deeper dives with a snorkel require more sophisticated protection for all equipment. During these shallow dives, flash may not be needed if the water is clear enough for adequate sunlight penetration.

Self-Contained Underwater Breathing Apparatus (SCUBA)

The need to dive deeper or stay submerged for longer than you can hold your breath requires use of more elaborate training and equipment, both for diving and photography. Scuba diving equipment is necessary, as is hard-case protection of the underwater photography equipment. At greater depth, both diver and equipment must be able to withstand the additional pressure. Beyond approximately 6 feet, flash will be required for illumination of the subject and proper rendition of color.

Equipment

In the 1950s, with the explosion of interest in diving, photographic equipment available on the market was not suitable for the new field of underwater photography. Divers and photographers interested in taking underwater photos had to create their own waterproof housings and special equipment. Today, you may choose from a plethora of excellent equipment available to fill all needs.

Three Approaches to Underwater Photography

When deciding on a camera to purchase for underwater photography, you have a choice of three approaches to take. Each has its good and bad points. The three variations are explained below.

Personal Adaptation of Regular Camera.   The first possibility is to use existing above-water equipment or to purchase a regular camera/lens combination and personally convert or adapt it to underwater use. At first, this may seem to be the easiest and cheapest way out. This may be true if you have considerable time, talent, and luck. Adaptation of above-water equipment to underwater use requires watertight housings capable of withstanding considerable pressure, even for shallow depth use. To prevent restricting your photographic capabilities and for overall convenience, underwater adjustment of focus, shutter speed, aperture, film advance, and shutter release functions should be possible from outside the housing. All controls and other access points that penetrate the housing must have watertight seals capable of withstanding the pressure.

Homemade housings have been made, and publications and craftsmen are available to assist the photographer. It still takes money and considerable time and effort. At the risk of offending all those who have successfully built their own equipment, there are alternatives that should be given consideration before attempting the homemade route.

Whether you build your housing or purchase it ready-made, a major contributor to the cost will be a curved-dome lens port. This curved port is necessary when using the extreme wide-angle lens. It eliminates the problem of blurred and distorted images with rainbow colors at the photo edges. If a wide angle is not to be used, the curved port is not required.

Commercial Adaptation of Regular Camera. In today's market, many professionally designed and manufactured watertight housings are available for various types of camera/lens combinations. These range from the small Instamatic type of camera up to the most sophisticated. The housings are constructed of a variety of plastics and metals with special glass or plastic lens ports suitable for quality photography. Metal housings are better as they minimize trouble with light reflections and condensation but are more expensive. Simple rubber or flexible plastic bags are suitable only for the shallowest snorkel operations.

Housings intended for smaller, simpler equipment are relatively inexpensive. Those that are designed for larger equipment and have more features are, naturally, more expensive. The less expensive housings may require setting exposures above the surface prior to diving. If your decision is to use your everyday photographic equipment for underwater use, a commercial housing is probably the best choice.

Before venturing into this, consider the following. Special tools are designed for every particular job. Others can be used, but they do not function as well nor do they provide the best results. The same is true regarding the use of above-water photographic equipment under water. It can be done and it will work with certain modifications, such as an extra-wide wide-angle lens which may not be suitable for use above water.

Figure 5.12 Underwater photo taken with inexpensive (less than $15.00) disposable waterproof camera.

Waterproof Camera.   The right tool for the job in this case is the waterproof underwater camera. No additional housings are required with these cameras, and they permit easier focusing and other adjustments of camera settings. The popular 35 mm format is available in waterproof equipment, ranging from a $15 disposable camera for use down to a depth of 8 feet, to the most sophisticated. Camera bodies adapt to a variety of lenses covering a wide range of focal lengths. This more sophisticated waterproof equipment fulfills the requirements for underwater photography from the surface to a depth of 150 feet, far deeper than you will probably ever have to venture. Figure 5.12 was taken with an inexpensive, disposable camera.

If your agency can justify and is willing to pay a little more for the highest-quality underwater photos, convenience for the diver-photographer, and reliability of equipment, the waterproof camera is the best choice in the long run. It is the best tool for the job.

Lenses

Focal Length.   The most useful lens that will produce the best results for investigative underwater photos is the close-up or wide-angle variety. If you intend to use your regular above-water camera, invest in a separate wide-angle lens for underwater photos. The wide capability needed under the water is much greater than that for wide angle photos taken in air.

Table 5.1 Comparison of Lenses: Focal Length and Angle of View Changes

Format	Focal Length		Angle of View	
	Above Water	Underwater	Above Water	Underwater
35 mm	21 mm	28 mm	92°	75°
	28 mm	37 mm	75°	60°
	35 mm	47 mm	63°	50°
	50 mm	67 mm	47°	36°
2¹/₄ × 2¹/₄ inch	38 mm	51 mm	93°	77°
	50 mm	67 mm	78°	62°
	60 mm	80 mm	68°	53°
	80 mm	106 mm	53°	41°

Water refracts light rays in a manner unlike glass or air, in that underwater objects are magnified. A shorter focal length lens will cover the same area underwater as a longer focal length accomplishes above water. The focal length increases and the angle of view narrows. A wide-angle lens tends to become a normal lens, and a normal lens tends to graduate toward a telephoto. For example, as shown in Table 5.1, a 21 mm lens has an underwater focal length equivalent to 28 mm, and the 21 mm angle of view is reduced from 92 degrees above water to 75 degrees underwater.

Lenses commonly used include 80 mm, 35 mm, 28 mm, 21 mm, and 15 mm. An extreme case would be a 7.5 mm fish-eye lens. This lens has very little use, if any, for underwater crime scene photography because of its inherent distortion. The 80 mm, 35 mm, and 28 mm can also be used above water.

Although a selection of various underwater lenses exists on the market, cost and limited usage will tend to restrict your purchase to one lens; a 35 mm f2.5 focus at nearly three feet. Local water clarity, however, may require getting closer and using a wider angle lens. Your local photo dealer can assist with this decision.

Aperture.   The reduced light penetration through water requires that lenses used for underwater photography have a large aperture; f2.8 or wider is recommended. The combination of large apertures and wide-angle lenses provides good depth of field.

It is highly recommended that a camera with a through-the-lens meter be used. If this is not possible, satisfactory results can be obtained down to a depth of 3 feet by taking a light measurement above the surface. Open the aperture one more f-stop for each additional 3 feet of depth. In extremely clear water, this may be changed to one f-stop for each 10 feet of depth. When using this method, bracket each shot a minimum of one stop each way; two stops would offer more assurance of obtaining at least one satisfactory photo in each series. Variations in water clarity, light penetration, and so forth do not lend themselves to a foolproof rule to provide exposure calculations for high-quality photos under all conditions. Weather, overcast or clear skies, clarity of water, depth of subject, surface calmness, and angle of the sun are a few variables that will determine the outcome.

Filters

Because of the usually shallow depths encountered, most crime investigation underwater photography will not require use of filters. For those who wish to experiment and those who do photograph at greater depths, the following general information is provided. Make your own tests and final decision.

Polarizing Filters.   The use and effect of a polarizing filter used with both black-and-white and color film have been explained in detail under the section entitled Categories of Underwater Photography. Refer to that section for details.

Filters for Black-and-White Film.   Contrast will be increased by using yellow, orange, or red filters. The disadvantage is that blue objects and background become darkened to the point of appearing to be black. It may be better to correct contrast during print development.

Filters for Daylight Color Film.   Water quickly absorbs the color red, leaving a bluish-green color. The greater the depth, the greater the loss of red, yellow, and green. When photographing with natural light at depth, color-compensating red (CC30R) for blue cast and magenta (CC30M) for green cast will eliminate the cyan bluish-green cast associated with underwater photography. Usually this is a problem with shots covering a considerable distance, not with close-up work. On the other hand, an overall blue or green color may be desirable and acceptable for those occasionally longer-range shots. The need for compensating filters is eliminated if artificial lighting such as electronic flash is used.

Film

Black-and-White Film.   When shooting black-and-white film in shallow water and/or good light conditions, a film speed of ASA 125 may be used. When depth increases and light diminishes, a faster film with a speed of around ASA 400 may be necessary. The faster film will have less contrast, but this can be remedied in the darkroom when developing prints.

Color.   The type of color film to use will depend on the end product desired. For color slides, a transparency film with a speed of ASA 64 is usually sufficient. The same speed applies to color negative film for those desiring color prints. These ratings should be considered as a minimum. Faster professional films, with speeds up to ASA 3200, are available and their use will be mandatory as underwater conditions deteriorate. Push processing by photo labs can provide results equal to those obtained by using faster films.

Light Meter

Some method of reading light intensity is necessary for quality underwater photography. The best is a metering feature built into the camera. The second best is to have a separate meter enclosed in the same waterproof housing as the camera. If not enclosed within, the meter should be attached to the outside to prevent loss. A separate hand-held meter may also be used, but it is inconvenient and must be protected the same as the camera.

Special underwater light meters are available on the market. An ordinary light meter may be used underwater if protected by a plastic enclosure or sealed inside a glass jar. Such arrangements should be watertight to around 30 feet in depth. Below this depth, it is advisable to use underwater meters designed and protected for the greater pressure.

Artificial Lighting

Natural sunlight is rapidly absorbed or scattered by the very nature of water. The angle of the sun, clarity, and surface condition have a great effect on depth of penetration. Even though underwater investigative photography is usually done at a relatively shallow depth, the use of artificial light is quite often essential for two reasons. The first is to illuminate the subject, the second reason is to obtain true color of underwater objects and surroundings.

Light from a flash produces all the wavelengths of the spectrum and, therefore, reflects true color without the use of compensating filters. This is a necessity at depths where daylight rays of red, orange, and yellow have been filtered out by the water, leaving predominantly blue and green rays. Even in the clearest waters, only blue and green wave lengths penetrate at a depth of 30 feet.

Electronic Flash. Correct illumination based on a preset aperture can be obtained through the use of a semiautomatic camera coupled to a dedicated flash. Although not an absolute requirement, the dedicated flash is helpful.

With a camera utilizing leaf shutters, the electronic flash can be synchronized to a variety of shutter speeds. It is not restricted to the required focal-plane shutter synchronization speed of 1/60 second.

Electronic flash does not have the disposal problem associated with used flashcubes or flashbulbs. The long-term cost of electronic flash usually is less than that of flashbulbs, especially if a large number of photos is being taken.

Flashcubes and Flashbulbs.   Some diver-photographers prefer flashcubes or flashbulbs over electronic flash, one of the reasons being that they can provide adequate, but not overpowering light. Flashcubes, having four individual mini-bulbs, put out sufficient light for most short-range underwater shots. If additional light is required, an adapter makes it possible to fire the larger M-5 bulbs in the same gun. A coiled sync cord permits positioning the flash gun in the most desirable location.

When photographing at a distance of less than five feet, blue bulbs should be used. The same applies to flashcubes, which should have a blue shield over the clear bulbs. However, to achieve truer, less blue color when photographing beyond five feet of distance, clear bulbs should be used. Another method is to remove the blue casting from bulbs and the blue shield from flashcubes.

Using flashbulbs with a focal-plane shutter camera permits flash synchronization at shutter speeds other than the 1/60 second required for electronic flash.

One last note on the subject is needed. It is the responsibility of the photographer not to litter the underwater environment with expended bulbs or cubes. Bring them out with you and dispose of them properly.

Positioning of Artificial Light Source

When photographing underwater with flash, the same problems are experienced as when taking flash photos during a blizzard or heavy rainstorm. Particles in the water are like snowflakes and raindrops: they reflect light back to the camera lens, obscuring the image with spots and haze. This is referred to as *backscatter*. Backscatter should always be considered a potential problem. It is rare that you will encounter water in its natural state that does not have suspended particles of one sort or another.

To eliminate the backscatter or blizzard problem, the same prevention tactics that apply above water apply under water as well. The flash attachment should be permanently mounted or hand held so that it will be close to the subject but off to one side, angling the light at 30 to 45 degrees toward the subject. This positioning also improves the quality of the photo by accentuating textures and depth perception and lessening color fade-out. Both flash and camera should be as close to the subject as possible to reduce the amount of material interference and obtain the best color. Distances of one or two feet are not uncommon.

Calculating Flash Exposure

When it is necessary to manually calculate the flash exposure, two rules of thumb can be used. Under favorable conditions, when the subject is relatively shallow, clarity of water and visibility are good, and the actual distance from lens to subject can be measured, divide the regular combination film-and-flashbulb guide number by three. For example, instead of using a guide number of 120 in air, use 40 for underwater. Divide the actual measured distance in feet into the underwater guide number to obtain the flash exposure.

The second method may be used when focusing the camera on the subject. The distance thereby indicated on the lens scale is the apparent distance to the subject as seen through the water by the camera. In this case, divide the regular above-water guide number of 120 by 3.9 or 4. The resulting underwater guide number will be approximately 30. Divide the focused apparent distance indicated on the lens scale into the underwater guide number for the flash exposure.

Do not neglect to bracket your exposures to compensate for inconsistencies in conditions.

Accessories

The accessories associated with underwater photography usually pertain to activities above water (e.g., keeping equipment protected from bumps, temperature extremes, water, and grit). A hard, foam-lined case should be used to protect and store the camera, lens, and associated flash equipment. Film must also be protected, as heat and cold can have drastic effects on it. Consider using an insulated container for both exposed and unexposed film.

The film and the interior of the camera must be protected from water at all times, especially during reloading. Dry yourself off before starting reloading operations, especially your hands, heads, and hair. A supply of clean towels protected by a plastic bag should be part of the accessories. Refer to Chapter 2 for information on spare batteries and other related accessories.

A supply of extra watertight seals should be kept on hand for emergency replacement. A simple, inexpensive seal can make the difference between success of a dive and loss of expensive equipment. Along with the seals, keep a supply of seal lubricant or grease.

Focusing Underwater

Water causes light to produce some appearingly strange effects. Water causes light rays to be bent or refracted, which in turn causes objects to appear larger and about one-quarter closer to you than they actually are. With through-the-lens viewing, the camera sees as you do, so focus on the subject as it appears to your eye, not where it is actually located. If you are not using a TTL camera, set the lens for three-quarters the actual measured distance between object and lens. Rangefinder cameras are more difficult to focus, because the camera and the photographer's eye do not always see the same way.

Another focusing problem arises when the watertight camera housing prevents the photographer from getting his or her eye close to the viewer. Focusing becomes an educated guess. A device similar to the wire viewer on a press camera is sometimes mounted outside the housing in an attempt to improve the guesswork. In most cases, it is not very successful.

Underwater Visibility

Underwater visibility problems are similar to those associated with aerial visibility, but more severe. Water, being denser than air, contains more suspended material and resists the transmission of light more than air does. Visibility may vary from 200 feet or more in clear tropical waters to less than 20 feet where plankton growth and suspended minerals are heavy. Silty, polluted, and oily water may have a visibility range of a few inches to zero. Even in supposedly clear water, light penetration decreases rapidly with increase in depth, making use of flash necessary.

No matter how clear you think the water is, all underwater photos should be taken at short range, preferably with a wide-angle lens. Unless you photograph in exceptionally clear water, even the shortest range telephoto lens should not be considered for investigative underwater photography. Scattering and absorption of light rays and particles in the water tend to obscure a distant subject, much like the haze problem associated with aerial photography. Figures 5.13 and 5.14 are composites of several photos taken during the fire investigation of a burned and sunken yacht in Cayuga Lake, New York, at a depth of 60 feet. Note the poor visibility and need for close focusing.

Cold Weather Underwater Photography

Not all underwater photography is timed for the warm summer months. It may be necessary to submerge during cold weather, even when the water is iced over. Cold itself will not hurt the equipment, but it may slow down some of its functions as well as your own. Obtain instructions and training from individuals certified in cold-water diving prior to attempting it yourself.

There is one consolation about underwater photography when the surface is iced over and the weather is below freezing: it is warmer underwater than above. If it was not above freezing temperature, it would be frozen solid. For example, lake water below the ice will be in the range of 39 degrees Fahrenheit. Obviously, it is necessary to be attired in suitable cold-water wetsuits and related scuba equipment. Lifelines are mandatory for safety and for finding your way back to the entrance hole. Disorientation and panic can occur quickly under the ice without such aids.

Operation of camera controls and other functions will be sluggish as lubricants become stiff. This problem can be reduced if the equipment is

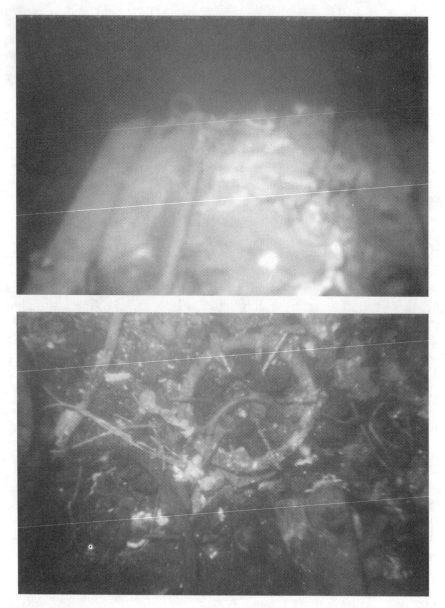

Figure 5.13 Underwater fire investigation photos of a burned and sunken yacht in Cayuga Lake, New York, at a depth of 60 feet; Ford engine (top) and stove burner grate (bottom).

winterized in advance by an authorized dealer or repair service. Power supplies for flash, motor drives, automatic camera functions, and so forth become drained faster and take longer to regenerate. Spares that have been kept warm should be available for replacement if needed.

Figure 5.14 Underwater fire investigation photos of a burned and sunken yacht in Cayuga Lake, New York, at a depth of 60 feet; toaster oven (top) and bilge pump (bottom).

Film becomes more brittle the colder it gets. It should always be advanced and rewound slowly without forcing it in order to prevent tearing it out of the sprocket, perforations, and generating static electricity, which will mark the film.

Try to avoid moving the camera equipment in and out of the water repeatedly. The more it is exposed to different temperatures, the greater the chance for condensation to form inside the housing and on the lens. The equipment should not be overheated (e.g., by setting it near a car heater) prior to submergence. Likewise, it should not be brought from the cold directly into a warm environment. Make both transitions gradually to allow the internal temperature of the equipment to neutralize.

Summary

The following tips will help the crime scene investigator to produce acceptable underwater photos.

1. It is as difficult to prevent movement of underwater cameras as it is to prevent vibration of aerial cameras. Use the fastest shutter speed possible under prevailing conditions.
2. If possible, photograph between 10:00 a.m. and 2:00 p.m., when the sun is high and the water surface is calm, for greatest light penetration.
3. Work as close to the photo subject as possible.
4. Use film with the greatest number of frames to minimize the need to surface to reload.
5. Bracket exposures by at least one or two f-stops.
6. Do not photograph straight down with the light source directly behind you, such as when snorkeling; shoot the subject at an angle for contrast and depth.
7. Become proficient with the equipment. Practice in natural outdoor bodies of water during summer and use indoor pools during cold weather.
8. Study other publications on the art of diving, diving equipment, photography in general, and underwater and related equipment.
9. Maintain all your equipment in the best possible condition.
10. Use a wide-angle lens and fast shutter speed.
11. Always test equipment for water tightness prior to submerging.
12. Think safety at all times.

Suggested Reading

B+W Filterfabrik. *The B+W Program.* Wiesbaden, Germany: 1978.

Bailey, A., and Holloway, A. *The Book of Color Photography.* New York: Alfred A. Knopf, 1979.

Bauer, E. A. *Hunting with a Camera.* New York: Winchester Press, 1974.

Bauer, E. A. *Outdoor Photography.* New York: Sunrise Books/E.P. Dutton & Co., 1974.

Cougin, J. *Conklin Creative Filter System*. Paris: 1978.

Eastman Kodak Consumer Markets Division. *Adventures in Color Photography*. Rochester, NY: 1976.

Eastman Kodak Consumer Markets Division. *Filters and Lens Attachments*. Rochester, NY: 1975.

Eastman Kodak Consumer Markets Division. *Kodak Master Photo Guide*. Rochester, NY: 1976.

Hedgecol, J., and Freisidder, J. *The Art of Color Photography*. New York: Simon and Schuster, 1978.

Hoya Corporation. *Hoya HMC Filters*. Tokyo: 1975.

Kinne, R. *The Complete Book of Nature Photography*. Garden City, NY: American Photographic Book Publishing Co., 1975.

Langford, M. *The Master Guide to Photography*. New York: Alfred A. Knopf, 1982.

Oberrecht, K. *The Outdoor Photographer's Handbook*. New York: Winchester Press, 1979.

Pfeiffer, C. B. *Field Guide to Outdoor Photography*. Harrisburg, PA: Stackpole Books, 1977.

Time-Life Books (Eds.). *Photographing Nature*. Alexandria, VA: 1981.

Vivitar, Ponder, & Best, Inc. *A Guide to Filters*. Santa Monica, CA: 1975.

Surveillance Photography

6

The methodology of surveillance photography is a secretive and continuous (or sometimes, periodic) visual documentation of activities involving persons, places, or objects of importance to an investigation. This type of photography is important in establishing identity and obtaining a permanent record of activities, in both criminal and civil court proceedings. Often surveillance will result in photographs of criminal activity in progress. Additionally, insurance industry surveillance may produce photographic documentation of fraudulent activity by an individual wrongfully claiming physical disabilities. This author has conducted numerous photographic surveillances involving fraudulent physical injury claims.

Before you embark on any surveillance assignment, know what photographic equipment is needed and how to use it. Do not forget the film! A faster film is usually desirable. ISO 400 speed film has been found to be very satisfactory. Several faster films are indeed useful in this photographic technique, including ISO 800, 1000, 1600, 3200, and 6400. Depending on the method of surveillance — whether stationary (remote or manned), on foot, or mobile — you must choose the equipment best suited for the occasion. Be sure it is in working order, and that all those involved know how to operate their assigned cameras, lenses, and accessories. This should also involve testing the film under similar light conditions in a controlled situation. You will know what to expect from your film only after you have shot it. Chances of reshooting surveillance subjects are not very likely. Once on the job, your primary concerns will be getting the necessary photographic documentation *and* not having your covert activities discovered by your subject. Keep in mind that everything you are doing is a means to an end. The primary purpose of surveillance photography is to document evidence of importance to a criminal or civil legal proceeding. If your covert activities infringe upon the subjects' rights to privacy, or if you do not have court authorization to conduct certain surveillance techniques, you may jeopardize the entire case because your photographic evidence may be ruled inadmissible.

Figure 6.1 The small "throw-away" cameras in 35 mm format are easily concealed in the palm of your hand.

Cameras and Accessories for Surveillance Photography

Because surveillance work by its very nature is secretive, the equipment should be compact and easy to use and should produce accurate photographic documentation. The best all-around format camera is the 35 mm. Except for rare occasions when a smaller, concealable camera (110 mm) might be needed, the 35 mm format provides the greatest versatility in lenses and films. A number of small "throw-away" cameras easily concealed in the palm of your hand are available in 35 mm format with ASA 400 film (Figure 6.1). They have fixed lenses and are acceptable for foot surveillance where "point-and-shoot" techniques are the only recourse. Usually, you move with the subject at a slow pace with, perhaps, momentary stops, and distance will be an average of 5 to 20 feet.

The camera may be as basic to use as the manual type, in which focusing, lens settings, and shutter speed are all controlled by the operator. On the other hand, because of activity or in the case of a mobile surveillance, it may be preferable to use an autofocus, programmable camera. However, keep in mind that the more automatic the camera, the more batteries it requires and, consequently, the more things that can and will go wrong. Depending on weather conditions, you may find it advisable to carry spare batteries and a backup camera. Cold weather, rain, and snow have an adverse effect on the more sophisticated cameras.

With the advent of the videotape format (Beta, VHS, or camcorder), 16 mm motion picture filming has been for the most part eliminated. Video is cheaper and faster, and it does not require processing. Many video cameras have playback (preview) capabilities, which allow you to review what you have recorded. The relatively low light level (lux) is also an advantage because most video cameras will produce satisfactory results under less-than-ideal lighting conditions, indoors or out. Depending on the proximity to your subject, you may also be able to record valuable and incriminating conversations on the sound track.

Digital format photography combines film and video capabilities in that one may preview the images before storing them for downloading later.

For the most part, auxiliary lighting, electronic flash, bulbs, or strobes are out of the question. You must rely on available light from nature and, if you are fortunate, a strategically located streetlight or other form of illumination normally found in the area. Two exceptions would be the use of a light intensifier or starlight scope and infrared photographic techniques. Adapters are available to fit almost any 35 mm camera or video recorder with these low-light accessories. These techniques produce acceptable photographic documentation in those scenarios when extremely low-level light sources exist (i.e., stars, moon, minimal street lighting). However, they are not without limitations. The light intensifier is not suitable for identifying color because the picture produced has a light green tint. As for infrared photography, total darkness is required when loading infrared film into the camera. This is best accomplished with a black, light proof change bag. A specially equipped strobe light with Filter No. 87 is used for illumination. Care must be taken to avoid detection of the lighting in extremely dark situations. Bouncing the light off the ceiling or walls greatly reduces the chances of seeing the flash. Again, the end result is a black-and-white photograph not suitable for color identification.

A rule of thumb for selecting lenses is to use a wide-angle lens (28-35 mm) for close proximity surveillance. This gives the best overall coverage and detail. Telephoto and variable zoom lenses (80 mm and up) are used for extended distance photographic documentation. If you are on a limited budget, select a variable focal length lens that gives you both wide-angle and various telephoto capabilities (28 to 200 mm, etc.).

There are many accessories for aiding in the reduction of blurred photographs frequently encountered in low-light, slow shutter-speed photography. Tripods, monopods, straps, and shutter release cords are essential for the use of long focal-length lenses. A telephoto lens over 100 mm shot at slow shutter speeds (less than 1/30 second) can produce noticeable camera vibration. In situations where you find yourself without the aid of such devices, leaning against a building or any sturdy vertical support will help

Figure 6.2a The use of your elbows as a support for the camera is an effective substitute for a tripod or other stationary objects.

immensely to reduce movement. You may also steady your camera by lying over the hood of the car or even prone on the ground. A technique that will aid in slow-shutter, low-light photography work is learning to time your breathing with the squeeze of the shutter release. If you are in a situation where the subject matter does not allow for supporting the camera in any of the previously mentioned ways, use your elbows with controlled breathing in the following manner (Figures 6.2a and b). Supporting the camera in both hands, place your elbows against your ribs. As you focus, regulate your breathing so that you exhale as you squeeze the shutter release *slowly*. Sometimes it helps to count backwards: 3-2-1-squeeze. Try the mirror test to check for steadiness: tape a small mirror to the front of your camera. In a darkened room, direct the light from a flashlight toward the mirror. Hold the camera as you would for taking pictures and direct the reflected light so that you can see it on a wall. As you squeeze the camera shutter, watch the spot of light; if the spot jumps, you are moving the camera.

Films

If there is one constant about surveillance photography, it is the less-than-ideal lighting conditions. To compensate, use fast (high speed) film. Although high speed film is considered to be that over ISO 400, there are times when film such as ISO 200 or even 100 will be acceptable. Table 6.1 shows some suggested camera/lens settings for given film speeds (ISO).

Figure 6.2b Support the camera in both hands and place your elbows firmly against your ribs. As you focus, regulate your breathing to exhale and squeeze the shutter release simultaneously.

Table 6.1 Suggested Film Speed/F-Stop/Shutter Speed Combinations

Film Speed	Aperture (f-stop)	Shutter Speed
ISO 100	f5.6	1/60 sec
ISO 200	f5.6 to 8.0	1/60 sec
ISO 400	f11	1/60 sec
ISO 800	f16	1/60 sec
ISO 1000	f16	1/60 sec
ISO 1600	f22	1/60 sec
ISO 2400	f16	1/125 sec
ISO 3200	f16	1/250 sec
ISO 6400	f16	1/300 sec

Color or black-and-white film is no longer a serious question to ponder. Today's color film technology is greatly improved. In fact, it has been well over ten years since this author used black-and-white film. For photographic documentation to be a true and accurate representation, there is no question that color film is the best choice.

There are, however, some other films applicable to surveillance photography. Kodak 2475 recording film (ESTAR-AH Base) is rated at ISO 1000. This film is particularly sensitive to the red-orange area of the light spectrum emitted by most low-light incandescent lamps.

High-speed infrared films must be handled (loaded and unloaded) in total darkness. The film is sensitive to a range of electromagnetic radiation

Figure 6.3 Most 35 mm SLR camera lenses have a preset infrared index mark near the infinity mark as indicated by the arrow.

of the spectrum not visible to the human eye. Because surveillance photography is frequently conducted under less-than-ideal circumstances, a very handy accessory to consider, if using infrared film, is a light proof change bag. It can be used anywhere, thus eliminating darkroom loading and unloading of the camera. The use of infrared film also requires a minor adjustment in focusing. The lens-to-film distance must be adjusted by 0.25% because infrared radiation and visible light are refracted differently by the lens. Today's 35 mm SLR camera lenses have a preset infrared index mark near the infinity mark (see Figure 6.3). It is usually indicated by a red or orange dot or line. To focus for infrared film exposures, focus with a normal light source and then rotate the lens to the infrared index mark. Next, place the No. 87 filter over the lens. Bracket your shot by taking several additional shots with larger and smaller *f*-stops.

Photographic Techniques for Various Types of Surveillance

Although most surveillance photography is done from a fixed, predetermined location, there are times when photographic documentation is desirable during a moving surveillance. Whether the surveillance is on foot, a bicycle, or some form of vehicle, the following are some tried and true methods.

Moving Surveillance on Foot

In a one-person cover, the investigator keeps the subject in view at all times, preferably without being discovered. The equipment involved must be kept to

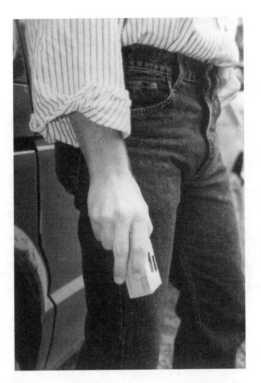

Figure 6.4 Candid photographs can be accomplished with the technique shown. With the camera concealed in your hand and held alongside your hip as you walk, aim the camera slightly upward.

a minimum, for both ease of use and inconspicuousness. The smaller and simpler the camera equipment, the better. Here is where the small "spy" format cameras come in handy. They are easily concealed and do not require focusing or setting f-stops. As mentioned earlier, the new throw-away cameras use ISO 400 film, and for under $10, they fit the need very nicely. They are fixed-focus cameras and cannot be used at distances closer than about five feet. The effective maximum range is approximately 20 feet, depending on available light. An effective technique for getting those difficult candid shots without giving up your anonymity is shooting from the hip (or its general area). It takes some practice to be sure you have the camera pointed in the right direction, but practice makes perfect. Use your natural hand preference (depending on whether you are right- or left-handed) and try shots in different directions: straight ahead, to the side, and to the rear. Hold the camera concealed alongside your hip, waist, or leg (Figure 6.4). As you walk, aim the camera in the direction of your subject. Depending on how close you are to the subject, try tilting the camera up slightly to avoid cutting off the subject's head (Figures 6.5 and 6.6). Use your imagination. It is the best tool in your bag of tricks for concealed photography. These small cameras can be used inside a pocket with a hole in it (Figure 6.7). How

Figure 6.5 If you are too close to your subject or the camera is not at the proper angle, the unfortunate results may look like this photograph. The subjects heads are missing and no identification is possible.

Figure 6.6 Practice with the camera tilted at various angles and try not to get too close to your subjects for best results.

Figure 6.7 These small cameras can also be concealed inside pockets of jackets and sweatshirts.

about a fake cast on your arm, or even a sling? In most situations of low or subdued lighting, such as a mall or well-lit parking lot, these cameras with ISO 400 film will produce satisfactory photographic documentation. These cameras do have limitations, however, particularly under long-distance and night photography conditions.

Two-Person Foot Surveillance

This technique affords better security against detection as well as less chance of losing the subject. Because one individual assumes the role of the tail or front person following the subject in close proximity, his primary responsibility is advising the second individual of the subject's whereabouts via two-way radio with an earphone. The second individual may remain some distance behind or even establish a checkpoint along the route as guided by the front person. From either of these vantage points, more sophisticated camera equipment can be used to get the necessary photographic documentation. Here, a 35 mm camera with telephoto or variable zoom lenses can be used with less suspicion on the part of the subject. You may even use the front person as a decoy to post near the subject: you pretend to be focusing on the decoy, but are actually including the subject in framing the photograph. This method also allows more latitude in choice of film. If you know the general time of day and location in advance, you can choose your equipment and film speed accordingly. Use a light meter to determine the actual light level and set your *f*-stop and shutter speed accordingly. For example, given a specific light level (overcast daylight) and knowing the subject will be approximately 100 feet away, you might use a 35 mm format camera with a 200 mm telephoto lens and ISO 400 color film. This would indicate an aperture setting of *f*-11 and shutter speed of 1/60 second. Do not forget one of the basic rules of forensic photography: *bracket your shot*. Take extra shots, one over the indicated setting (*f*-16 at 1/60 second) and one under (*f*-8 at 1/60 second).

Moving Surveillance with Vehicles

Whatever the vehicle (car, truck, van, boat, or aircraft), it will afford more opportunities to use a variety of photographic equipment — 35 mm cameras and videotape are very adaptable to this technique. In a vehicle, you may conduct part of the surveillance from behind or in front of the subject, or you can be stationary. Whatever the position, use your photographic ingenuity to get the one picture that will make your case. You can hand-hold your equipment or mount it in or on the vehicle.

There are many different types of mounts on the market that can be adapted to your vehicle. A big, adjustable tripod can be snugly fitted over the console of most vehicles with bucket seats (Figure 6.8). Figure 6.9 shows a table-edge mount which can be modified to fit on the edge of some dashboards or the window glass. When a camera is mounted on a door window, its height can be adjusted (Figure 6.10). A very inexpensive mounting material is Velcro. Affix one piece to the bottom of your camera and the other to the dashboard.

There are any number of ways to remotely trigger a camera mounted in a van, on the grill of a vehicle, or in cargo on the back of a pick up truck. Cable release, timed, or radio-transmitter triggering devices are just a few methods to use in conjunction with a motor drive or power winder on your camera. Also, do not forget the timer mode found on most modern cameras. This function allows you to trigger the shutter after about 10 seconds have elapsed without touching the camera.

The average automobile has several rearview mirrors, which can produce excellent reflective images of the subject. Use your 35 mm camera with a normal 45-55 mm lens or variable zoom lens, 28-70 mm up to 35-105 mm. Focus on the surface of the mirror (Figure 6.11).

Aerial surveillance techniques do not require special equipment. Many modern automatic focus 35 mm format and video cameras with high-speed

Figure 6.8 The use of a tripod over the console of most vehicles with bucket seats is very effective in stationary or moving photography from a vehicle.

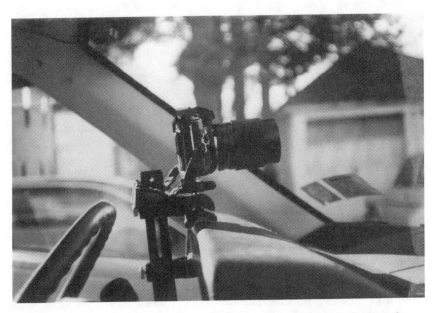

Figure 6.9 There are many commercially available mounting devices that can be modified to fit the dashboard of a vehicle.

Figure 6.10 There are also mounts that will work on window glass. When mounted on the door window, the height can be adjusted with the use of the window.

Figure 6.11 The use of rearview mirrors in surveillance photography can produce very effective reflective images of the subject.

film are fast enough to capture acceptable identification photographic documentation. Refer to Chapter 5, Aerial and Underwater Photography, for details of aerial techniques.

Fixed Surveillance

This form of surveillance may be either active or passive. An active situation requires the presence of an individual operating the camera/video equipment. Passive surveillance uses remote activation — for instance, infrared light, timers, or a radio transmitter — to activate a camera/video camera with a power winder or motor drive for situations that prohibit the presence of an individual.

Setting up this type of surveillance requires forethought. You must consider accessibility of your cover and visual obstructions. Again, a very important consideration that is easier to evaluate is the available light. Take some light level readings with a light meter and try a few test rolls of film to find the best photographic/videographic results. For example, your subject of interest is indoors, across the street from your vantage point. The light level reading should be taken at the source where the subject is located. Check the light level reading both inside and out near the window to see if light is lost because of the window glass (multipane, tinted, etc.), and use the lowest light reading. Try to get the photograph with the light source in front of the subject, avoiding a silhouette effect that would prevent successful identification. Obviously, this has to be done without drawing attention to your activities.

This type of photography requires telephoto and variable zoom lenses. Photographic surveillance work over distance will often encounter obstructions. Screens, fences, shrubs, and other interference can be eliminated by opening up the f-stop and focusing on the subject.

It cannot be stressed enough that success comes with practice and testing of your equipment and film. The use of high-speed film and push processing are commonplace. Push processing, which was mentioned in previous chapters, is a photographic laboratory technique that increases the film's effective speed. A typical roll of ISO 400 color film can be pushed to ISO 800 or ISO 1600. For each increase (push), you can increase the shutter speed by one setting. Pushing ISO 400 to ISO 800 would allow you to increase your shutter speed from 1/60 second to 1/125 second.

What's New?

As mentioned in the first edition, video image capturing has become commonplace with today's advances in computer and digital photographic technology. Refer to Chapter 10, Digitial Photography.

Suggested Reading

Duckworth, J. E. *Forensic Photography.* Springfield, IL: Charles C. Thomas, 1983.

Eastman Kodak. *Adventures in Existing-Light Photography.* Rochester, NY: 1977.

Giovia, S., Jr. *Surveillance Equipment and Techniques.* Hackensack, NJ: Bergen County Narcotics Task Force, 1987.

Mazzucca, V. *Aerial Surveillance Techniques* (unpublished). Available from T.L.I. Helicopters, Leonia, NJ.

Siljander, R. P. *Applied Police and Fire Photography.* Springfield, IL: Charles C. Thomas, 1976.

Photographic Aspects of Physical Injuries and Fatalities

7

In matters of trauma to the human body that may be of importance to a legal proceeding, it is critical that the evidence be documented in color. Preserving the physical evidence of violence to the body, whether accidental or intentional, requires strict attention to the smallest detail of trace evidence. If a person is suffering only from injuries that will heal in time, then accuracy in preserving the injuries photographically is paramount. In legal proceedings, it usually takes several years before any evidence is presented in a court of law. Obviously, the injuries will be healed or minimized over time and original photographs of the injuries represent the only graphic evidence.

Several considerations previously mentioned regarding documentation of the victim at the scene are repeated here to orient you with specific reference to close-up photographs of physical injuries. If possible, the following photographs should be taken:

1. Points of entry into structure/vehicle.
2. Any trace evidence at entry points to connect assailant and victim.
3. Victim's body in relation to any physical evidence (weapons, bloodstains, furniture, vehicles, etc.).
4. If incident scene is outdoors, overall photographs of scene to orient victim's location to points of reference such as buildings, vehicles, lighting, highway markers/signs, etc.
5. Indoor scenes should include complete photographic documentation of the room where the victim was found, particularly all four walls and ceiling from the perspective of victim's location. Include close-ups of any furniture or room contents that may be of evidentiary value.
6. In both exterior and interior scenes, be sure to thoroughly document evidence of activity by the victim and assailant prior to, during, and after the assault. This may include evidence of a struggle such as overturned furniture or broken windows, furniture, or other contents.

Figure 7.1 The position of a victim in a motor vehicle accident can often be identified by matching injuries with a particular object in the vehicle.

7. In a motor vehicle accident, be cognizant of items inside or outside the vehicle that may have caused a particular injury to the victim. The unique shape of the injury, its location on the victim, and the item on the vehicle responsible for the injury, when pictured together, can tell an important story about probable cause and responsibility (Figure 7.1).

8. Bloodstains at the scene can be the deciding factor in the final analysis of whether the event was an accident, suicide, or homicide. Photographic documentation of this evidence is the best method of preservation. Connecting photographs to additional bloodstain evidence on the victim and assailant, and the victim's wounds is critical.

See Chapter 8 for detailed techniques on the photographic preservation of bloodstains.

How do the previously mentioned photographic situations relate to the documentation of bodily injuries? You are telling a story, reconstructing the sequence of events that resulted in the injury or death of a victim or assailant. You cannot focus on an injury at the hospital or fatal wound at an autopsy without first laying the foundation for the sequence of events that led to the end result. You have to orient those who were not at the scene and are charged with determining the facts of the case in a court of law.

Some Factors to Consider

Because the subject of trauma to the body is so critical, its accurate photographic documentation must be accomplished on the first try; more often than not you will have only one opportunity. Two important considerations are lighting and film.

Lighting

Because you may not have any control over the ambient lighting conditions, you should be prepared to take corrective action, such as using specific film or filters. Lighting can be critical to the appearance of some injuries, and the use of certain film may adversely affect the results. For example, fluorescent lighting (frequently used at autopsies) can convey a greenish tint to your photographs. Also, postscene photography of injuries or fatal wounds is frequently done in bright white or stainless steel surroundings. These situations can produce problems with wash-out of detail (overexposure; Figure 7.2).

In low-light situations, such as motor vehicle/pedestrian accidents at night, often the only lighting may come from the vehicle's headlights. In such cases, the assignment would dictate the use of electronic flash or floodlighting to illuminate the scene.

The use of a light meter to take incident readings at the body's injury sites can improve photographic results (see Figure 7.3). Using the manual mode of your camera and the suggested f-stop and shutter speed will produce the desired photographic results. For example, the average incident reading of the light meter advises a shutter speed of 1/30 second and aperture setting of f 11. Because using the shutter speed of 1/30 second is inadvisable without additional support, a tripod may be in order. With a tripod, you can also bracket the shot with additional exposures of 1/15 second and 1/60 second at the f 11 aperture. If you use the built-in light meter of your 35 mm SLR camera, set it on automatic or program mode and get closer to the subject for your reading.

In the automatic mode, depending on your camera, you may select either the shutter speed or aperture setting. The program mode selects the best average exposure from the wide variety of selections preprogrammed into the camera. To reduce the problem of overexposure encountered with electronic flash, there are a few helpful techniques. One is to use a white reflective surface off which to bounce the flash held at an angle above the subject. A matte finish will soften the lighting (Figures 7.4a and 7.4b). A second method

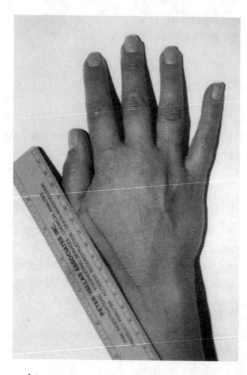

Figure 7.2 Photographing most scene injuries and fatal wounds is done in the presence of bright light or reflective surfaces that can produce a wash-out of the detail (overexposure).

is to cover the flash head with a layer of white tissue or a handkerchief. This will cut the light by as much as one or two stops, depending on the number of layers you use (Figures 7.5a and 7.5b). Also, remember that most electronic flash units have variable light-output settings for such photographic situations. Some units also have a diffuser to clip over the flash head for close-up subjects. In any case, read your owner's manual for helpful hints and instruction in the use of your equipment. In another technique, you can use the flash extension cord to remove the flash unit from the camera and hold it higher above the subject (Figures 7.6a and 7.6b). Be careful with this method; you may create unwanted shadows if the flash angle is too acute.

To bracket your shot when using an electronic flash, remember that your 35 mm SLR camera is synchronized with the flash at a predetermined shutter speed, usually 1/60 or 1/125 second. You can take the additional bracketing photographs by adjusting the f-stop one above and one under the suggested exposure. For example, the suggested f-stop is f 8; bracketed exposures would be one under, at f 5.6, and one over, at f 11. Follow the suggested settings on your flash unit or in the owner's manual.

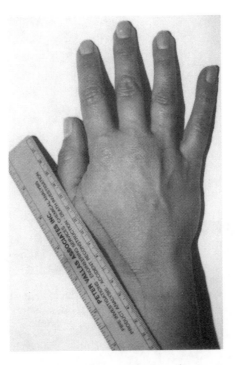

Figure 7.3 Satisfactory photographic results can be accomplished by using a light meter to take incident readings at the body's injury site. This can be done by using the light meter on an SLR camera to produce results similar to the above.

Film

Color is preferred over black-and-white film for documenting injuries. The color or change in color of certain trauma injuries can be an important factor. If inflammatory graphic photographs might not be acceptable in a certain jurisdiction, then it may be prudent to take a backup set in black-and-white.

As for selecting a particular film speed for the job, rely on your lighting source to help in the decision. A good, all-around film both in color or black-and-white is ISO 400. Other new products include ISO 800 and 1600 color reversal (slide) film and ISO 3200 and 6400 black-and-white. Remember, the higher the ISO rating (film speed), the better the chance of sacrifice in quality (increased graininess), particularly when enlarging photographs for courtroom presentations.

Generally speaking, your photographic subject will exert little or no movement, and with adequate lighting, you can use a lower ISO film speed. Also, with close-up photography, keep in mind the depth of field. Using

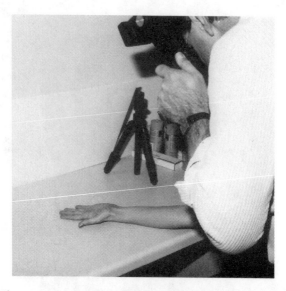

Figure 7.4a The use of a white reflective surface held at an angle above the subject will aid in bouncing flash lighting to reduce overexposure.

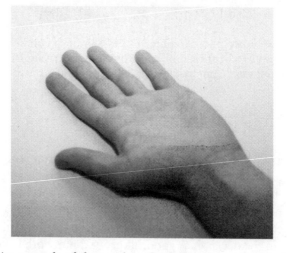

Figure 7.4b An example of the results achieved with the bounced flash lighting technique shown in Figure 7.4a

aperture settings of f11 to f16 should suffice for most situations. Adequate lighting should produce satisfactory shutter speeds of 1/30 to 1/125 second.

An additional technique worth noting involves the use of high speed infrared 4143 film and infrared reflectance photography to document invisible subcutaneous injury. Such injuries result in pooling or flow of blood often not visible on the surface (see Chapter 8).

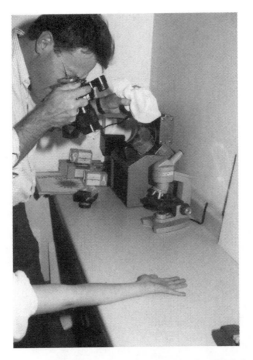

Figure 7.5a The use of a handkerchief folded over the flash head is effective in reducing overexposure of subject matter.

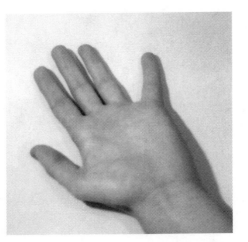

Figure 7.5b This photograph shows the results of use of the handkerchief technique shown in Figure 7.5a.

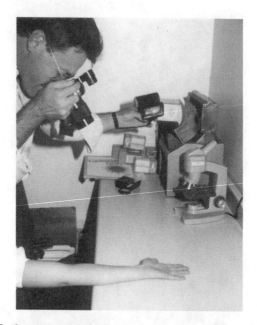

Figure 7.6a A flash extension cord will allow you to remove the flash unit from the camera and hold it above the subject matter.

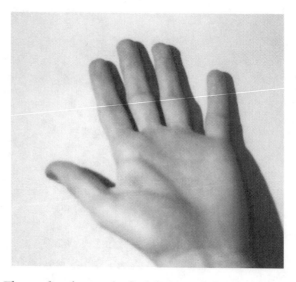

Figure 7.6b The results of using the flash lighting technique shown in Figure 7.6a.

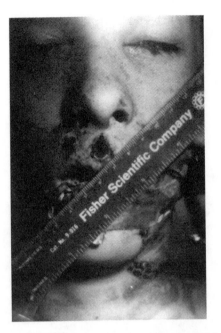
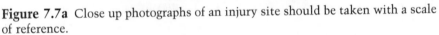

Figure 7.7a Close up photographs of an injury site should be taken with a scale of reference.

General Methodology

The following is a generally accepted list of steps to follow in the photography of injuries.

1. When in doubt about the correct exposure, always bracket your shot.
2. After overall photography of the victim, do a series of close-ups of the body, head to toe, with straight-on shots and profiles of the head.
3. After on-scene authorities charged with responsibility for the victim give approval to move the victim, photograph the process of removal as well as the area where the victim lay.
4. Get photographs of all injuries to the body, both with and without a scale of reference (Figures 7.7a and 7.7b).
5. Close-up photographs of injuries should include a scale of reference. They should follow photographs of the injury from normal distance. This is to avoid distorting the size or shape of the injury, and prevent misinterpretation.
6. Photograph all clothing involved.

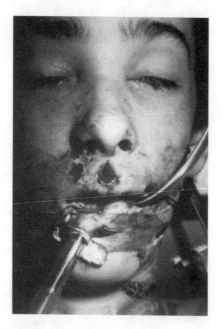

Figure 7.7b The injury site should also be documented without a scale of reference.

Accidental Injuries

In most cases, the victims will still be alive. They may also be in shock and/or a great deal of pain. Your duty of photographing the injuries may have to take a backseat to emergency medical treatment. Although your job may not seem of paramount importance to the victim, relatives, or emergency personnel, your photographs of the extrication process or the precarious position of the victim may prove extremely important in future court proceedings. For example, take the case of one of my colleagues who responded to an industrial accident. The victim was a man who worked for a large commercial bakery. During his routine work assignment, he would pour material into a hopper with an auger in the bottom. The man lost his balance, tumbled into the hopper headfirst, and became impaled on the auger. At the scene, my associate positioned himself at a vantage point that did not interfere with the rescue efforts. The results were a series of dramatic photographs documenting the cause of injuries, the rescue efforts, and injuries sustained (Figures 7.8a and 7.8b).

Be careful when using auxiliary lighting around the victim, particularly electronic flash. It may frighten the victim, and it could even cause further injury if the victim should make sudden movement when startled or if he has an eye injury.

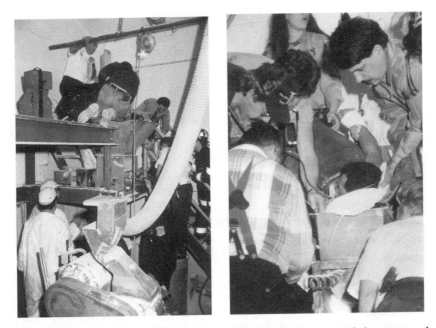

Figures 7.8a and 7.8b Graphic documentation of the cause of the injury, the rescue effort, and injuries sustained.

Assault

The same general rules apply as previously described under the heading of Accidental Injuries. In addition, the medical personnel in hospitals may be helpful when photographing injuries to private areas. A nurse or physician can be a helpful witness later if present during photographing of injuries sustained in or near the private areas of the body (groin, anus, or breasts). Never touch a victim's injuries.

Autopsy

As mentioned earlier, the background at an autopsy will tend to be light in color, resulting in unwanted reflection. To prevent overexposure, and because movement of the subject is now not a factor, you can use slower shutter speeds, a tripod, and ISO 100 speed film for most situations. The f-stop setting will vary depending on the light source and how close the camera is to the subject.

Sometimes it is practical and courteous for the photographer to use a variable zoom lens. A 28 mm wide-angle to 70 or 80 mm telephoto lens with macro capabilities is all you need to document your overall and close-up photographs. Using this method, you stay out of the way so the pathologist can do his job.

As the autopsy progresses, be sure to photograph step-by-step the examination of various injuries. This includes overall shots of the injury prior to any incisions or probing, and then close-ups of the wound site showing unique characteristics such as powder stippling, jagged edged incisions, or contact bruises from close-proximity firearm discharge. It is important to photographically differentiate between entrance and exit wounds from gunshots. This has often been the critical evidence that contradicts or confirms witnesses' statements as to accidental, suicidal, or homicidal intent.

Another unpleasant but nonetheless important subject at an autopsy is the photographic documentation of the body's state of decomposition. This is an important consideration, particularly when determining the type and state of development of insect larvae (maggots), which are very useful gauges in establishing the time of death.

If the subject was the victim of a fire, there are additional evidentiary considerations to document. In addition to the points of interest covered in Chapters 2 and 4, several points are unique to fatal fire victims. Fire by its very nature is destructive, and being able to recognize the difference between fire-caused injuries and other trauma takes experience and the benefit of witnessing many autopsies.

Injuries to the body such as skin splitting, blistering, pugilistic attitude, presence or absence of soot in the airway, and various degrees of burns (Figures 7.9-7.11) all play important roles in evaluating the cause and responsibility for the victim's demise. Many victims of foul play, who were initially thought to have succumbed to the ravages of fire, were later found to have been the victims of a homicide or suicide. A series of photographs documenting the condition of the face (nose and mouth), airway (trachea), and lungs can confirm whether the victim was alive or dead prior to the fire. The absence of combustion by-products (soot) in the air passages would confirm a victim's death occurred prior to exposure in a fire scene (See Color Figure 1.*) Another important photographic confirmation of a victim's status in a fire would be good color photographs of the internal organs (lungs, heart, etc.) showing the characteristic bright cherry red coloring caused by inhalation of carbon monoxide (CO) during the fire.

One additional subject that may be associated with an autopsy would be exhumation of bodies already interred for a period of time (Figure 7.12). I have witnessed not only the exhumation but also the subsequent autopsies of severely decomposed subjects. These photographic sessions are conducted in surroundings ranging from the most primitive, makeshift morgue in a

---

* Color figures follow page 206

Figure 7.9 Injuries such as the skin splitting require an experienced medical expert to differentiate between fire-caused injuries and wounds caused by blunt trauma or sharp objects such as knives.

tent at a cemetery to a typical hospital morgue. Again, a series of photographs showing the condition of the subject from the time the casket or vault was opened until completion of the autopsy should be taken.

Child Abuse/Neglect

This crime is receiving increased publicity and attention, not only by the legal community, but also the general public. In recent years national attention has been focused on this historically secretive crime. Reports of children being physically and sexually abused in day-care centers, at home, and in school have shaken the country and the family unit. I have investigated cases involving everything from scalding with hot water, to cigarette burns, to death by satanic ritual. There appears to be no limit to the trauma, pain, and suffering endured by innocent children at the hands of strangers, neighbors, more aggressive siblings, and, most frequently, parents or guardians.

The purpose of this preamble is to caution those who encounter this very sensitive photographic assignment. Your work will be under the scrutiny of

Figure 7.10 Blistering of the skin can aid in evaluating the injuries or death of a fire victim.

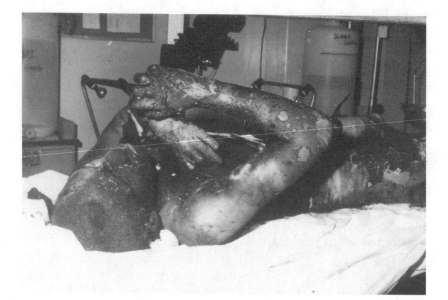

Figure 7.11 The pugilistic attitude of the fire victim's body is a normal consequence of exposure to heat and flame.

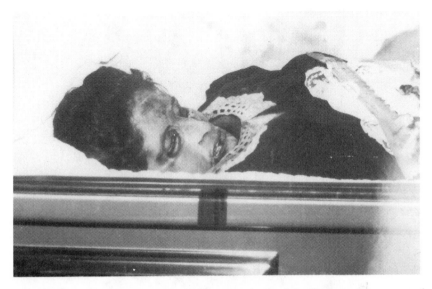

Figure 7.12 Although photographing an exhumed body may be extremely unpleasant, it is important to document the subject at the time of opening the casket or vault until completion of an autopsy.

many people. Because the objective is to document evidence of injuries and the objects responsible, you may find yourself in hostile surroundings with uncooperative victims and suspects.

Photographing children should be done preferably in the presence of a pediatrician or nurse. Never put yourself in the position of being alone with the victim during a photographic session. The same general rules previously mentioned regarding lighting and scale of reference also apply to photographing children.

Homicide

Because homicide victims are usually autopsied, it is not necessary to repeat the procedures noted in the Autopsy section. There are, however, some additional considerations important to photographic documentation of intentionally inflicted fatal wounds.

I become very frustrated every time I read about documentation of a cause of death that was bungled by poor — or worse, absent — investigation efforts by supposedly professional legal or medical personnel. My associates and I have been called upon many times to review cases of reported accidental or suicidal death only to uncover obvious evidence to the contrary.

Fortunately, in many cases, photographs and/or physical evidence were still available for our review. Even if the authorities were not sure what they

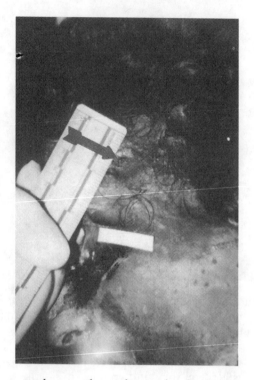

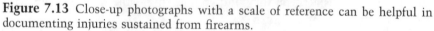

Figure 7.13 Close-up photographs with a scale of reference can be helpful in documenting injuries sustained from firearms.

were documenting, at least they took the time to preserve the scene, body, and whatever physical evidence was in the immediate vicinity with photography or videography.

However, for every homicide that we or others in the profession have resolved, how many victims have gone to the grave with their secrets?

It has been said that "dead men tell no tales," but in reality the opposite is true. Proper photographic documentation of the wounds and bloodstains can provide an amazingly accurate account of the events that transpired. Consideration of the type of wounds (gunshot, stabbing, ligature, or blunt instrument) and their location are of paramount importance in assessing the mechanism of death.

Both entrance and exit sites of gunshot wounds to the head, chest, or back should be documented. Close-up photographs with a scale of reference can help document the caliber of weapon, proximity of firearm (discharge distance), angle of trajectory, and position of assailant (Figure 7.13).

Close-up photographs of entrance wounds may document evidence of powder stippling (tattooing) caused by a relatively close discharge distance. These distances have been established for various caliber firearms including handguns, shotguns, and rifles. The lack of this evidence indicates a greater discharge distance (usually several feet) and usually precludes suicide. A contact wound, usually indicated by a bruise around the entrance site in the shape of the barrel, may be caused by either homicide or suicide. Be very careful in photographing these wounds and include a scale of reference.

Another important series of photographs should be taken of the hands (front and back) to document presence or absence of bloodstain backspatter. (See Chapter 8 on photographing bloodstain evidence.)

Stab wounds require a critical eye when documenting their number, location, and angle. The approximate depth as well as which hand the assailant used can be determined. Again, it is important to note and document other wounds in conjunction with stab wounds. Knife wounds to the palms of the hands, forearms, and fingers are usually defensive wounds. Sometimes the shape of the puncture wound can provide proof of the type of weapon — for instance, the X-shaped puncture from a Phillips-head screwdriver.

Homicide by ligature (strangulation) is often an attempt to simulate suicide by hanging. It is extremely important to carefully photograph the material still in place around the victim's neck. All too often, however, during the initial contact by emergency personnel, this evidence is discarded or cut off the victim before the investigator arrives. If still present, take particular care in documenting the material used, type of knot, and location of constriction. Note and document scratches and/or gouges around the bruise from the ligature. Often these injuries are self-inflicted by a homicide victim while struggling to free the ligature around his neck. This can be confirmed by close inspection of the victim's fingernails.

Homicides by hanging are relatively rare. Occasionally, accidental ligature death results from autoerotic behavior, generally in young men. Pay close attention to the details of knots and other forms of bondage, as well as any collection of sexually related paraphernalia in the immediate area of the body.

Manual strangulation (by hands) will produce characteristic subcutaneous tissue injury, which may not be initially visible to the eye; however, pronounced bruises are usually noted during autopsy. Photograph the bruises caused by fingernails and thumbs on the victim's neck, from the front as well as from both sides.

Suicide

The logical, common sense approach is to treat suicide as a homicide until proven otherwise. The photographic documentation is exactly the same for this mechanism of death as for homicide or accidental death. However, some additional types of injuries associated with suicide should be noted and photographed carefully.

Self-inflicted gunshot wounds are, almost without exception, very close range discharges. The short distance creates certain limitations on the angle of impact and, consequently, the spatter of bloodstains. The most common target is the head, and depending on the caliber of the firearm, the trauma can range from destruction to minute, single-entrance wounds that may go undetected in the hair and/or scalp. Remember your scale of reference when photographing these wounds; it is important in the later identification of gun caliber.

Again, as mentioned in reference to homicide firearm cases, it is important to photograph the hands of the victim. A characteristic of self-inflicted gunshots is the high-velocity blood spatter found on the thumb and index finger of the hand. Usually, the hand used to hold the handgun will have the predominant pattern. If a shotgun or rifle is used, both hands may show the characteristic backspatter of bloodstains (See Color Figure 2.*)

Suicide with a cutting instrument — whether a knife, razor, or piece of glass — usually leaves evidence commonly referred to as *hesitation marks*. These marks are usually numerous and parallel to each other.

Ligature strangulation as a means of suicide is very common. Anything that can be used as a ligature (e.g., rope, wire, shoelaces, belt, clothing, or bedding) is readily available. The photographic documentation includes the position of the body; standing in a doorway (flexing knees), sitting, kneeling, and even lying down are all typical suicide postures. Thoroughly document the type of knot without undoing the knot and, if necessary, the removal of the ligature. It is preferred that the ligature be cut at a point where the knot will not be altered.

Regardless of the method of suicide, always look for a suicide note. A very large percentage of suicide victims leave notes. Photograph the place where it was found. I once investigated a suicide where the victim left a 10-page note by the typewriter. Photograph all pages of the note, in case something happens to them. If the note is handwritten, find another copy of the victim's handwriting for comparison purposes. (See Chapter 8 for techniques of photographing documents.)

Suggested Reading

Duckworth, J. E. *Forensic Photography*. Springfield, IL: Charles C. Thomas, 1983.

Moenssens, A. A., Inbau, F. E., and Starrs, J. S. *Scientific Evidence in Criminal Cases*, 3rd ed. Mineola, NY: The Foundation Press, Inc., 1986.

* Color figures follow page 206

Evidence Documentation

8

Forensic photography is essential for documentation of physical evidence. Whether the photography is done during the collection and preservation at the scene or during evaluation in the laboratory, it permanently records the evidence at the scene. Enlarged photographs can be used for convenience in comparison of microscopic or fragile artifactual evidence. Photographs of physical evidence make the task of evidence analysis by several individuals at one time more practical. Obviously, photographic documentation reduces the consequences of damage or inadvertent loss of the evidence.

The subject of scene photography has been covered with great detail in previous chapters. Here we are concerned only with the scene documentation of the physical evidence after all preliminary work has been completed. The primary purpose is to identify the evidence at the scene in relation to important points of proof. Photographic documentation should include a scale of reference in one photograph to indicate the item's dimensions. A second photograph should be taken without the scale of reference to show the evidence as it was found.

Close-up photography should be done at the scene, particularly of evidence that may be destroyed or altered, such as bloodstains, latent fingerprints, or footprints. Any items of evidence that need further scrutiny can be taken to the laboratory to be photographed under ideal lighting conditions.

Some details of evidence, such as latent fingerprint ridges, tire marks, paint chips, glass, footprints, hairs, fibers, and bloodstains, require further scrutiny under a variety of special lighting and photographic examination techniques.

Image Magnification

The process of magnifying the images of small objects or areas of interest on larger objects can be accomplished by several methods. These photographs can be made with a 35 mm camera and, depending on your pocketbook, any of the following accessories.

Macro Lens

A wide variety of macro lenses, including macro-zoom lenses are available. A very versatile lens with both macro as well as zoom telephoto capabilities is a 28 to 70 mm lens with macro capabilities. There are several variations of this lens, but whatever your choice, it will be equally useful in the field and laboratory. It eliminates the necessity of carrying and interchanging lenses, which is inconvenient in a scene situation.

Lens Reversing Ring

This method involves reverse mounting of the normal lens so that the rear lens element is closer to the object being photographed.

Supplementary Close-Up Lens Set

These are usually sold in sets of 3 and the designated power of magnification is noted in diopters. A diopter is the magnification power of the lens with a focal length of 1 meter. The lenses are usually 1, 2, or 4 diopters and may be used singly or in combination. If you use them in combination, the highest diopter (power) lens should be placed next to the camera lens (lens + 4 + 2 + 1 = 7). This is a simple, inexpensive technique that does not require exposure compensation.

Adjustable Bellows

This device attaches to the camera body and allows you to use a variety of lenses ranging from normal 150 mm to macro. The bellows moves the lens farther from the film plane as a practical method of magnification. However, this method usually requires longer exposure time.

Extension Tubes

These also come in varying lengths and may be used in combination. As with bellows, they fit between the camera body and lens and perform basically the same function.

Infrared and Ultraviolet Illumination

These techniques are useful for recording latent evidence not readily visible. With the right combination of film, filters, and illumination, altered or illegible documents, old, weathered bloodstains, fingerprints, and many different material artifacts can be uncovered and preserved.

Infrared techniques were discussed in earlier chapters. Infrared radiation requires special high-speed infrared film, which must be handled very carefully (in total darkness) to ensure success. Remember to use a No. 87 filter over the camera lens to allow only the infrared light rays to be recorded. Gunshot residue analysis, document examination, ink comparison, and hair and fiber analysis have all found success with infrared illumination.

Ultraviolet light can be recorded on all types of film, both black-and-white and color. On color film, it appears as a light to bright blue. The usual light sources (electronic flash, arc lamps, and certain fluorescent bulbs) provide ultraviolet light. To record only the ultraviolet light, use a No. 18A LJV filter over the camera lens. Use a moderate to high speed film for recording ultraviolet radiation (ISO 200 to 800). The use of ultraviolet luminescence in document examination is very successful in uncovering erasures.

Still another technique, similar in principle but more frequently used in forensic engineering, is fluorescent dye penetration analysis for detecting material defects and failures.

Nondestructive Evaluation in Forensic Investigations

The science of forensic investigation improves as modern engineering technology gives birth to new, state-of-the-art instrumentation. It is of critical importance during forensic investigations, particularly in the beginning stages, that the evidence not be destroyed or altered by destructive testing in order to establish its material characteristics. Unfortunately, in past years a number of investigations in the field of forensic science were inconclusive because the reconstruction ability of the particular case was hindered by missing information. Unforeseen or careless use of destructive types of testing often prevented the preservation of the evidence for additional investigation that might have established the probable cause. Unintentional damage caused during testing has the potential to mask information vital to the investigation. It is essential to select the specific technique and technology that will provide the investigator with a quick, accurate answer and the proper, realistic, and truthful conclusion.

As technology advanced in the twentieth century, composite materials, plastics, and ceramics invaded the field of nondestructive examination, which was previously dominated by metals. Objects such as piping and castings for the transportation of liquids and chemicals, as well as electronic components, were once metallic but now are often plastic or ceramic. Common household items previously made of metal have been replaced in many instances by inexpensive plastics, that may suffer from improper or poor manufacturing quality-control procedures sometimes at the expense of the consumer.

During product liability investigations, it is extremely important to be able to segregate the probable cause from intentionally caused damage, inherent material defects, or failure caused by inherent material defects during normal or abnormal operating conditions. Visual examination and photographic documentation precede all other investigative techniques in order to establish a focal point, which is then pursued in order to establish a probable cause for a failure or an accident.

In numerous investigations, especially with regard to failure of ceramics and plastics, the most important visual aid could be provided by one of the nondestructive testing techniques, such as liquid penetrant inspection. Initial inspection by the unaided or optically aided eye, while unable to reveal the cause of crack initiation, would reveal the direction of a crack's progression in a plastic pipe or valve or in a utility-supplying ceramic enclosure. During visual and fluorescent liquid penetrant inspection and photography, the point where the failure occurred becomes evident with the aid of ambient or ultraviolet light. This provides a high-contrast image of the failure's characteristics and establishes, in addition to the origin of the crack defect, the pattern of crack progression, the direction of the crack progression, and whether it was caused by impact, a short-term failure, or a fatigue-induced failure. The last is normally found when cyclic stresses are applied to a material, rendering it susceptible to failure after an extended period of time (See Color Figure 3.*)

Liquid penetrant inspection involves the use of colored or fluorescent dyes suspended in a liquid to detect surface discontinuities. The penetrant is trapped in these discontinuities by capillary action on the surface of the part being inspected. After removal of the excess liquid, discontinuities are revealed by applying a developer that draws the trapped penetrant to the surface. Liquid penetrants are relatively easy to use and involve very simple principles; however, the inspection procedure and photographic documentation must be controlled. The penetrant inspection technique is widely used and is applicable to both metallic and nonmetallic materials, but should not be used on porous materials or materials that will be chemically altered by the penetrant. In some cases, extreme care must be taken to prevent an explosive reaction between the inspection materials and the materials that were or will be used in service. Vessels designed to contain liquid oxygen, for example, must be totally free of reactant penetrant, or the penetrant involved must be inert.

Penetrants can be used to locate only surface defects, and such defects must be sufficiently large to trap the suspended dyes. Some shallow defects, such as fine grinding cracks, may not allow penetrants to enter. The dimensions that can be detected vary widely, depending on the inspection techniques and materials. Cracks having a width of only 0.01 micron have been

* Color figures follow page 206

detected in laboratory tests using fluorescent penetrant techniques. In practice, however, the minimum detectable crack width should be considered larger than 0.01 micron. With colored dye penetrant, the minimum crack width should be 50 microns in any investigation.

The liquid penetrant process is relatively simple. There is no electrical system involved, and the equipment is simpler and less costly than for most nondestructive inspection methods. The liquid penetrant method does not depend on ferromagnetism, and the arrangement of the discontinuity is not a factor. The penetrant method is good for detecting surface flaws not only in nonmagnetic fields, but also in a variety of other nonmagnetic materials. Penetrant inspection is also used with items made of ferromagnetic steels in some instances. Its sensitivity is greater than that of magnetic particle inspection. The major limitation in liquid penetrant inspection is that it can detect only those imperfections open to the surface. Some other method must be used for detecting subsurface defects or discontinuities. Another factor that may inhibit the effectiveness of liquid penetrant inspection is the surface roughness of the object being inspected. Extremely rough or porous surfaces are likely to produce false indications. The physical principle of liquid penetrant inspection depends merely on the liquid effectively wetting the surface of a solid specimen, flowing over the surface to form a continuous and reasonably uniform coating, and then migrating into cavities open to the surface.

The cavities of interest are usually exceedingly small and are often invisible to the unaided eye. The ability of a given liquid to flow over the surface and enter surface cavities depends principally on the cleanliness of the surface, configuration of the cavity, size of the cavity, surface tension of the liquid, and finally, the ability of the liquid to wet the surface.

The cohesive forces between molecules of a liquid cause surface tension. An example of the influence of surface tension is the tendency of free liquid, such as a drop of water, to contract into a sphere. In such a drop, the surface tension is counterbalanced by the internal hydrostatic pressure of the liquid. When the liquid comes into contact with the solid surface, the cohesive force responsible for surface tension competes with the adhesive force between the molecules of the liquid and the solid surface. These forces generally determine the contact angle between the liquid and the surface molecules.

If the contact angle is less than 90 degrees, the liquid is said to "wet" the surface or to have good wetting ability. If the angle is equal or greater than 90 degrees, the wetting ability is considered poor. Closely related to wetting ability is the phenomenon of capillary rise and depression. If the contact angle between the liquid and the wall of the capillary tube is less than 90 degrees — that is, if the liquid wets the tube wall — the liquid meniscus in the tube is concave, and the liquid rises in the tube. If the halo is equal to

90 degrees, there is no capillary depression rise. If the angle is greater than 90 degrees, the liquid is depressed in the tube and does not wet the tube wall, and the meniscus is convex. In capillary rise, the meniscus does not pull the liquid up the tube; rather, the hydrostatic pressure under the meniscus is reduced by the distribution of surface tension. In a concave surface, the liquid is pushed up the capillary tube by the hydraulically transmitted pressure of the atmosphere at the free surface of the liquid outside the capillary tube. The height to which the liquid rises is directly proportional to the surface tension of the liquid and the cosine of the angle of contact, and is inversely proportional to the density of the liquid and to the radius of the capillary tube. If the capillary tube is closed, the wetting liquid will still rise in the tube; however, there will be extra pressure resulting from the air and vapor compressed in the closed end of the tube, so the capillary rise will not be as great.

When using fluorescent liquid penetrant, certain procedures must be performed. First, the piece to be inspected must be completely clean and free of grease or any other blockage to the possible crack defect, which might not be visible to the free eye. The second most important thing is that the liquid penetrant should be applied and remain on the surface for approximately 15 to 30 minutes, allowing a good contact and capillary action into the most minute crack defects. After the "dwell time" (penetration time) of 15 to 30 minutes, the dye penetrant will have to be removed in a dark area where the ambient light is 10 percent or less under 3600 to 3800 angstrom unit ultraviolet light. Keep in mind that the inspector must be in the darkened area for at least seven minutes prior to the inspection so that his eyes can get accustomed to the darkness. Some of the penetrant can be removed by either solvent or by water, depending on whether it is solvent- or water-soluble. When you use water-washable penetrant, which is very popular, it is very important that you do not wash out any of the penetrant from the existing crack defects to avoid loss of definition. That is why the inspection has to be performed under 3800 angstrom wavelength ultraviolet light.

The item can initially be inspected while the washing is done, but to be certain about the total surface characteristics of the material, a period of air drying is required. If a dryer is used, do not exceed 107°C. The application of a nonaqueous developer would remove the trapped fluorescent dye by hygroscopic properties and display them on the inspected item's surface, making it possible to photograph the results of the inspection. Ultraviolet imaging photography does not necessarily require ultraviolet or infrared film. High-speed film, such as ASA 400, with a cable release seems to be sufficient after the camera is focused. It is extremely important that the camera remain motionless; therefore, a tripod is recommended.

Metallurgy as an Aid in Forensic Investigations

Metallurgical evaluation of an item, unlike the previously discussed inspection methods, is destructive to the material being tested. The science of metallurgy is essential in studying the structural characteristics or constitution of a metal or alloy in relation to its physical and mechanical properties. One important phase of this study is known as macroscopic investigation, which involves the visual observation and photographic documentation of the gross structural details of the metal, either with the unaided eye or with the aid of a low-power or binocular microscope. Because the attending magnifications are of low order, usually under 10×, macroscopic observations are somewhat limited as to the kinds of metallurgical data they reveal. This circumstance is considerably important in many instances. However, some metallic characteristics are best determined by such studies.

The most important part of metallography deals with the microscopic examination of the prepared metallic or nonmetallic specimen, employing magnifications with an optical microscope from 100× to as high as 2000× magnification. With state-of-the-art scanning electromicroscopy, we obtain greater than 20,000 to 30,000× magnification.

Such microscopic studies are of much broader scope than macroscopic examinations under appropriate observation conditions. They will reveal to the trained metallographer an abundance of constitutional information concerning the inspected item. Such structural characteristics as grain size, the size, shape, and distribution of secondary phases and nonmetallic inclusions, segregation, and other heterogeneous conditions will be clearly defined. All those factors profoundly influence the mechanical properties and behavioral characteristics of the metal. When photomicroscopic examination determines these or other constitutional features and the extent to which they exist in a microstructure, it is then possible to predict, with considerable accuracy, the behavior of the metal when used for a specific purpose. Of equal importance is the fact that, within limits, there is reflected in the microstructure an almost complete history of the mechanical and thermal treatment that the metal has received. It has been only through diligent microscopic study and photography of metals that many perplexing problems of physical metallurgy have been solved. It may be safely predicted that contributions to the field of physical metallurgy in the future will depend in part or solely upon structural evidence revealed by photomicrography.

It is our experience that little can be learned regarding the original structural characteristics of a metal specimen, such as electrical wiring, that has been subjected to or caused extreme heat. The wire will be rendered into a molten condition by the formation of molten beads at the ends or throughout its longitudinal axis. Therefore, only a microscopic examination will reveal whether the characteristics of the material show that the wire was victimized by induction overheating by an external fire, or that the wire was indeed the major contributing factor by causing electrical overload, such as a short or other previously undetectable anomaly.

None of this information can be learned unless the surface of the item to be examined is first prepared so that it is flaw-free to the naked eye. This requires rigorous preparation. With the use of the modern metallurgical microscope and its precision optical parts, that allow resolution as great as a fraction of a wavelength of light, it becomes evident that perfect specimen preparation is of the greatest importance. Improper preparation is likely to remove all important inclusions, erode grain boundaries, or temper hardened steel, so that upon microscopic examination the specimen will appear entirely different from a specimen is truly representative of the characteristic of the metal. Obviously, an examination of such a poorly prepared specimen will lead only to erroneous interpretations and unreliable conclusions.

In general, the procedure of specimen preparation first requires a flat, semipolished surface, which is obtained by grinding the specimen with a series of emery papers in decreasing grit size, or by grinding on suitable abrasive laps, followed by final fine polishing with one or more cloth-covered lap wheels. These operations ultimately produce a flat, scratch-free, mirror-like surface, which is required before it can be etched and the metallographic structure appropriately revealed and photographed.

Specimen preparation is a relatively simple procedure in principle, but in actuality, many difficulties may be encountered when carrying out the manipulations. At the outset, it must be emphasized that specimen preparation is still a technical art and carrying out the manipulations requires skill and dexterity on the part of the technician. Such skills can be attained and mastered only after continued practice. However, with state-of-the-art equipment in modern metallurgy, automatic and computer-controlled polishing equipment is already available. It is still up to the operator whether or not the automatic polishing system renders the prepared sample acceptable for study. The technician should never assume that automated polishing will solve all problems. After final preparation of, for example, an electrical copper wire that has suffered in service, the inspection can be performed by etching it with a properly prepared solution of, perhaps, water ammonium hydroxide and hydrogen peroxide to bring up some of the grainy structure of the material. The inspector or the metallographer will have to pay close attention to the revealed microstructure, noting the sizes of the grains, the difference in the sizes of grains near the surface as well as at the core of the wire itself, and whether the grain boundaries are separated or homogeneous. All these characteristics will provide information to the

Color Figure 1 Documenting the presence of soot in the airway of the fire victim is important in establishing whether the victim was dead before the fire or succumbed to the toxic products of combustion later during the fire.

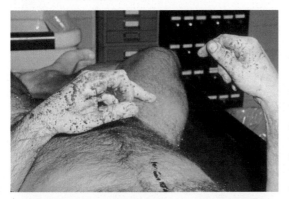

Color Figure 2 It is important to photograph the hands of a gunshot victim. As shown in this photograph, the hands of a suicide victim frequently show the characteristic backspatter of bloodstains.

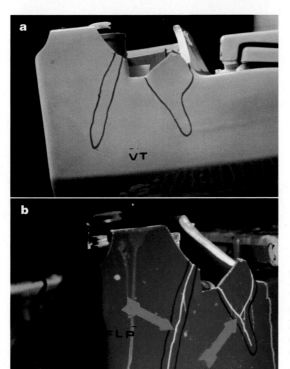

Color Figure 3a and 3b During visible (a) and fluorescent liquid penetrant (b) inspection and photography, the focal point where the failure occurred becomes evident with the aid of ambient or ultraviolet light.

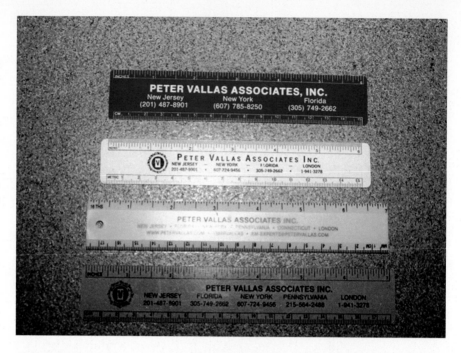

Color Figure 4 Experience has shown that colored rulers scaled in millimeters and inches work well to eliminate glare and provide a good guide for color reproduction.

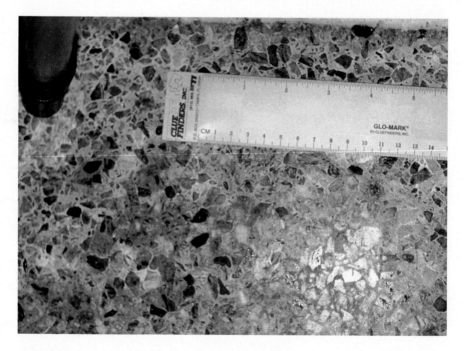

Color Figure 5 Luminol reagent is applied on objects or areas containing traces of suspected bloodstains. See Color Figure 6.

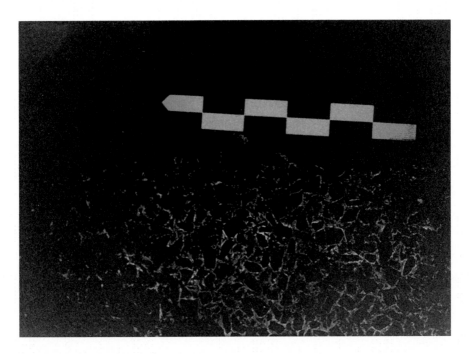

Color Figure 6 A bluish white luminescence or light production on a suspected area observed in the dark is a positive test.

Color Figure 7 Some examples of Luminol use include light tracing of blood on dark floors as depicted here on the bottom step and concrete floor of a carport, and areas where previous attempts to clean bloodstains are suspected.

Color Figure 8 Although not detectable with black and white film, it is possible to obtain a double image of the Luminol reaction and the object using 400 ASA color film.

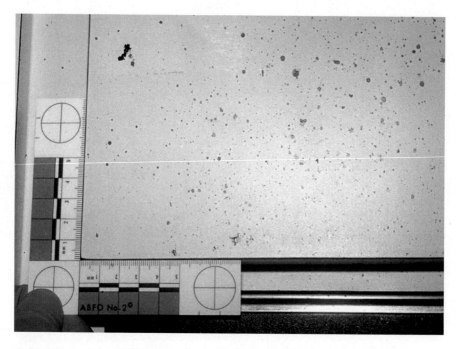

Color Figure 9 Impact spatter photographed with photo-macro graphic reference scale with three cross-hair circles useful for compensation of distortion.

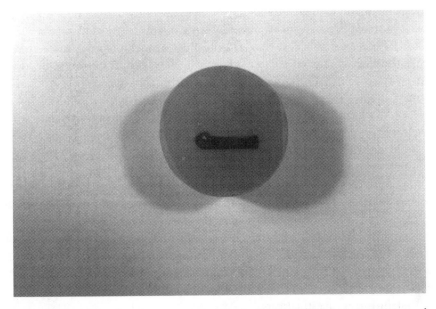

Figure 8.1 During visual examination and photographic documentation of a sample prior to micro preparation, we can already have a fairly good idea of the probable cause of failure. The purpose of preparing a micro sample, such as this beaded end of an electrical conductor, is to confirm theory rather than base a conclusion on an assumption.

metallographer, which will also serve as evidence for the determination of the probable cause of the wire failure.

Visual examination and photographic documentation of a sample may provide a fairly good idea of the probable cause of failure. The purpose of preparing a micro sample is to confirm that theory, not to base a conclusion on an assumption. Normally, when a wire is melted by greatly excessive current or overload, it tends to melt all the way through and lengthwise at the same time. When the wire finally falls apart, the current stops and the wire cools. Often there will be offsets where the wire started to fall apart when the current stopped. This can be found in copper, aluminum, or any other kind of wire (Figure 8.1). When evidence of overcurrent is found, fuses or circuit breakers should be checked. Arc marks indicate that the circuit was energized. Small, isolated arcs are not likely to start fires unless a very easily ignitable fuel is present. Massive arcs, such as those found in entry cables and service equipment, can start fires fairly easily. Fire melting can obliterate arc marks or any other effects that were present at the start of the fire. Thus, failure to find characteristic marks in fire-melted wires does not necessarily mean there were no arcs. This is a problem especially with aluminum wiring because it melts at relatively low temperature (1200°F). Fire melting can usually be distinguished from arc marks because fire affects a wider area. Fire melting of copper wire gives a gradation ranging from light oxidation to distortion of the surface or blistering to flow of metal. Under some conditions, the flow of melted copper leaves a surface with a thin neck. Beads in the pointed end are characteristic of melting on the surface above an unmelted core. Fire melting of copper wire is a function of the duration of the fire, the location of the wire, and the amount of protection of the wire.

In a normal building fire, the temperature in the upper part of a room or building will be higher than at lower parts. Melting of wire in the upper parts of the room or building is unusual and in the lower parts, almost nonexistent. Caution should be taken, as fire can cause arcing of a building's electrical wiring. This arcing can continue to destroy electrical wire from the original point of the fire-induced arc back toward the power supply. This arcing may or may not trip the circuit protective device. Careful investigation needs to be used here, as this arcing or melting can be mistakenly considered as the cause of the fire rather than a consequence of it. Consequences of the electrically caused fire or wiring victimized by fire can be easily distinguished by metallurgical investigations.

The responsibilities of the metallurgist are to be able to determine the condition of the sample, which suffered a type of melting or other deformation by fire — perhaps by arcing — to determine the probable cause, and to construct an unbiased report stating the cause within reasonable scientific and engineering probability. Based on the foregoing discussion, it should become obvious to the reader that a clue alone is not sufficient to classify a fire as electrical. The clue must be validated by proving the necessary physical cause and condition where present. If clues cannot be validated, the fire cause should not be listed as electrical. The physical condition at a fire scene, which provides clues may be caused by a fire of other than electrical origin.

It would be in the best interests of the forensic investigator to have at least a basic knowledge of nondestructive evaluation and metallurgical concepts. Such knowledge provides a reasonable choice for the particular type of investigative procedure which a specific case may require. The end result is an accurate and unbiased test result. Testing laboratories throughout the United States provide specialized education or assistance in the fields of nondestructive and destructive testing, fire investigation, and supplemental training to the forensic investigator. In view of the fact that the investigator's opinion will subsequently lead him to the witness stand during subrogation or litigation proceedings, he should be well prepared from the first day he sets foot on the scene until the day he sets foot on the witness stand. Without proper training, the investigator will be awkward and unqualified to contribute to the investigation, even if years of experience have provided him with a so-called gut feeling.

Thermographic Imaging

Because our senses are capable of recognizing changes in temperature, we have always been aware of thermal energy. Its physical nature became understood only as recently as 1800, when Sir William Herschel discovered the evidence of light outside the visible part of the electromagnetic spectrum. Herschel was the royal astronomer under King George III of England and made his discovery while experimenting with optical filters. A thermometer coincidentally placed in the vicinity made him aware of the evidence of radiant energy outside the range of visible colors. Because this energy occurred beyond the red, he named it *infrared* energy.

Several other scientists further explored the phenomenon of heat radiation during the remainder of the nineteenth century and developed instrumentation to accurately measure changes in radiant energy. The first "heat picture," using the principle of displaying differences in superficial heat emission from an object's surface, was created by Sir John Herschel (the son of Sir William Hershel) in 1840, when he exposed a thin oil film to infrared radiation, which caused a color pattern through the change of the oil film's refraction characteristics.

In the 1900s, infrared radiation took on practical significance with the application of very sensitive infrared radiation detectors for military reconnaissance purposes. These detectors were capable of detecting the heat emitted by a person from as far as 300 meters away. The further development of military night vision equipment remained secret while considerable progress was made in the production of increasingly sensitive detectors capable of registering small amounts of infrared radiation over very long distances. The general public became aware of the existence of this technology when infrared scanning systems for medical diagnostics were developed in the 1950s. The "thermograph" was capable of composing a black-and-white image in which variations in brightness corresponded to the intensity of heat emission from the human body, generally taking 15 minutes of slow scanning to build up the thermal pattern on photographic film.

The television type of scanning system introduced in 1965 used a cryogenically cooled photovoltaic detector capable of producing real-time heat pictures on a cathode-ray tube 16 times per second. Reduction in the size and weight of the apparatus made it possible to pursue and develop a market for this dynamic technology. During the decade following the unveiling of this advanced equipment, thermography was gradually recognized as a valuable tool for research and many aspects of industrial process operations. The electric utility industry recognized the benefits of heat detection as a way of preventing power failures after the total loss of electric power on the entire Eastern Seaboard of the United States, which was caused by the failure of a transmission line that triggered a chain reaction. Because component failure in a power distribution system is preceded by heat buildup caused by the reduced conductivity of a mechanically defective joint, the benefit of regular preventive maintenance through thermal imaging was quickly appreciated, and the practice of thermographing transmission and distribution systems was adopted throughout the industry.

Few stimuli can transfer more information to the human brain than can a good picture. The great power of sensitive infrared thermography not only generates good pictures, but the pictures graphically illustrate phenomena that are normally invisible, providing a powerful analytical tool for the solution of industrial problems.

Temperature is one of the most important variables of concern to industry. A significant portion of plant investment is spent on measurement and control of process temperature. Critical equipment is protected by temperature sensors coupled to alarm systems. Thermography is a remote means of measuring temperature and temperature differences. There is no contact between the event studied and the infrared sensing device. Temperature information is provided visually in the form of a picture, with gray scale variations representing temperature differences. With inframetrics equipment, temperature differences may also be presented across a section of the observed item (line scan mode). In either case, a real-time representation of the thermal events under study is developed in a form most readily accepted and understood by the observer. Thermography has limitations, as do all temperature sensing and measurement techniques. The observed radiometric temperature is affected by background temperature and emissivity. Thermographic information can be corrected for these factors, however.

Serious industrial investigative work requires thermally sensitive equipment and the ability to document observations photographically, with sufficient gray scale and spatial resolution to make the record understandable to the untrained eye.

After the documentation of several thousand electrical faults, conventional wisdom on electrical system problems is beginning to be at variance with experience. We often hear of electrical fires caused by short circuits related to insulation problems. However, less than one percent of low voltage electrical problems result directly from insulation failure. Problems almost always develop at connections. Resulting heat can cause insulation to deteriorate and fail with a resulting short circuit. The insulation alone was not the start of the problem, rather; a nearby connection was. In all of these cases, the thermographic process allowed the operator to precisely pinpoint the source of the problem, measure how serious the problem was, and generally recommend a cure.

Electrical preventive maintenance inspection using infrared equipment has become a highly competitive business. Electrical systems analysis was one of the earlier applications for infrared thermography.

In many ways, thermography remains an ingenious solution looking for problems to solve. A practical tool for industrial, research, medical, and forensic applications, thermography has become a critical and valuable source of information with unique possibilities.

Industrial Preventive Maintenance Inspections: Why Inspect?

Hidden facility and equipment problems exist in virtually every industry and plant. Unfortunately, very few are discovered and corrected through conventional maintenance procedures. Many go unnoticed until there is an operating failure, sometimes involving an on-the-job injury. At minimum, a failure means unscheduled repairs or equipment replacement and costly downtime.

The High Cost of "Hidden Costs"

In industrial plants, downtime costs $5000 to $50,000 per hour, or more. In addition to such unbudgeted costs, many plants incur energy losses from leaking steamlines and traps or from refractory problems, wet insulation, or electrical problems. Such situations are virtually invisible. Because they are ongoing, energy-related problems are generally even more costly.

The Right Equipment. Results depend on having the most sophisticated equipment available. Baird Infrared Technology, Inc., of Wilmington, Delaware, a specialist in industrial diagnostics, uses sensitive quantitative infrared imaging radiometers made by Inframetries, a U.S.-based company, the leader in this field. Inframetries radiometers are so advanced they can provide precise temperature resolution to 0.1°C.

Comprehensive Documentation

Real-time data are useful in spotting immediate problems. Potentially serious problems should be discussed with management before leaving the plant.

Preventive Maintenance Case Histories

Preventive maintenance inspections are conducted in a wide variety of industries and manufacturing operations. The following projects illustrate the kinds of situations that can be pinpointed.

1. While training a nondestructive engineering (NDE) group in infrared preventive maintenance, a potentially dangerous induction heating problem (232°C) was discovered in the isophase bus system at a nuclear plant. An outage resulting from this problem would have cost $1 million per day.

2. The temperature of a bolted pad connection on the load side of a 500 kv substation at a nuclear plant was 78°C higher than its neighbor. A failure would have caused a $1 million per day shutdown and could have caused extensive damage.

3. During start-up inspection of a major corporation's new computer center, a critical 6000 amp bus connection was found to be overheating by 90°C while under light load. Full load operation in this condition would have led to a $1 million burnout from outage and repair costs.

4. A utility power plant main unit 125 MVA transformer was discovered to have a hot bushing connection. Failure would have caused extensive damage and a shutdown.

5. In a city-owned utility system, significant revenues were lost from a customer whose meters were not functioning. Thermographic inspection pinpointed the problem as bad transformers.

6. A secondary bushing connection on a main substation transformer was found at 51°C above normal only one year after being found normal. A burnout would have shut down 28 production lines.

7. A 49°C rise on a high voltage bushing on a printing plant's main transformer could have shut down the operation if it had failed.

Equipment and Design Evaluation

When coupled with powerful computer-driven thermal analysis equipment, the new high-performance infrared imaging systems provide many new opportunities for electronic equipment evaluation.

1. By using economical infrared imaging techniques, clients have been helped to materially increase the salvage rates of expensive multilayer boards, both populated and unpopulated.

2. Infrared analysis techniques can be used to prove the thermal design of electronic components, ranging from microchips to complete assemblies.

3. In populated circuit boards, infrared inspection allows quantification and documentation of VCC-to-ground short circuits and even excessive current draws.

4. Sophisticated masking techniques permit fault screening of many different types of printed circuit boards against standard reference images.

5. Utilizing infrared imaging techniques, forensic investigators are able to recover residual evidence, predominantly in the electrical field, by establishing the probable presence of inherent wiring and structural defects. Reenergization of evidence should provide immediate and ample data to reveal electrical malfunctions in computer systems, circuit boards, and structural wiring systems.

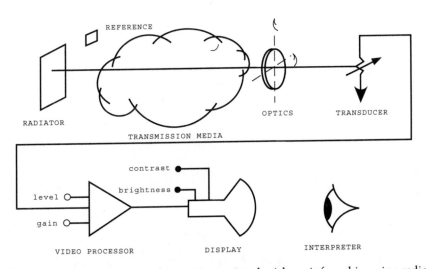

IFRARED IMAGING RADIOMETERS

Figure 8.2 The seven basic elements associated with an infrared imaging radiometer system are shown in the above illustration.

In fire investigations the question is, was the fire caused by electrical malfunction or did the fire cause the damage to the electrical system? Particularly in product liability cases, the search for the correct answer is essential. In order to establish the major contributory factor as well as the minor contributory cause for an assumed electrical fire, infrared imaging should provide the necessary tool for the evaluation.

In view of the severity of the problem normally accompanying investigation for probable cause, it is also mandatory that the investigator be well versed in the discipline he uses to determine cause within reasonable scientific and engineering probability.

Basic Radiometries Pertaining to Infrared Imaging Radiometers

The basic elements associated with an infrared imaging radiometer system are depicted in Figure 8.3. It is assumed initially that each of the seven cascaded elements shown has some meaning to the reader without explanation. The purpose of the treatise that follows is to expand upon this initial understanding with a series of brief discussions pertaining to the fundamental physical relationships of the elements involved. An attempt has been made here to introduce the subjects with simplistic mathematical expressions to allow the reader to quickly reach an overview understanding of the physics involved.

Unfortunately, the elements shown in Figure 8.2 tend to interrelate and, therefore, it is not possible to discuss each element independently. To the

MEASUREMENT MODES

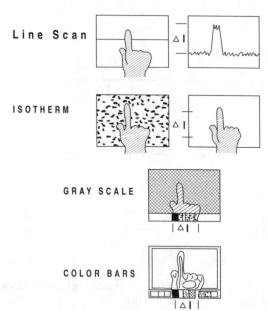

Line Scan

ISOTHERM

GRAY SCALE

COLOR BARS

Figure 8.3 Since the image is a crucial part of an imaging radiometer system, the measurement reading must be displayed in a manner that will complement the image, as shown above in the four commonly used methods of displaying the measurement without destroying the image content.

extent possible, the order of presentation start with the radiator in the upper left and works through the system to the interpreter in the lower right.

Thermographic imaging depends primarily on heat absorption and its point of origin. All bodies above a temperature of absolute zero (−270°C) continuously generate and emit electromagnetic radiation by virtue of the motion of the constituent atoms and molecules. Infrared radiation (heat radiation) is part of this electromagnetic spectrum, with wavelengths ranging from 0.76×10 meters to 10 meters (0.76 to 1000 microns). Thermal agitation of these molecules within a material increases when temperatures increase and decrease. When the temperature is reduced to absolute zero, no electromagnetic radiation is emitted because all molecular activity ceases.

Referring to Figure 8.2, the topics covered pertain generally to the radiator; the transmission media, optics, and transducer; the optics, transducer, video processor, display, and interpreter; and the radiator through the interpreter.

Table 8.1 is a listing of the basic equations used to characterize the elements of the imaging radiometer system. For the most part, they are commonly used expressions and are referenced in the glossary. Unfortunately, the topics cover a rather diverse set of disciplines and no single text compiles cursory material for all subjects involved with imaging radiometry.

Table 8.1 Basic Radiometric Relationships for Thermographic Applications

Fig. #	Name	Relationship	Units	Ref.
2, 3a	Spectral radiance	$N_\lambda = \dfrac{\varepsilon(1.2 \times 10^4)}{\lambda^5(e^{1.4 \times 10^4/(\lambda T)} - 1)}$	watts/cm² microns	35; 1–18
3a, 3b	Photon energy	$P = hc/\lambda = 6.6 \times 10^{\delta\lambda}\, c/\lambda$	joules/photon	5; 57
3b	Photon spectral radiance	$Q_\lambda = (\lambda/hc)N_\lambda$	photons/sec – cm² microns	35; 1–18
2, 11	Kirchoff's Law	$\varepsilon + \rho + \tau = 1$ for steady state where $\alpha = \varepsilon$	unitless	5; 106.2
4	Stephan-Boltzman law	$N = \int_0^\infty N_\lambda d_\lambda = 6T^4 = 5.67 \times 10^{-12} T^4$	watts/cm²	35; 1–18
4	Stephan-Boltzman photon law	$Q = \int_0^\infty (\lambda/hc)N_\lambda d_\lambda = 1.52 \times 10^{11} T^3$	photons/sec – cm²	35; 1–18
	Greybody transmission	$\tau = e^{-at}$	unitless	5; 30
7, 8	Spectral transmission (atmosphere)	$\tau_\lambda = e^{-a_\lambda t}$	unitless	5; 30
9	In-band radiance	$N_{\Delta\lambda} = \int_{\lambda_1}^{\lambda_2} \varepsilon_\lambda N_\lambda d_\lambda$	watts/cm²	36; 1
9	In-band photon radiance	$Q_{\Delta\lambda} = \int_{\lambda_1}^{\lambda_1} \varepsilon_\lambda (\lambda/hc) N_\lambda d_\lambda$	photons/sec – cm²	36; 1
10	In-band photon radiance for small ΔT	$Q_{\Delta\lambda} = \varepsilon_{\Delta\lambda}(\lambda/hc)C_{\Delta\lambda}T^{h_{\Delta\lambda}}$	photons/sec – cm²	37; 9
10	In-band photon contrast with ΔT	$\Delta Q_{\Delta\lambda}/\Delta T = \varepsilon_{\Delta\lambda}(\lambda/hc)h_{\Delta\lambda}C_{\Delta\lambda}T^{(n_{\Delta\lambda}-2)}$	photons/sec – cm – °k	37; 9
12, 13	In-band photon radiosity	$J_{\Delta\lambda} = (1-\varepsilon)Q_{\Delta\lambda}T_\beta + \varepsilon Q_{\Delta\lambda T_5}$	photons/sec – cm²	Eq. IV-1
14b	Lambert's law	$Q(\phi) = Q_\Delta Cos\phi$	photons/sec – cm²	5; 113
18	Lambertian photon radiance	$Q = Q/\pi$	photons/sec – cm² str	5; 113
19	Resolution element (IFOV)	$IFOV = ld/f_1 = w$	milradian	—
19	Detection photon irradiance (w/o atmosphere)	$R = (w^2D^2)(Ap/D^2)(J_{\Delta\lambda}/\pi)$	photons/sec	—

Table 8.1 Basic Radiometric Relationships for Thermographic Applications (*continued*)

Fig. #	Name	Relationship	Units	Ref.
20	Reflection at optical element surface (normal incidence)	$\rho = (h-1)^2/(h+1)^2$	unitless	35; 7–10
20	Transmission through an uncoated optical element (normal incidence, parallel faces)	$\tau = 2n/(n^2+1)$	unitless	35; 7–10
23	Detector spectral responsivity	$R \approx \lambda/\lambda_p\, R_p$ for $\lambda < \lambda_p$ $R \approx 0$ for $\lambda > \lambda_p$	υ watt-micron	—
24	Detector spectral photons responsivity	$R_q \approx R_{qp}$ for $\lambda < \lambda_p$ $R_q \approx 0$ for $\lambda > \lambda_p$	v-sec/photon-micron	—
26a & b	System response (with atmospheric radiance)	$v_c = R_q(\varepsilon_a Q_a + \gamma_a R)$	volts	—
10, 13, 28	System contrast with ΔT	$\Delta v/\Delta T = R_q\, \tau_e\, \Delta R/\Delta T$	volts/°K	—
28	Thermal resolution (Noise equivalent temp. difference)	$NETD = (v_{pp}/6)/((\Delta v/\Delta T)$	°K	—
27, 28, 32a & b	Gaussian noise – rms	$v_{rms} = v_{pp}/6$	volts	—
29	Minimum detectable temp.	$MDT = NETD/T_e^{1/2}F^{01/2}$	°K	38; 22
30	Spatial frequency @ IFOV	$f_0 = 1/2$ IFOV	cyc/mr	—
31	Minimum resolvable temp. diff.	$MRTD \to MDT$ for $f < f_0/5$	°K	—
32	Contrast	$\Delta Q/Q = \dfrac{Q_{MAX} - Q_{MIN}}{Q_{\Delta VE}}$	unitless	—
32	Shade of gray	$I_1 = \sqrt{2}I_0$	lumens	—
32	Accuracy	$Q \pm \delta Q$		3; 49
32	Precision (repeatability)	$\delta Q_4/Q_0$		3; 49
32	Dynamic range	$\Delta Q_s/Q_n$ (20 log $\Delta Q_s/\delta Q_n$) $NEQ = \delta Q_n$	db	—

Table 8.2   The Radiance Collected by a Radiometer from an Opaque Surface is Dependent upon the Following Parameters:

I. Radiating Surfaces	
1. Temperature of unknown	T_t
2. Emittance of unknown	ε_t
2.1 Material	
2.2 Texture	
2.3 Geometry	
2.4 Viewing angle	
3. Background radiation onto unknown and reference	T_b
4. Reference temperature	T_r
5. Reference emittance	ε_r
5.1 Material	
5.2 Texture	
5.3 Geometry	
5.4 Viewing angle	
II. Transmission media	
Path absorption (neglect)	
Path radiance (neglect)	
III. Radiometer response	
6. Calibration curve	$N(T)$
6.1 Spectral response	
6.2 Instantaneous surface area viewed	
6.3 Optical collecting area	

Two fundamental aspects to the utility of the imaging radiometer are measurement (quantitative) and recognition (qualitative). *Measurement* refers to the ability to quantify the radiance that leaves the radiator surface and thereby infers its temperature. *Recognition* refers to the ability of the eye to observe temperature patterns on the radiator surface. These patterns then frequently provide important insight as to the overall status of the surface.

In many applications, it is important that the imaging radiometer be non-contact and produce this information without disturbing the thermal conditions of the surface. In other cases, where the surface is moving relative to the observation point, the remote aspect of imaging radiometry is mandatory.

Measurement

Even though the physical relationships are well understood, many parameters are involved when the complete imaging radiometer system is considered. Sixteen of these parameters are listed in Table 8.2. Many of them are difficult to quantify. Further, they often vary with time, materials, geometry, and measurement conditions. Consequently, there is often a practical limit to the overall accuracy and precision that can reasonably be achieved with an imaging radiometric system.

The transmission medium is the most restraining element in the complete system illustrated by Figure 8.2 in that it is the most difficult to control. It can be controlled by restricting the spectral bands over which the optics and transducer operate. With proper spectral restriction, the response of the radiometer can be limited to regions where the transmission medium is essentially nonabsorptive.

If spectral restriction or filtering were imposed upon the system to an extent that dependence upon the transmission medium is completely eliminated, only a relatively small portion of the total radiant energy leaving the radiator would actually reach the transducer. Consequently, a significant sacrifice in the imaging radiometer sensitivity would occur. Therefore, a spectral window is usually employed, which results in the transmission medium exerting some influence on the radiometric measurement. Because most imaging radiometer applications today do not require highly accurate measurements, transmission media errors can often be neglected. In these cases, the operator merely uses the system calibration curves for quantification. Calibration curves are normally generated by the instrument manufacturer at distances from a radiator black body standard of less than 1 meter. At these short distances, the atmosphere transmission medium is essentially negligible.

Because the image is a crucial part of an imaging radiometer system, the measurement reading must be displayed to the operator in a manner that will complement the image. Figure 8.3 shows four commonly used methods of displaying the measurement without destroying the image content.

Line Scan

Line scan allows the operator to select a horizontal line in the scene and then display a temperature profile of this line. It provides a convenient, easily readable vertical temperature scale. The scene must normally be stationary, which means in part the radiometer should be mounted on a tripod, not hand held. One useful alternative is to videotape record in a dynamic situation and perform line scan analysis in stop-action playback.

Isotherm

Isotherm injects a "sparkle" pattern overlay on the image which is representative of a temperature contour. A calibrated panel control allows the operator to move the sparkle pattern to different radiance levels. In this way, the radiance differences or temperature differences of various points of interest throughout the scene can be determined. The isotherm mode is particularly useful for real-time assessment when there is motion in the scene and/or the radiometer is hand held.

Gray Scale

Gray scale is an indirect method of measurement, seldom used because of the convenience offered by isotherm and line scan modes. When a gray scale is displayed with the image, a unit of length along the gray scale is representative of a known radiance difference. Therefore, if a displayed image is photographed with its gray scale, different gray tone points on the gray scale can be correlated with equal gray tone points in the image to quantify radiance levels.

Color Bars

Color bars are images analogous to multiple isotherms. Each color represents a preset span of radiance. Usually color bars are displayed with the image along the gray scale. The colorized image normally does not present as much information to the operator as does the gray tone image mode. It is often helpful when observing a surface area with small monotonic temperature gradients. These gradients might not be detected as a gradual change in gray tone, but in a colorized mode, the color pattern will accentuate these changes by changing color abruptly when the adjacent color radiance level is reached. For the same reason, color bars are also helpful when small changes in temperature must be observed over a period of time.

Recognition

The imaging portion of an imaging radiometer can be regarded as a frequency converter. It shifts the frequency of the invisible infrared photons to the frequency of visible photons, which the eye can observe directly. The picture quality desired for the frequency converter can be likened to a television picture.

The eye is very subjective. In the late 1930s and early 1940s, a great deal of effort was wisely devoted to establish basic TV communication requirements for optimized transmission and display of electronic pictures. Television has flourished partly as a result of the efficiency established by these initial efforts. We are all well conditioned to TV and receive most of our daily information through this medium.

There are four basic aspects associated with electronic picture display which deserve introductory comment: the number of pixels (picture elements), the contrast, the brightness, and the frame rate. The values used for these parameters as optimized for TV represent good reference points to consider when working a trade-off design for an imaging radiometer.

Pixels

A standard television display repeatedly produces a picture having some 100,000 resolution elements or pixels. In this context, an element is analogous to one square in a checkerboard having 100,000 squares.

Contrast

The contrast available on a standard TV display is usually five to seven shades of gray where a shade of gray represents a 20.5 change in the cathode-ray tube (CRT) intensity. What appears to be white on the display is five to seven shades of gray (5.66 to 11.31 times) greater than the intensity that appears black.

Brightness

The brightness desired on a TV display is dependent upon the ambient light level in which the observer views the picture. When viewing in an interior room, a brightness setting near 2×10^{-14} photons/sec/cm^2 would be normal. Under these conditions, the intensity would appear to the eye to be close to the midrange of the monitor's gray scale. If the monitor contrast provides a display with six shades of gray, three might be less than the midrange gray, toward black, and three greater, toward white.

Frame Rate

A television picture is repeated at a rate of 30 frames per second. A frame consists of two interlaced fields, each of which is displayed at a rate of 60 per second. This rate with the interlace was chosen to match the persistence of the eye. It provides a flicker-free image. If the frame rate is reduced with differing amounts of interlace, the picture often has a pulsing or flickering appearance.

Referring to the Video Processor in Figure 8.2, the maximum useful gain for an imaging system is reached when electronic noise begins to mask the picture. This is the condition one observes when attempting to watch a TV program from a distant station — "snow" on the picture tube.

Associated with the maximum gain setting is a corresponding minimum useful input signal. This minimum input is referred to as the sensitivity of the instrument. It is expressed as a number representative of the energy content of the minimum usable input signal.

Sensitivity is one of the parameters that must be treated differently for visual TV and infrared imaging radiometers. With visual TV, the signal detected by the TV camera transducer is primarily reflected light. Should the signal modulation be too low for good contrast pictures, the light level incident on the scene can be increased until the desired picture quality is achieved. On the other hand, with imaging radiometers, the signal detected by the infrared transducer is self-emitted radiance, and there is no way to increase contrast without increasing the temperature of the surface under study.

Considering the limited radiance available, the scanner/transducer portion of the infrared imaging radiometer is often designed with restrictions on the number of pixels allowable. This is done because the temperature sensitivity of an image radiometer improves rapidly as the pixel count is reduced. Consequently, industrial imaging radiometers will normally be observed to have somewhat poorer picture quality than visual TV.

Military imaging radiometers, on the other hand, often have picture quality comparable to visual TV. These military systems must use significantly more complex scanner designs within multi-element detector transducers numbering in the hundreds in some cases. This represents significantly more cost than the single element transducers commonly used in industrial systems.

The level control on the video processor is somewhat similar to the brightness control shown on the display in Figure 8.2. As mentioned previously, the brightness control on the display is used to set the midrange gray tone for optimum viewing at different ambient light levels. On the video processor, the level control is used to adjust the video output signal driving the display. When the level is properly adjusted, the average (or midrange) temperature or radiance on the surface under study is displayed as a midrange gray tone. It should be recognized that this level adjustment will become more critical as the video processor gain is increased to display smaller temperature spans.

The input signal level is another parameter that, like sensitivity, has notably different design characteristics for visual TV systems and infrared imaging radiometer systems. For visual TV systems, black, relative to white, essentially represents the absence of photon arrival at the transducer. There is usually very little reflected radiance from the black part of the surface when compared with the white part of the surface. Consequently, for visual TV, the contrast is high between black and white. On the other hand, with infrared imaging radiometers, the average or quiescent radiance level is typically very large with relatively small changes representing the differences between black and white.

There are many advantages when an electronic imaging system can be designed to have a video output format that is compatible with established TV standards. We are well accustomed to TV and its ever-increasing application base. Over the past decade, partly because of value, prices of TV components have remained quite stable against inflationary trends of other items we commonly use.

Additionally, many types of peripherals are available for electronic data processing of TV images. These techniques can conveniently assist the eye with the interpretation of the imaging radiometer's display. They can be expected to become quite useful as more applications involve significant quantification to draw more sophisticated conclusions from the thermal patterns that are produced.

It is important to elaborate on the word *thermography*. It is defined in current dictionaries as an electronically produced image representative of thermal patterns on a surface. It is synonymous with the displayed output produced by the imaging radiometer except there is no requirement for thermography to produce quantitative information. The instrument used to produce an infrared electronic image is sometimes referred to as a *thermograph*. In this chapter, we have elected to refer to the instrument as an *imaging radiometer* to denote a quantitative feature in conjunction with an image.

Radiometric Characteristics of a Surface

An exchange of energy can occur between surfaces by radiation coupling. The net energy transfer between surfaces is shown to be related to the differences in the fourth power of the absolute temperatures of the surfaces. Further, the radiant energy is identified to be electromagnetic in nature, and therefore no medium is necessary to transport the energy, as is the case for conductive and convective energy transfer.

Because it is electromagnetic, radiant energy travels at the speed of light and has the same characteristics of emission, reflection, transmission, and absorption as the eye commonly observes in the visible portion of the electromagnetic spectrum. Radiant energy has wavelike properties that cover a fairly wide spectrum of frequencies and corresponding wavelengths.

The dominant wavelengths most closely associated with radiant energy transfer on Earth are largely between 2 and 20 micrometers (μm). This is true for essentially all practical surfaces encountered in the temperature range of 200 to 2000 Kelvins (K). These are *mid-infrared* wavelengths. In general, the *near-infrared* wavelengths are shorter and the *far-infrared* wavelengths are longer.

The sun exhibits a surface temperature around 6000°K. Its dominant wavelength is near 0.5 μm. The eye is conveniently adapted to the sun's peak radiance, and the visible wavelengths roughly cover 0.5 to 0.7 μm. The near-infrared falls just beyond 0.7 μm. Sensors used in the near-infrared, like the eye in the visible spectrum, largely rely on the observation of reflected radiance from very hot subjects.

The concept of an ideal or black body radiating surface was introduced earlier in this chapter. The ideal surface has no reflection or transmission. It is a perfect emitter and absorber. It is analogous to a black surface in the visible portion of the spectrum. It is most important for radiometrics because it obeys a unique mathematical expression formulated in 1901 by Max Planck.

In an industrial radiometric application, the problem is usually approached in the reverse order. The radiometer first observes and measures the apparent radiance from a surface. Knowing this apparent radiance and the empirical response of the radiometer, the actual surface temperature can be determined. The determination involves the use of the radiometer output reading along with three appropriate physical relationships: in-band radiance, surface emissive power, and radiance directional dependence.

To summarize, the radiometer actually couples to, or receives, some relatively small portion of the total radiant energy leaving a surface. The radiometer acts as a transducer that electronically converts this radiant energy to a quantified output reading. The operator then applies knowledge of the basic physical relationships involved to compute the temperature of the surface from the radiometer reading. Further, the response generally varies both with different instrument designs and with different measuring conditions and environments.

Artifactual Evidence

Bloodstains

Photographic documentation of physical evidence at the crime scene is an essential part of the overall investigative effort and reconstruction of the events that occurred. The circumstances and nature of violent crimes involving bloodshed frequently produce a variety of bloodstains that, when carefully studied and evaluated with respect to their geometry and distribution, often yield information of considerable value to the ultimate reconstruction of the crime scene. Crime scene investigators responding to death cases and nonfatal, violent crimes frequently do not appreciate the valuable information available from the careful examination and interpretation of bloodstain patterns. As a result, the photographic documentation of the victim, scene, physical evidence, and assailant with respect to bloodstains may be incomplete and lacking in detail for subsequent evaluation and courtroom presentation. Persons trained in bloodstain pattern interpretation may be consulted on a case for the prosecution or defense after the event has occurred and the crime scene is no longer available. Reconstruction of the scene and ultimate conclusions regarding bloodstain patterns in a given case may be limited in scope, and important details in a case may be impossible to resolve because of poor photographic technique used at the time of the original scene investigation. Furthermore, investigators trained in bloodstain pattern interpretation must depend upon good photographic documentation of bloodstains when testifying in court.

The examination and serological studies of bloodstains in the crime laboratory, such as the precipitin test for human origin, ABO grouping, genetic marker profiling, and DNA studies, must also include photographic documentation of bloodstains on clothing and other items of physical evidence before bloodstains are removed from the material submitted for examination. Samples of suspected blood that are cut or otherwise removed from articles of clothing or other physical evidence may represent portions of an important bloodstain pattern. Sometimes the bloodstained area may be minute in size and quantity, as with high-velocity impact blood spatter. Total removal of these small bloodstains for serological testing may be required. In such cases it is extremely important that the bloodstains be photographed properly; otherwise the interpretative value of those bloodstains is irretrievably lost.

The following is a general outline for the interpretation of bloodstain evidence. Items in boldface type specifically involve photography. It is important to recognize that the study and interpretation of bloodstains at a crime scene should be integrated within the systematic approach to the examination of all types of physical evidence and crime scene reconstruction. A complete analysis of bloodstains at a crime scene where numerous, complex stain patterns exist may require hours or days of work involving measurements, projections of angles of impact, sketches, diagrams, and often extensive photography. Good photographic documentation of the bloodstains, both of overall bloodstain patterns and individual bloodstains, is crucial.

Scene

1. Secure scene and exclude unauthorized persons.
2. Avoid alteration of bloodstains.
3. **Photograph victim and associated bloodstains prior to moving victim.**
4. **Photograph weapon if present and secure it.**
5. Note environmental conditions.
6. Conduct preliminary evaluation of overall bloodstains and patterns.
7. Move body cautiously.
8. Collect trace evidence.
9. Complete search for and recognition of bloodstains and patterns.
10. **Photograph bloodstains, including close-up views and reference scale.**
11. Take bloodstain measurements, including locations, widths, lengths, angles of impact, convergences, and origins.
12. Make preliminary sketches and diagrams.
13. Perform preliminary blood testing if desired.
14. Collect, tag, identify, and collect bloodstained items.
15. Perform string reconstruction if desired.

Assailant

1. Examine assailant and his environment.
2. **Photograph and document clothing and other physical evidence.**
3. Obtain appropriate blood samples.

Autopsy of Victim

1. **Photograph body, clothed and unclothed, including injuries.**
2. Secure clothing, physical evidence, and blood samples.
3. Obtain autopsy report, x-rays, and medical data.

Laboratory Reports

1. Blood identification and individualization.
2. Trace evidence, ballistics, and other physical evidence.

Bloodstain Reconstruction

1. Final diagrams and bloodstain experiments.
2. Bloodstain interpretation of scene, clothing, and other items.
3. Correlation with autopsy and laboratory reports.

Crime scene photography, including documentation of bloodstain patterns, is easily and effectively accomplished with the use of a 35 mm camera with a 35 to 50 mm lens for overall photographs, close-up or macro lens capability, flash attachment, and a high-quality color film. Color 8 × 10 or full frame 8 × 12 enlargements are good size photographic reproductions for analysis and courtroom presentation. Color slides are also very useful for courtroom presentation. Color slides may be produced from original scene photographs with the use of a copy stand with photo lamps. Good results have been obtained with the apparatus shown in Figure 8.4. Reflecting the light from a white cardboard reduces the amount of glare on the subject photograph. Color slide ASA 100 film is utilized with the camera set at ASA 125 with the lens setting at automatic. The exposure time is adjusted to 1/15 second or the closest setting that will allow a reading of f-8 to f-11 on the internal light meter of the camera. These parameters have been effective in reducing overexposure of the slides, which can be a problem.

Personal experience has shown that Polaroid reproductions have limited value for crime scene work and bloodstain pattern interpretation. Black-and-white photographs have use with Luminol (described later) but generally do not suffice for bloodstain pattern interpretations, because stains other than blood will appear similar to bloodstains and tend to confuse interpretation.

A most important tool for the forensic photographer is a measuring device scaled in millimeters and inches, to be included in photographs or slides of bloodstain patterns or individual stains in order that the sizes of the

Figure 8.4 Color slides may be produced from original scene photographs with the use of a copy stand and photo lamps. Reflecting the light from the white cardboard reduces the amount of glare on the subject photograph.

bloodstains are well documented. Experience has shown that blue or gray six-inch rulers work well to eliminate glare and provide a good guide for color reproduction (See Color Figure 4.*)

Indoor and Outdoor Crime Scenes

The indoor crime scene is, for the most part, protected from the elements and easily preserved for extended periods. An exception is when the incident occurred in a public place and there is pressure to clean up the scene as quickly as possible. Bloodstains present at outdoor crime scenes may be altered in appearance by the nature of the terrain and weather conditions. Photography of the outdoor crime scene should be accomplished as soon as possible to minimize changes or obliteration of bloodstains and other physical evidence caused by prevailing conditions. It may be necessary to photograph an outdoor scene at night with the use of a strong light source. The use of a ladder or truck with a boom is useful for overall photographs of the outdoor scene. If weather is not a problem, significant bloodstains should be rephotographed in the daylight hours.

* Color figures follow page 206

Whether indoors or outdoors, it is important to limit access to any crime scene. This is especially true for bloody scenes, to avoid tracking of wet blood or alteration of existing bloodstain patterns to the extent that proper interpretation would be compromised.

Bloodstain evidence at the crime scene should be documented with high-quality color photographs and/or slides prior to moving the body or otherwise altering the scene. A scale of reference should be utilized. It is important to coordinate the photography of the victim and visible injuries with photographs of bloodstains and patterns on the body and clothing. Overall views from above should be taken as well as close-up photographs of small bloodstains on the body, with a ruler in place. Bloodstains on the body of the victim should be photographed in conjunction with the bloodstains in the immediate area of the body before the victim is turned or moved. When the body position has been altered, the area should be rephotographed to document any alterations of previously formed bloodstains or the creation of new or artifactual bloodstains.

Much of the critical bloodstain pattern photography of the walls, ceilings, floors, and other objects may be best accomplished after the overall scene photography and photographic documentation of the body have been completed and the body has been removed for autopsy. Bloodstain patterns should be photographed with the camera held at 90 degrees to the bloodstains. When individual bloodstains are photographed at close range, the general area of these bloodstains should be recognizable from prior photographs taken from a greater distance so that a point of reference is established (Figures 8.5 and 8.6). If bloodstain convergences and points of origin are established through measurements and string reconstruction, these procedures should be photographed.

Photography of Road Surfaces and Vehicles

Prompt examination and photography of road surfaces for evidence of bloodstain patterns during the investigation of pedestrian-vehicle accidents may reveal impact sites that can assist with pinpointing the victim's original location. It is important to photograph bloodstains on the exterior of a vehicle where impact occurred or contact was made with a victim, especially on the tires and the undercarriage of the vehicle. The undercarriage should be photographed while the vehicle is on a lift in a garage.

Photographic documentation of bloodstains in the interior of a vehicle may assist in the determination of the locations of persons in the vehicle prior to impact. The question of who was the driver and the positions of passengers may be resolved.

Photography of the exterior and interior of vehicles is often enhanced by the use of a strobe or flash unit utilized in daylight. This technique helps to eliminate the shadows in wheel wells and other structures of the vehicle.

Figure 8.5 The general area of bloodstains should be recognizable in overall photographs so that a point of reference is established.

Figure 8.6 Individual bloodstains should be photographed at close range with the camera held at 90 degrees to the bloodstain.

Photography of Bloodstained Clothing

The bloodstained clothing of a victim should be carefully removed after initial photography at the scene and the postmortem examination. The garments should not be folded or packaged in a damp condition. The best procedure is to hang and air dry clothing over clean paper prior to packaging it in paper bags. This will minimize the alteration of bloodstains and the production of additional bloodstains or artifacts.

Examination of a suspect's clothing for bloodstains and trace physical evidence often provides valuable evidence that associates that person with a victim. Assailants frequently acquire bloodstains and spatters on exposed parts of their bodies, such as the face and hands, which should be photographed promptly. In a recent case investigated by the Palm Beach County Sheriff's Office, a man reported that he discovered the body of his friend upon returning home. The victim had been beaten to death with a portion of a stop-sign post. An alert investigator recognized the small, medium-velocity blood spatters characteristically produced by beatings below the knees on the trousers worn by the man and photographed them at the scene. Also, the man's hands were bloodstained and were photographed at the scene. On his bloodstained right hand was a void area in the web of the palm, which demonstrated that he had been grasping an object at the time the hand was bloodstained. These photographs provided key evidence that led to the man's arrest and his eventual guilty plea. Photographic documentation of bloodstains on clothing should be accomplished before any suspect bloodstains are removed for serological testing. The use of a mannequin is helpful in documenting the orientation and location of bloodstains as they were when the victim or assailant wore the garments (Figure 8.7).

The Use and Photographic Documentation with Luminol

Luminol is a well-known chemiluminescent compound that is utilized as a presumptive, catalytic test for the presence of blood. It utilizes the peroxidase-like activity of heme for the production of light as an end product, rather than a true color reaction. Luminol reagent is applied on objects or areas containing traces of suspected bloodstains. A bluish-white luminescence or light on the suspected area observed in the dark is a positive test. Luminol is best utilized for the detection of traces of blood that are not readily observable at crime scenes. This would include light tracking of blood on dark floors and carpeted area, cracks and crevices in floors and walls, and areas where an attempt to clean bloodstained areas is suspected. The patterns of blood resolved with Luminol may be as important as the detection of blood itself. The sensitivity of the Luminol test is as high as approximately one part in five million, and it works very well with aged and decomposed bloodstains. The Luminol test is easy to perform and adaptable to crime

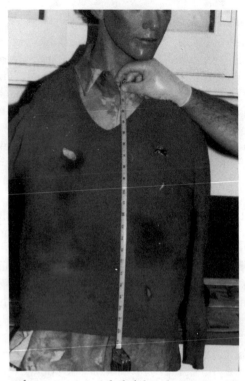

Figure 8.7 The use of a mannequin is helpful in the proper orientation and location of bloodstains as they were when the victim or assailant wore the garments.

scene work. Reagents and supplies are relatively inexpensive and can often be obtained from a local crime laboratory. Commercial kits for Luminol testing are more expensive. They are packaged in vials for individual test use and reagent preparation is simplified. It is important to recognize that Luminol is a presumptive test for blood. Further analysis of positive areas must be made before the stains can be confirmed as blood. Certain surfaces, such as painted walls, porcelain, and metal, and cleaning agents such as hypochlorites may react with Luminol.

Many investigators confirm a positive result with an additional presumptive test, such as phenolphthalein, which can be accomplished after the Luminol spray has been applied to the surface. Preferences in procedure for further serological testing of Luminol-reactive areas should be obtained from a local crime laboratory.

One of the advantages of Luminol is that the procedure lends itself well to photographic documentation and is especially valuable when large bloodstain patterns otherwise not visible are resolved. The following is a list of equipment required for the use and photographic documentation of Luminol:

1. Luminol reagent and spraying device
2. Luminescent measuring device
3. 35 mm camera with 50 mm lens, bulb shutter setting, and wide-open lens setting (i.e., f-1.8) capability
4. Shutter release cable
5. Tripod
6. Flash unit
7. ASA 400 black-and-white or color film (print or slide)
8. Timer
9. Appropriate protective clothing, gloves, and goggles

Procedure. Prior to the use of the Luminol reagent, the surface or object should be photographed in position using a flash unit with the luminescent ruler in place. This will assist with the location of the positive luminescent areas that will be in a dark background. With the exception of some overall views, the camera angle on the tripod should be perpendicular to the surface of interest. The camera lens f-stop should then be set at the widest aperture and the exposure setting at the B (bulb) position. With the shutter cable release attached, the equipment is ready for use.

With the room or location darkened, the Luminol reagent is applied, using the spraying device in a slow, even motion avoiding saturation of the sprayed surface. As fine a mist as possible is optimal. The surface can be resprayed during the time exposure to enhance the reaction. An exposure time of 30 to 45 seconds will generally produce satisfactory results. Experimentation with this timed exposure may be desirable. Two or three investigators may be required for this procedure: one to spray Luminol, a second to operate the camera, and possibly a third to operate the timer and lights. (See Color Figures 5-7.*)

It is possible to obtain a double image of the Luminol reaction and the object. This occurred quite by accident in a recent case when, at the end of the exposure time, the room lights came on while the bulb setting was still activated. The shutter cable was released within a second afterward and the resulting photograph, initially thought to be worthless, showed both the subject (a jacket) and luminescence quite well in a single photograph. (See Color Figure 8.*)

Charles Eden of the Broward County, Florida Sheriff's Office, Forensic Services Division, published an article in the *Journal of Forensic Identification* that demonstrated the use of a light source during the Luminol spray period. This light source permitted visualization of the area subjected to Luminol as well as the positive luminescent reaction in the same photograph.

---

* Color figures follow page 206

Summary

The value of bloodstain evidence as an important tool for crime scene reconstruction is enhanced by good photographic documentation. Photography provides a permanent record of bloodstain evidence which is easily conveyed to a jury through enlarged photographs or slides. Photographic evidence must stand up to the scrutiny of opposing experts and counsel as well as acting as a visual aid to a jury who must ultimately weigh the evidence and reach a verdict in a court of law.

Fingerprints

Because they are unique to every individual, the importance of preserving latent fingerprints is paramount. They are left on a multitude of surfaces, and the best method of preserving these artifacts of identification is photography. It must be done prior to any attempts to lift the print or remove the object on which it is found. Two photographs of the latent print are a good practice — one as it is found and one with a scale of reference.

Depending on the background color (light or dark), the use of filters may be in order to help bring out the definition in the latent prints. Sometimes prints are found on multicolored backgrounds (beer and soft drink cans). The best technique is to try observing the object through different color filters until you find one that gives the best contrast between the latent print and background. A red filter No. 25 over the camera lens will eliminate a red-colored background.

If the latent print is on glass, a mirror, or other highly reflective background, alternative lighting techniques are in order. Usually the most effective method is cross-lighting, either at 45 degrees or a more oblique angle. It may also be helpful to use an opposite color background, such as black or dark blue behind a light-colored (white or gray) powdered latent print.

Another procedure successful in multicolored background situations is to use fluorescent powder and ultraviolet light exposure. Either an electronic flash or long-wave ultraviolet lighting will be satisfactory. With the suspect area dusted for prints using a fluorescent dusting powder, expose the area with an electronic flash. Tape a No. 18A LTV filter over the flash. This will provide only ultraviolet light, which will be picked up by the 35 mm camera with ISO 100 to 400 film. Again, remember to hold the flash unit off the camera and at an oblique angle. The area must be darkened as much as possible. With the camera on a tripod, take several photographs (bracketing) at f-stops above and below the suggested lens opening.

One additional lighting technique for fluorescent photography is a long-wave ultraviolet light source close to the subject for maximum illumination. This also must be done in a darkened environment and several exposures (bracketing) are in order.

It is very important to remember that latent prints may be smeared or altered when attempting to dust them on certain surfaces. If you have found that certain surfaces are more difficult than others when raising latent fingerprints, then perhaps one of the following techniques may be helpful.

Cyanoacrylate (Super Glue) Fuming

This is a very simple yet effective technique that permanently fixes the latent print on any surface. It is usually done in the laboratory in a fuming tank (aquarium) for small objects. Place the object (gun, glass, cartridge, etc.) in the glass fuming tank with a small quantity of cyanoacrylate. Cover the tank and place a safe heat source — heat lamp or large light bulb — next to one side of the tank. The heat accelerates the process. Usually within several hours, the latent prints appear as light white (dried glue) ridges. These are permanent and can be dusted without fear of destruction.

Freezing

A latent print may be stabilized by putting the object (particularly metal) in a freezer or spraying it with a CO_2 fire extinguisher. Next, blow on the suspected area with your warm breath, creating condensation and enhancing the latent print image.

These procedures are also applicable for photographic documentation of footwear prints and glove and clothing impressions.

Imprints

Shoes, bare feet, tires, and clothing often produce imprint patterns on hard surfaces such as linoleum, which cannot be lifted or preserved other than by photography. To photograph them properly, place your camera on a tripod with the film plane parallel to the floor or ground surface (Figure 8.8). Use a scale of reference in the photograph and fill the image area as much as possible. If and when a suspect is found, photograph the item (shoe, foot, tire, etc.) and make an overlay comparison of the negatives for the perfect match.

Remember when photographing a tire imprint to document the entire circumference of the tire. This can be accomplished with a series of overlapping photographs.

Microevidence

Small items such as paint chips, electrical wire beads, glass fragments, hairs, fibers, wood chips, and matches require careful handling and patience. Obviously the ideal environment for this work is the forensic laboratory. The big secret to success in creating convincing demonstrative evidence is a combination of camera perspective and lighting angle. Because much of this evidence

Figure 8.8 Photograph footwear and tire impressions with the camera film plane parallel to the surface. Be sure to use a scale of reference in the photograph and fill the image area as much as possible.

is so small and fragile, it requires some type of mounting for protection against further damage or loss. The mounting technique can also be beneficial for lighting from various angles to produce the best photographic documentation.

Glass fragments are best preserved and photographed on a clear adhesive material or even Plexiglas or glass sheets. They can then be photographed with a variety of lighting techniques: cross-lighting, back-lighting, and oblique reflective lighting (Figures 8.9 and 8.10).

Matches and the book they were torn from can be compared and photographed with oblique cross-lighting reflected off a white surface to reduce shadows (Figures 8.11a and 8.11b).

Hairs and fibers, by their physical nature, are very difficult to document photographically. Hairs are found on some obscure surfaces, textured fabrics, wood, metal, and so forth. Creative lighting is needed to visually separate the hair from the background surface. Cross-lighting and 45 degree angle illumination from two sides will usually render a satisfactory photograph (Figure 8.12).

Paint chips and wood fragments provide valuable comparison evidence to demonstrate that two pieces have the same origin. Usually there is very little depth of field to work with, so you must concentrate on photographing the surfaces from an angle that shows the matching layers of paint or wood grain. Mount the pieces on contrasting color paper so the edges are at the same level when focused through the lens (Figures 8.13a-d).

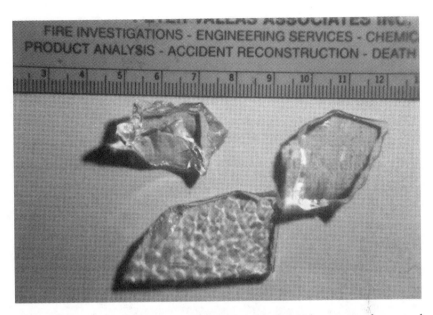

Figure 8.9 Glass fragments can be preserved through macro photography techniques.

Figure 8.10 Cross-lighting is one of a variety of techniques used to preserve glass fragment evidence.

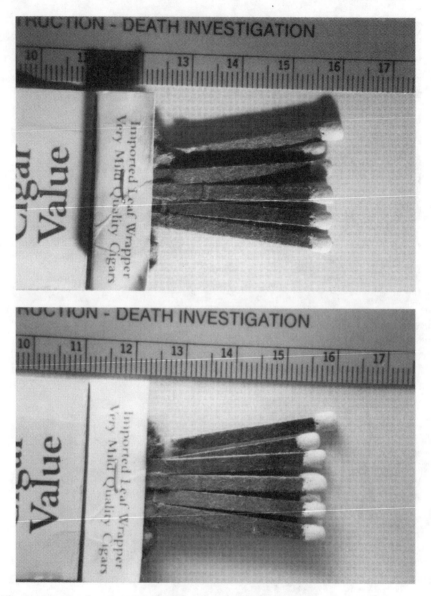

Figures 8.11a, b The oblique cross-lighting technique is very effective in comparing and documenting matches and the book from which they originated.

High-Speed Photography

To appreciate the capabilities of this special photographic technique, consider the average camera's fastest shutter speed, 1/1000 of a second. This may be adequate for stopping the action of a vehicle during an accident reconstruction

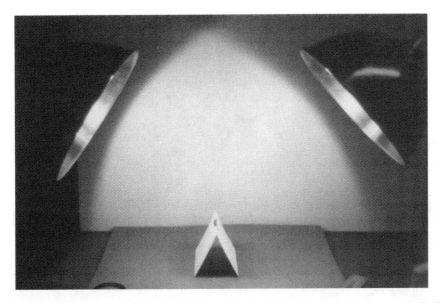

Figure 8.12 Some of the best laboratory photographic work is accomplished with cross lighting from two sides.

reenactment, but stopping extremely high-speed subjects, such as a bullet in flight, requires strobe lighting. This very brilliant and brief light source produces exposure times as fleeting as a microsecond. To understand this in simple terms, consider that the bullet travels about 1100 feet per second. During the 1-millisecond exposure of a camera shutter, the bullet travels approximately 13 inches. During the 80-microsecond exposure of a high-speed movie camera, it travels about one inch. In 3.0 microseconds of a strobe lighting, the bullet travels only 0.04 inch. To study high-speed events such as bloodstains caused by gunshots requires a series of high-speed photographs in a fleeting moment. A series of single flash photographs is very difficult if not impossible to successfully document the desired results. The most satisfactory and easiest method of documentation is multiple flash exposure on a single frame. Strobe lighting is capable of producing multiple flash exposures. This equipment has been in use commercially for many years for the visual analysis of industrial machinery.

This technique also has its applications in forensic science, not only with single image exposures but also with high-speed videography. The short duration flash of the strobe stops rapid movement that would normally be blurred.

Lighting

The synchronization of the strobe lighting with the subject being photographed (e.g., a bullet in flight) is the most critical function in this technique.

Figures 8.13a through d Illustrate a technique used to document minute pieces of physical evidence such as paint chips.

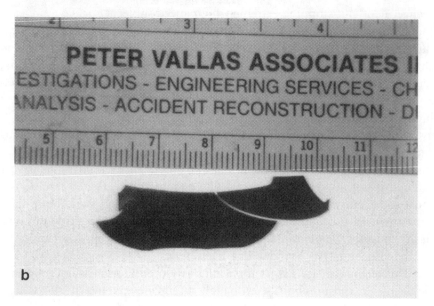

Figure 8.13b

If the flash activates prematurely or late, the subject will be "stopped" in the wrong position or missed entirely.

The easiest method involves darkening the room so that only the strobe light has to be synchronized with the event. If your camera is equipped with

Figure 8.13c

Figure 8.13d

a bulb setting, it can be left open during the recording of the motion of the subject. The strobe flash is activated by the action of the subject being photographed. Because high-speed flash lighting is a relatively low-intensity light source, it requires large aperture settings, fast ISO film (400 or higher), and almost total darkness.

Subjects photographed at high speed often do not contrast well against their background. To improve your chances for clear, sharp images, use either a light or dark background, depending on the subject. Light-colored backgrounds may produce excessive reflections when the light source is at the wrong angle to the camera and subject. It may be preferable to use a dark, nonreflective background. Side lighting (at an approximate 45 degree angle) bounced off a light-colored, reflective material helps to eliminate overexposed image washout.

Methods of Activation

There are numerous techniques for triggering the strobe, camera, and subject action simultaneously. The simplest method is a manual activation of the camera shutter under low ambient light conditions. Other activation methods include mechanical contacts and optical and audio sensors. The easiest method for activation is use of mechanical contacts. A few examples include a wire-carrying current broken by a bullet, two pieces of aluminum foil (with current-carrying wires attached) that become pressed together by the motion of the subject, and the most common method, in which a piece of paper with metal foil coating on either side causes activation when the bullet passes through it, making contact with both foil coatings simultaneously.

An example of this technique can be applied as follows. A bullet traveling at approximately 1100 feet per second was stopped as it passed through a target. The 35 mm camera is positioned about 10 inches from the target. A 28 to 70 mm variable lens is set at f-8 aperture. The strobe light unit is positioned about 12 to 14 inches from the target. The foil contacts are positioned a couple of inches in front of the gun barrel.

Firearms and ammunition create problems with reflections off shiny surfaces. The light source has to illuminate from both sides at a 45 degree angle, or axial lighting is used at 90 degrees to the subject reflected off a glass positioned at a 45 degree angle between the camera and the subject (Figures 8.14a and b).

Summary

Because physical evidence plays such an important role in the litigation arena, how it is handled, preserved, and presented in court is of paramount importance to the forensic photographer. Photographic documentation is recognized by both experts and laymen when it comes to evaluation of this medium of demonstrative evidence. No other evidence brings the evidence to the jury and the jury to the scene like the graphic portrayal accomplished with forensic photography.

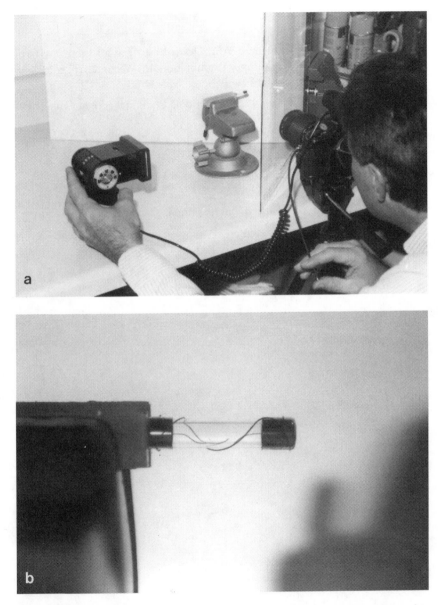

Figures 8.14a and b illustrate axial lighting at 90 degrees to the subject reflected off a glass positioned at a 45-degree angle between the camera and the subject. This method is useful in reducing reflections off shiny surfaces.

Suggested Reading

Coyne, M. Photographic Documentation in Death Investigation: From the Crime Scene through the Forensic Autopsy Examination. In: Wecht, Cyril, ed. *Forensic Sciences*. Vol. 2. New York: Matthew Bender, 1988:35A-1-35A-85.

Eckert, W. E., and James, S. H. *Interpretation of Bloodstain Evidence at Clime Scenes*. New York: Elsevier, 1989.

James, S. H. *Interpretation of Bloodstain Evidence at Crime Scenes*, 2nd ed. CRC Press, Boca Raton, 1998.

MacDonell, H. L. Preserving Bloodstain Evidence at Crimes Scenes. *Law and Order* 1977, 25:66-69.

MacDonell, H. L. *Bloodstain Pattern Interpretation*. Corning, NY: Laboratory of Forensic Science, 1997.

Legal Aspects of Visual Evidence

9

Because it is often impractical, if not impossible, to take the jury to the scene of the crime or incident, the next best alternative is to bring the scene into the courtroom. For more than 130 years, the best method has been photographic documentation of the scene. Forensic photography is the accepted methodology, and because of its success, the legal foundation for admissibility has been significantly simplified.

There are two basic requirements for the admissibility of photographs. First, someone must have personal knowledge to testify as to the accuracy of the depiction of the subject in the photograph. Second, someone must identify the equipment used as well as its capability of producing a true and accurate representation. In recent years, it has been my experience that this process has become less complex. Generally, all that is required is confirmation by a witness that he saw the object or subject at the scene and, further, that the photographic documentation is a fair and accurate representation.

Historical Foundation

For the most part, the requirement for accurate photographic representation includes photographs, slides, videotapes, movies, and x-rays. The acceptance of this broad medium as evidence in court has been well established.

The first photographs (Daguerreotypes) were used in a civil case by the Supreme Court in *Lueo vs. United States*, 23 Howard 515 (1859), to decide the authenticity of photographs in comparing signatures. The first recorded criminal case introducing photographs as identification evidence was *Udderzook vs. Commonwealth*, 76 Pa. 340 (1874). Color photographs were introduced in civil litigation in *Green vs. City and County of Denver*, 3 Colo. 390, 142 P.2d 277 (1943), involving color photographs of spoiled meat in violation of the health ordinance prohibiting the sale of putrid meat to the public. Criminal cases have shown the importance of color since the 1960s, in a case that depicted the graphic wounds of the victim, *State vs. Conte*,

157 Conn. 209, 251 A.2d 81 (1968). Slides have been admissible since the notable *State vs. Sheppard* case, 100 Ohio App. 345, 128 N.E. 2d 471 (1955), upheld in a rehearing, 352 U.S. 955 (1956). Color slides depicted the victim's wounds. Motion pictures were accepted in 1916, *Duncan vs. Kieger*, 6 Ohio App. 57. The use of videotapes as evidence of defendants' statements and confessions has been upheld as early as 1969, *Parramore vs. State*, 229 So. 2d 855 (Fla., 1969).

Points of Objection

The main goal of any challenge would address the fair and accurate representation of the photographic evidence. (See Color Figure 9.*)

Accuracy of Color

The true color reproduction may be a point of contention if the color is a critical issue. Questions may be directed at the lighting, filters, and processing, any or all of which can alter color balance. Use of a standard color balance bar in the corner of the photograph allows comparison with the original bar used to produce the photograph.

Alterations of Negatives and Prints

Any deliberate attempt to alter the photographic evidence is inexcusable and, to the untrained eye, difficult to detect. Usually the deception is one of two types. One is eliminating evidence such as scars, cracks, or defects from photographs by filtering. The second is through the use of double exposure; objects or people can be added to a photograph with multiple negatives. Careful scrutiny of the highlights and shadows in the photograph or negative can reveal these attempts at deception.

Computer Generated Images

Today's computer technology brings with it new enhancement capabilities to apply to problem photographs. It also brings the chance of misunderstanding because of many individuals' fears of the unknown. It is imperative that supporting testimony from the computer imaging expert provides the proper foundation for acceptance of this type of evidence.

Enlargements

For the normal viewing distance for 35 mm format film, 8 × 10 enlargements are the standard. However, to avoid a challenge for cropping important evi-

---

* Color figures follow page 206

dence from a negative, use full frame enlargements which are 8 × 12. If larger prints are used (poster size, 24 × 30) the objection may be that the subject is larger than life-size and therefore not a fair and accurate representation. It may be necessary during the laying of the foundation to explain the purpose of the enlargement, thus avoiding some objections. (See Figures 9.1 and 9.2.)

Errors in Printing

The most common printing error is the reversed print. Complex negatives or those without obvious indicators such as lettering can be very misleading. The normal combination of photographs and diagrams used for orientation of the jury to the scene could be totally confusing to even the most astute juror if a critical photograph was reversed. To avoid potential problems with admissibility, always have the negatives available in court for comparison purposes.

Equipment

Cross-examination about your camera and accessory equipment is rare today. In the past 16 years, I have been questioned only once about my camera equipment. The best way to avoid confusion and objections is to know your equipment. It is also a good idea to have your equipment with you in court. The best evidence is demonstrative in nature — if you get the opportunity, show it to the jury.

Inflammatory Photographs

Photographic documentation that shows graphic details of gruesome wounds, injuries, or deceased victims may raise objections on the grounds that it may prejudice the jury. The relevancy and factual content are important to the admissibility of graphic photographic evidence. Nudity is another area where proper foundation will avoid unnecessary objections. In a series of rape assaults on college women, the photographic documentation of puncture wounds to the breasts was admissible based on the fact that the weapon (a sharpened screwdriver) responsible for wounds inflicted on four different women was a common modus operandi of the defendant.

Lighting

The use of lights in many disciplines of photography is for artistic purposes and can produce very interesting yet deceptive results. Forensic photography uses available lighting in every applicable situation. There are, however, many indoor or night situations where electronic flash and floodlighting are necessary. Fire scenes are typically shot with several flash techniques because of the tendency for charring to absorb light (fill-in, cross-lighting, painting). It is advisable to photograph the situation in both available light and with flash to show the necessity of auxiliary light.

Figure 9.1 Example of a full frame (35 mm) 8 × 12 inch enlargement.

Figure 9.2 Same photograph as in Figure 9.1; however, it has been cropped to 8 × 10. Note the potential for missing crucial evidence.

Marking Photographs

The use of a particular photograph to emphasize a point with more than one witness is often done by marking the photograph. The marks may consist of lines, arrows, numbers, circles, and so forth to draw attention to a particular point in the photograph. To preserve the integrity of the photograph, it may be helpful to use clear acetate overlays on which the witnesses can make their marks. Another method would involve duplicate prints of the subject, one to be used for marking by the witnesses.

Another type of mark that may be objectionable is a defect in the negative that produces artifacts on the print. These marks can appear as light or dark spots or even clouded images. If the photograph is critical, it will be necessary to produce the negatives for review by your adversaries. To counter their argument that it is not a true and accurate representation, you might point out that no photograph is an exact representation considering that it is only two dimensional.

Misleading Photographs

In addition to objections that arise over color, optical distortions, markings, or time lapse are several other areas relevant to objectionable content of photographic documentation. Some photographs may be confusing to a juror if unnecessary or irrelevant objects are crowding the photograph. Likewise, if the photograph is taken too close, segregating the object from the rest of the scene, it can be just as misleading. Therefore, it is suggested that additional overall photographs be taken for orientation to the overall picture.

A single photograph portraying one point of view, particularly when related to subject material over a period of time, could be misinterpreted by jurors. For example, an intersection where a pedestrian-vehicle accident occurred was shown in a photograph as having relatively light pedestrian traffic. The correct photographic series showed the actual time frame when the accident occurred — some three to four hours later than the single photograph of the same intersection.

Photocopies (sometime referred to as laser copies) produced on color photocopying machines appear as very good likenesses at first glance. However, the limited quality of color shading is most noticeable and the paper (typically bond) cannot compare with photographic paper. Recently, an adversary attempt was made in court to substitute 8 1/2 × 11 color enlargements from a color photocopier for 8 × 10 color prints. These enlargements were initially introduced and marked into evidence several days prior to the court date. You can imagine the surprise I created when I announced that what was handed to me for identification was not a photograph enlargement but rather nothing more than a color photocopy. I proceeded to point out three obvious indicators: first, the paper was typical bond, not photographic glossy or matte finish; second, the copy size was $8\frac{1}{2} \times 11$, not 8×10; and finally, the color was flat with no graduation or tone. If enlargements are used in court, the negatives or slides used to make them should be made available.

Optical Illusions

Avoid using excessively wide-angle lenses (greater than 28 mm), which create fishbowl distortions at the edges of photographs. Telephoto/zoom lenses are useful in many instances, for example, in surveillance, where close-up identification is desirable, but you must avoid subjects in the foreground, as they can detract from the objective by appearing closer in the photograph than they actually were. Also, consider the composition of your photograph in relation to accuracy. Vertical lines will appear longer than horizontal lines of the same length. Lighter-shade objects will appear larger than dark objects. If the photograph is to fall within the guidelines of a true and accurate representation, do not let distortion detract from your objective to present the truth.

Scale of Reference

When the photographic evidence portrays size or distance, it is suggested that two photographs of the same subject be taken — one as it is found and a second with a scale of reference. The scale can be a standard ruler, yardstick, tape measure, or specifically designed rule, usually six to seven inches in length, marked in both inches and millimeters and blue or gray in color. A scale of reference photographed with bloodstain evidence is far more effective in differentiating between high-velocity (diameter less than 1 mm) and cast-off blood spatter.

Sight Perspective

If the photograph depicts an observation made by a particular witness, be sure the photograph was taken from that person's perspective. It is important to take the photograph as near as possible to the same angle and eyesight level as the witness. This is particularly important in motor vehicle accidents, in which the sight perspective of a driver or pedestrian can be very important because of any obstructions. (See Figure 9.3.)

Time Frame

The lapse of time between the event and when the photographs were taken is subject to objection based on time of day, weather conditions, time of year, or changes of appearance in the scene caused by actions of individuals (moving furniture in a room, construction or demolition of buildings, etc.).

If a substantial period has elapsed, additional care may be required to lay the foundation for admission of the photographs as relevant. The witness must show that the photograph is fair and accurate in aiding his testimony.

Figure 9.3 Example of the sight perspective from the driver's seat during accident reconstruction.

Presentation Strategy

The primary purpose of photographic evidence is to aid the jury in relating witness testimony to other forms of physical evidence. The objective in preparing demonstrative evidence for court is to have it viewed by jurors while testimony is given. All too often the photographic evidence is taken for granted, and the normal 3 × 5 prints are passed among the jurors during testimony. Not only is this confusing to the jurors, but it can be very distracting to the witness. There are several alternative techniques to maximize the effectiveness of photographic evidence.

Enlargements are routinely accepted. One method of presentation I encourage my client to promote is allowing me to walk before the jury slowly with each enlarged photograph as I testify to its content and relevancy. Occasionally, a juror will stop you for a moment or ask you to point out the subject you are addressing. Such evidence stays with them long after you have left the courtroom and they have retired to deliberate. The original print (and sometimes negatives) should also be available for comparison of content and accuracy.

An alternate technique with enlargements is to mount poster-size photographs on a stiff backing material (foam-core board, illustration board) and display them on an easel near the jury. The witness can then direct the juror's attention to points of interest during testimony. The disadvantage is the lack of personal contact with the jury developed with the previous technique.

Presentation of slide transparencies in court has become widely accepted. The advantage of a large photograph directing everyone's attention to one visual display at a time may be outweighed only by problems with courtroom dynamics. Older courtrooms may not allow adequate darkening for proper viewing of slides. More recent courtroom design, however, has provided for proper room darkening as well as strategically mounted screens for optimum viewing. An important footnote to proper preparation is always have a backup projector and spare bulbs for the unexpected failure. One additional suggestion — for the convenience of the jurors, have a set of prints made from the slides that can be passed around later during deliberation.

Modern photographic documentation brings the technology of video-tape into the courtroom with ever-increasing frequency and great success. When properly prepared and introduced, nothing is closer to the truth than a moving documentation, particularly with audio backup. It is as close to lifelike as our technology has come, keeping everyone's attention directed to one subject at the same time.

The latest introduction to the field of demonstrative evidence is computer graphic enhancement of photographic images. This technique, while relatively new in its application to the area of forensic photography, has been accepted in several judicial proceedings. It is important to lay proper foundation for the accuracy of the work and the expertise of the individual who produced the work. The three-dimensional capabilities of this medium hold tremendous promise for the areas of accident and crime scene reconstruction. This author and associates are presently involved in researching and collecting data for potential use of this technique in fire scene reconstruction.

Summary

The technology of modern photographic equipment has significantly reduced the margin of error in producing court-acceptable photographs. If you read the owner's manual provided with your camera, use the suggested film speed (ISO), and practice, you should encounter little concern about the acceptability of your work in court.

There are times and situations where special techniques for photographing evidence may require additional testimony to lay the foundation for its admissibility. The need may arise for additional explanation of methodology, equipment, and technician's experience. This is often the case with techniques such as microscopy, macro photography, ultraviolet photography, photogrammetry, and videography.

Remember, whatever your level of experience, do not ever testify to something you did not do or do not know. Even if the photographic documentation is accurate in every respect, if you did not prepare it or do not have first-hand knowledge of the subject, it can be ruled inadmissible if you are found to be untruthful in your testimony.

Suggested Reading

Moenssens, A. A., Inbau, F. E., and Starrs, J. E. *Scientific Evidence in Criminal Cases.* 3rd ed. Mineola, NY: The Foundation Press, Inc., 1986.

Digital Photography

10

In today's field of photography, the diversity of equipment and technology shows that traditional photography and digital imaging are becoming closer and closer in quality. With each passing day, the quality of the two mediums becomes harder to differentiate. Professional photographers are using film and flat bed scanners as well as photo discs and CDs to transfer their photographs into computers for enhancement and quicker e-mail transfer to their market (news media, studios and other markets). The photographers using digital equipment (cameras and digital camcorders) are also downloading and e-mailing their pictures by the computer format (Figure 10.1).

Even though the two technologies make it easier for the amateur and professional photographer to compose creative images with improved quality, these images are the result of creative manipulation and enhancement through computers and other digital services. The fact remains that in the field of forensic photography, the underlying number one criterion is that the image be a true and accurate documentation of the scene or subject.

Digital Photography Basics

Digital photography's universal format is its greatest advantage in that images can easily be transferred between multiple devices and applications. An example of these applications is the addition of images to word processing formats, e-mail, posting on web sites, or the simple editing of these images to manipulate or improve them. The down side to digital imaging is its ability to be manipulated, which will inevitably prevent it from widespread use in the courtroom. Conventional photography will continue to be the primary format utilized though the traditional prints, negatives and slides, which can be scanned into a digital format for convenient access, use, a25nd distribution. An additional benefit of digital photography versus conventional formats is the money saved on the purchase of film, developing, waiting time for processing, and less use of film and toxic chemicals used for processing. The utilization of digital photography allows you to view the images immediately.

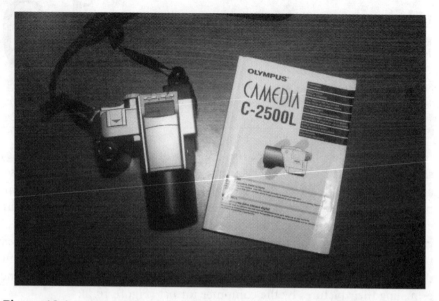

Figure 10.1 Example of a digital camera that looks and functions similarly to conventional cameras.

This is extremely helpful if the image was not taken properly, or was underexposed, or overexposed. A photo can be erased and re-imaged.

In insurance and law enforcement, digital photography has more applications, but with these applications come limitations and restrictions.

For the law enforcement field, digital photography should be a backup to conventional photography. Since digital photography can be enhanced and manipulated, it would obviously have to be backed up to show through conventional means that the evidence or scene had not been manipulated. Digital photography, however, can be used for quick processing and distribution among agencies as well as cataloguing and easy access to information without having to wait for the distribution of conventional prints.

For the insurance policyholder, digital photography would prove an easy way of documenting contents in homes, but for the field adjuster and investigators who are typically on the scene after a type of loss, this method could be used to capture the images needed and almost immediately download them to their own home or business system for review and consultation. These images can be sent while the adjuster is in the field and, upon receipt, an investigator or engineer may be able to direct the field adjuster, claim representative, or special investigation unit investigator to a particular area of concern for immediate documentation. This could prove to be valuable in cases where spoliation of evidence may be a concern, or hazard conditions exist, for example where a building must be razed to prevent possibility of collapse and other hazards to the safety of the community and/or passersby.

Although most, if not all, digital photography cannot yet meet the resolution of conventional print photography, (see Figures 10.2a through 10.2f) the transmittal of these images to Websites, e-mails, and in-house representatives is limited by the viewing medium (printer or monitor). A lower resolution digital camera would be satisfactory in capturing these images, which are only as good as the viewing medium they are portrayed on.

What Makes up Digital Imaging?

The components of digital imaging are image sensors, resolution, and color. The image sensor for a digital camera is a solid state device. The image sensors are small, approximately one inch by one inch, silicone chips that contain hundreds to millions of photo-sensitive diodes referred to as photo sites. Each of these individual photo sites records the intensity of the light to which it is exposed, which causes the photo site to react by accumulating an electric charge — hence, more light, the higher the charge. This intensity of light at each photo site is recorded as a set of numbers that is used to determine the color and brightness of what you see on a printed page or a monitor. This visual display is an accumulation of many pixels. Pixels are small dots arranged in grid patterns to portray color. Groups of pixels are arranged to constitute a complete picture.

Resolution

The quality of resolution is dependent on the number of pixels used to make up an image. Visualize a standard 35 mm negative and a standard 3 × 5 print showing great clarity. Typically, if the 35 mm film is blown up into a poster size print, the clarity greatly decreases and becomes grainy. The more pixels a screen or printer has, and the smaller they are, the greater the detail. The standard way of portraying resolution is total number of pixels, pixels per inch (PPI), or dots per inch (DPI). Camera resolutions are dependent on the image sensors, which contain the small photo sites. Each photo site represents one pixel in the image to be viewed. The solid state image sensor in the camera, which contains the photo sites, determines the resolution by how many photo sites are on the surface of the sensor. The resolution is related in the sensor dimensions and pixels or by total number of pixels, such as 1200 × 800 pixels, 960,000 pixels, or by file sizes such as 30 megabytes. Low end cameras can produce 640 × 480 pixels. Better cameras producing one million or more pixels are referred to as megapixel cameras. Multimegapixel

Figures 10.2a through 10.2f show the differences in quality and sharpness between 35 mm format photographs and digital images of the same fatal tractor accident. Figures a, c, and e are the 35 mm photographs. Figures b, d, and f are the digital images.

Figure 10.2b

Figure 10.2c

Figure 10.2d

Figure 10.2e

Figure 10.2f

cameras allow over two million pixels on the image sensor. One downside to the higher resolutions is that they require larger files to store the information (images). Some of these cameras may even have adjustable resolution.

When investigating a camera's resolution, beware of the claims of enhanced resolution. This is known as interpolated resolution. Software built into the camera or scanner evaluates the pixels surrounding each new pixel to determine what the color should be for an apparent higher resolution image. Interpolated resolution does not add any new information or delete any information from the image; it only enhances. What to look for in a camera or scanner is optical resolution. This is a set number of image sensor photo sites.

Digital Cameras

Digital cameras have one of three types of electronic shutters that control the exposure. This concept is the same as that utilized in traditional cameras. The first is an electronically shuttered sensor that uses the image sensor to set an exposure time. A timing circuit tells it when to start and stop the exposure. The second is electro-mechanical shutter, which is a mechanical device that is controlled electronically. The third is an electro-optical shutter, which is an electronically driven device in front of the image sensor, which changes with the optical path transmittance.

Monitors

Resolution on a display monitor is depicted by screen width and height in pixels such as 640 × 480. The first number, 640, is the horizontal number of pixels across the screen. The second number, 480, is the vertical number of pixels down the screen. The images are of low resolution in comparison to a print format. For convenience, easy access, and organizational purposes as well as distribution, monitor images are highly valuable. A monitor does not have the capability of producing an image as clear as those produced by printers and scanners.

Printers and Scanners

Prints and scanners are classified by the number of dots per inch (DPI). Images can be produced in ranges up to 1700 DPI.

Special Notes

Cameras to pay particular attention to are those equipped with CMOS image sensors versus CCD image sensors. CCD image sensors are charged-coupled devices. They originated over 20 years ago. They captured light onto small photo sites on the surface and got their name from the way the charges read after an exposure. The charges on the first row are transferred to a read-out register. From there, the signals are sent to an amplifier and then onto an analogue digital convertor. Once the row has been read, the charges on the read-out register are read and deleted. The next row enters the read-out register and so on. These charges on each row are then coupled to those rows above. Each row is read individually. The largest problem with CCDs is there is not enough *economy of scale*.

CMOS image sensors are complementary metaloxide semi-conductors. The cost of fabricating the CMOS is approximately a third of the fabricating cost of the CCD. This process is the same as the way pentium chips, which contain approximately ten million active elements, are manufactured. The performance of the CMOS image sensor compared to the CCD is similar in the quality shown in below- and mid-range CCD image sensors. The high end image sensors of the CCD are still dominant. The use of CMOS image sensors allows for the addition of image stabilization and compression, which not only makes the camera smaller, lighter and cheaper, but also requires less power so the batteries will last longer. The CMOS image sensors can switch modes immediately between still photography and video. Video, however, generates huge files. The downside to CMOS is low light conditions.

Summary

Like their predecessors, digital cameras have their place and are making progress in the field of forensic imaging. Digital photography and videography impose new technology and methodology in the field of photographic documentation.

It is essential that the forensic photographer become proficient in whatever medium is chosen. This includes obtaining the training, background, and references necessary to support the photographer's position in a legal matter.

Suggested Reading

Russ, J., *Forensic Uses of Digital Imaging*, CRC Press, Boca Raton, FL, in press.

Glossary

AC (alternating current) In the United States AC is 120 volts, 60 cycles.

AC adapter Multipurpose accessory. Converts standard household alternating current (120 v/60 Hz) or foreign AC current (110 v/220 v/240 v) to 9.6 v direct current (DC) power. Also recharges batteries.

Accelerant Something that increases the speed of a process (e.g., gasoline and fire).

Accessory Helping in a secondary way; something extra.

Accessory shoe A nonelectrical fitting on top of a camera that supports accessories. See *hot shoe.*

Acetate Cellulose; a film base.

Actinic rays Light rays of short wavelengths occurring in the violet and ultraviolet parts of the spectrum which produce chemical changes, as in photography.

Adapter back An auxiliary back for a camera that permits the use of different size film than the camera was originally constructed to use.

Adapter ring A device that makes two different-sized pieces of equipment compatible, lens and filter using a Series-7 holder, for example.

Aerial perspective Effect of depth produced by haze in a photograph. Distant objects are recorded with lighter zones and with colors distorted toward blue, giving a three-dimensional impression.

Animation Incremental sequence of still images that, when shown in rapid succession, simulate movement.

Anti-aliasing A technique or system to reduce or eliminate *jaggies*, the jagged visual effect caused by the pixels in diagonal lines of low-resolution displays.

Aperture Adjustable opening, also referred to as *f-stop*, which controls the amount of light that is focused on the film.

Aperture preference The automatic exposure system used on some cameras, in which a specific aperture is selected but the shutter speed adjusts automatically to expose the film to the correct amount of light.

Artificial light Any light other than daylight.

Artificial light film Color film balanced for use in tungsten artificial light, usually 3200°K. Packs are usually marked "tungsten" or "Type B."

ASA American Standards Association, formerly a standardized rating number for film based on its sensitivity to light (see also *DIN* and *ISO*).

Audio The sound portion of a television signal.

Audio dubbing Addition of sound to previously recorded tape.

Autofocus Automatically sets the focus (distance) from scene to camera.

Auto iris Automatically regulates the amount of light entering the camera.

Automatic Self-thinking, or in the case of a mechanical device, preprogrammed and self-regulating.

Automatic camera A camera with a built-in exposure meter that automatically adjusts the lens opening, shutter speed, or both for proper exposure.

Autopsy Examination and dissection of a dead body to discover cause of death.

Auto white balance Electronically adjusts camera color levels.

Auxiliary lens A lens element added to a regular lens to shorten or increase the focal length.

B (1) Bulb setting on the shutter ring indicating that the shutter will stay open as long as the shutter release button is depressed. (2) Professional 1" reel-to-reel format videotape.

Background The part of the scene that appears behind the principal subject of the picture.

Backlighting Light shining on the subject from the direction opposite the camera, distinguished from frontlighting and sidelighting.

Backscatter The light reflected back to the camera in underwater photography caused by flash reflection off particles suspended in the water.

Backspatter Blood directed back toward its source of energy. Backspatter is often associated with gunshot wounds of entrance.

Battery pack Rechargeable, portable power source.

Bayonet mount A casting on the rear of a lens corresponding to an appropriate fitting on the camera body.

BETA Sony format ½" videotape.

Blur Unsharp image caused by movement or inaccurate focusing.

Bounce Lighting A light source reflected off of another surface and then onto the subject.

Bracketing Using the recommended aperture (f-stop) and shutter speed and decreasing and increasing the aperture for additional exposures.

Buffer An area of memory in which information is stored while the computer is on.

Bulb A shutter speed setting used to hold the shutter open for extended periods with the use of a shutter release cord or continuous pressure on the shutter release button.

Burn An afterimage produced on a TV screen caused by excessive light falling on the recording camera's tube.

Burn pattern The visible path of fire on a surface or surfaces.

B&W Black and white.

C Professional 1" reel-to-reel format videotape.

Cable release A flexible, enclosed wire used to release the shutter mechanism.

Cadmium sulfide cells (Also *Cd*) Used in exposure meters to indicate amount of light entering meter.

Camera A photographic apparatus used to expose sensitized film or plates to reflected light images formed by a lens. Also, an electronic device to change film or live action into video signals.

Camera angle The photographer's point of view of a subject or scene as viewed through the lens or viewfinder.

Cartridge A lightproof container that is loaded with film in the dark and can be handled and placed in the camera in the light.

Cassette A film cartridge or magazine.

Cast Overall bias toward one color in a color photograph.

CCD Charged coupled device.

Changing bag Bag made of opaque material that allows film to be loaded into cassettes or tanks outside a darkroom.

Circle of confusion An optical term describing the size of an image point formed by a lens.

Close-up A photograph taken close to the subject, often requiring an auxiliary lens. Macro and micro are degrees of close-up.

Color The sensation produced in the eye by a particular wavelength or group of wavelengths of visible light.

Color balancing filters Filters used to balance color film with the color temperature of the light source and to prevent the formation of color casts. An 85B filter is used with tungsten film in daylight, an 80A filter with daylight film in tungsten light.

Color compensating (CC) filters Comparatively weak color filters used to correct for small differences between the color temperature of the illumination and that for which the film was manufactured.

Color conversion filters Fairly strong color filters used for exposing film in light of a type markedly different from that for which the film was made.

Color negative film Film that records the colors of the subject in complementary hues that are subsequently reversed again in the printing paper to give the correct colors.

Color reversal film Film that produces a direct positive by effectively reversing the negative image during processing. Transparency (slide) film is of this type.

Configuration The arrangement of various computer options and settings, including the tools, colors, and current drive path.

Contrast The difference in intensities of light falling on various parts of a subject.

Contrast filter A colored filter used to make a colored subject stand out either lighter or darker (for black-and-white film).

Correction filter Filter used to alter colors to suit the color response of the film.

Coupled exposure meter Exposure meter built into the camera and linked with the aperture or shutter speed controls, or both.

Coupled rangefinder A rangefinder connected to the focusing mechanism of the lens which is focused while measuring the distance to the subject.

Criminalistics The scientific recognition, identification, preservation, and interpretation of physical evidence.

Cropping The elimination of part of an original image on a single negative during printing because of automation or enlargement.

Crosshairs Two lines, one vertical and the other horizontal, used to accurately specify a point on the computer screen.

CRT Cathode ray tube (video picture tube).

Cyan A blue-green (minus red) color.

Daylight color film Color film designed to be used with daylight or a light source of equivalent color temperature, including blue flashbulbs and electronic flash. The film is balanced to 5400°K.

DC (direct current) Voltage supplied by a battery to power portable equipment.

Default The minimum settings necessary for computer software to operate.

Definition Clarity, sharpness, resolution, and brilliance of an image formed by the lens.

Dense Dark negative or positive film on paper that is overexposed, over-developed, or both.

Depth of field The zone between the foreground and background which appears in sharpest focus for a particular lens, distance, and aperture.

Depth of field scale Scale on a lens barrel showing the near and far limits of depth of field possible when the lens is set at any particular focus and aperture.

Diffuser A material used to soften the original light and to disperse it to a degree.

DIN Deutsche Industrie Norm, the European equivalent of ASA rating of film's sensitivity to light (see also *ISO*).

Directory The disk tree structure that holds groups of image files.

Distortion Incorrect rendering of the shape of an object.

Documentary photography The taking of photographs to provide a record of situations with the aim of conveying information.

Electronic flash Lighting unit utilizing the flash of light produced by discharging a current between two electrodes in a gas-filled tube.

Electronic viewfinder (EVF) A small TV monitor attached to a video camera for viewing of recorded images.

ELP Extra long play.

Emulsion In photography, a suspension of a salt of silver in gelatin or collodion used to coat film.

Enhance To develop or bring out from a latent form.

Enlargement A print made from a smaller negative or slide through magnification.

EP Extended play.

Existing light That light present at any one time in a given area no matter what the source.

Expert Witness A witness determined by a judge in any court to be qualified as an expert in a certain field, based on qualifications.

Exposure The subjection of sensitized film to the action of light for a specific period.

Exposure index Method of rating film speed developed by the American Standards Association, now known as the American National Standards Institute, Inc. (ANSI).

Exposure meter An instrument measuring the intensity of light on a particular speed film and determining the correct f-stop and shutter speed.

Exposure setting The lens opening and shutter speed selected to expose the film.

Extension cord An auxiliary wire used to maintain electronic contact between the camera and strobe.

Extension tube A device that increases the distance between the lens and the sensitive film in the camera and changes the lens capability.

Eyepiece The optic device installed on a camera, microscope, telescope, and so on used to look through the instrument.

Fade A decrease in a video or audio signal intensity.

Fade-in/fade-out Gradually changing video from dark to picture or picture to dark.

Fast film Film designed to be very sensitive to light. Such films have high ASA ratings.

Fast lens Lens with large aperture requiring less light.

Fatality An accident or crime that results in a death.

FF Fast forward.

Field of vision The area a photographer can see through the viewfinder or lens.

File Information (text or graphic) that is given a name and stored on a computer disk. MS-DOS file names can have up to eight letters or numbers and may optionally include a three-character extension following a period, such as BLOCK-2A.TGA.

Fill-in Secondary illumination to keep shadow areas from photographing too dark; also known as the *fill light*.

Film A sheet or strip of celluloid coated with light-sensitive emulsion for exposure in a camera.

Film plane Portion of the camera body that holds the sensitized film in place during the exposure process; portion of the camera where the image is focused.

Film speed A means of representing numerically the response of a photographic emulsion to light.

Filter A glass, plastic, or gel that absorbs or transmits certain light rays.

Filter factor The number by which the correct exposure without the filter must be multiplied to obtain the same effective exposure with the filter.

Finder A viewer through which the picture to be taken may be seen and centered.

Fingerprint powder A powder (silver, gray, black, red, or fluorescent) dusted on a latent print with a brush to enhance or bring out the print.

Fish-eye lens Wide-angle lens with angle of view as wide as 180 degrees. Depth of field is practically infinite.

Fixed focus A simple camera that has a short focus and a small-aperture lens that is not adjustable.

Flash A general term for any auxiliary, sudden brilliant light. A unit holding flashbulbs is referred to as a *flash*.

Flash bar An Instamatic light source consisting of eight or ten AG lightbulbs and requiring no external battery

Flashbulb Plastic-coated expendable glass bulb containing metal foil that burns to emit light of an intensity ranging from 3800°K (clear bulb) to 5000°K (blue bulb). Duration of the flash ranges from 1/20 to 1/200 second depending on the type.

Flashcube An Instamatic light source consisting of four AG size flashbulbs in a cube form and requiring a battery for firing.

Flash sensor Electronic unit actuated by light flash.

Flash synchronization Method of ensuring that flash light duration and maximum shutter opening coincide. There are often two settings on a camera, C and M. C is the setting used for electronic flash in which peak output is almost instantaneous on firing. M is for expendable bulb flash, which normally requires a delay in shutter opening of about 17 milliseconds to allow the bulb output to build up.

Flood Light source providing a wide, diffused beam of light.

Fluorescence Property possessed by various substances that glow when exposed to light of a short wavelength.

Focal length The distance in millimeters (mm) from the center of the lens to the point where the image comes into critical view.

Focal plane shutter A shutter that operates immediately in front of the focal plane. Usually contains a fixed or variable-speed slit in a curtain of cloth or metal which travels across the film to make the exposure.

Focus Point at which converging rays of light from a lens meet.

Focusing The adjustment of the lens-to-film distance to produce a sharp image of the subject.

Font A collection of letters and numbers of one style and point (height) size.

Forensic science The application of scientific disciplines to legal matters.

Format Size, shape, and general makeup of negative, slide, photographic print, camera viewing area, or video equipment.

Frame An individual picture on a roll of film or one full on-screen image of displayed computerized information.

Frame buffer A separate area of memory where an image or frame is stored in a computer.

f-stop (f-number) Focal setting for the diaphragm that controls the size of the aperture; the higher the f-stop, the smaller the aperture opening.

Fully automatic Combination of camera aperture and speed settings that can be automated to provide complete automatic exposure for a picture.

Gain select Increases sensitivity to light during video recording, used when sufficient illumination is not available.

Gamma A process that improves the video image by correcting for the lack of picture clarity.

Genlock Synchronization of a computer's image capture board by an external video source.

Glare Intense light reflected off highly reflective surfaces such as water, glass, and very light-toned subjects.

Grain Individual silver particles or groups of particles in the emulsion which, when enlarged, become noticeable and sometimes objectionable.

Graininess The grainy appearance of photographic enlargements. More prominent on higher speed films.

Guide number An indication of the power of a flash unit, enabling the correct aperture to be selected at a given distance between flash and subject. The number divided by the distance gives the f-stop that should be used. A film speed is specified with the guide number and recalculation is needed for different speeds.

Gun Any device for igniting flashlamps or flash powder.

Half-inch The width of the tape used in all home video recorders; also the format name.

Haze filter Lens filter that reduces the effect of atmospheric haze. Red reduces most, green the least. A blue filter induces haze.

Hot shoe An electronic device usually found above the 35 mm camera's eyepiece to hold a strobe unit. It is activated when the shutter is released.

Hot spot A concentrated area of light on a subject that creates a reflection and at times destroys detail or image.

Hue The name by which one color is distinguished from another (e.g., blue, red).

Identification Recording of sufficient visual detail to allow recognition of a particular individual.

Illumination A specific amount of light present in any given area. Expressed in lux or footcandles; the lower the lux of equipment, the less light required for a good picture.

Image (1) The photographic representation of an object or scene formed by optical and/or chemical action. (2) A two-dimensional array of pixels representing a three-dimensional computer-generated scene.

Image aspect ratio Ratio of the width to the height of a displayed computer-generated image.

Infinity A distance from which the light appears to reach the lens in parallel rays.

Infrared Invisible band of wavelengths on the electromagnetic spectrum beyond visible red.

Infrared photography Recording of images produced by infrared radiation.

Instamatic A designation of a particular brand-name camera normally associated with 126 size film.

Interchangeable A camera lens that can be removed and replaced by another lens.

Iris The opening of a camera lens that controls the amount of light let in.

ISO International Standards Organization; the rating number that replaced the ASA/DIN rating.

Jaggies The undesirable "stair-stepping" (aliasing) effect of diagonal edges in a computer image. Reduced by *anti-aliasing*.

Kelvin (K) Unit of temperature measurement used to measure the color temperature of light.

Latent image The image on a film that is invisible until developed.

LCD Liquid crystal display.

LED Light-emitting diode. An electronic display of numbers or letters.

Lens The camera's light-gathering device consisting of one or more glass elements.

Lens cap A cover used to protect a lens from dust and damage when not in use.

Lens elements A number of lenses or elements in combination to achieve the overall function of that particular lens.

Lens speed The largest lens opening (smallest f-number) at which a lens can be set. A fast lens can transmit more light and has a larger possible opening than a slow lens.

Light A form of radiant energy that makes up the visible part of the electro-magnetic spectrum.

Light meter Alternative term for *exposure meter*.

Light source General term for any source of light used in photography, whether natural or artificial.

LP (Long play) VHS recording speed that is half as fast as SP.

Lumen Photometric unit equal to the luminous flux on one square foot of surface from a standard candle one foot away.

Lux A measurement of available light; the sensitivity of a video camera is expressed in lux. Generally, ten lux equals one footcandle of light. A footcandle is defined as the amount of light given off by a candle held one foot away from the subject. Standard lighting is 150 footcandles (1500 lux). The lower the lux of the equipment, the better for shooting in low-light conditions.

Macro lens Lens designed to work at close distances permitting image magnification.

Macrophotography Photography usually involving close-up capabilities, whether with lens or bellows, with a magnification from life size (1:1) up to 50 times (50:1).

Magenta A reddish-blue (minus green) color.

Manual A booklet published by a manufacturer covering functions of a particular piece of equipment.

Master A high-quality tape that serves as the source for subsequent copies; also, a video unit used for playback in a dubbing operation.

Menu A screen display containing a list of selectable items.

Microphone A device used to convert voices into audio signals.

Microphotography Photography using a compound microscope allowing high-order magnification.

Monitor A TV set designed to accept audio and video signals.

Monochrome Single colored; for instance, black-and-white photographs and sepia- or other-toned images in one color. Similar light rays of one color wavelength (i.e., a single, pure color).

Motor drive Device for advancing the film and retensioning the shutter by means of an electric motor.

Multiple flash The use of more than one flash unit, usually operating simultaneously.

Nanometer A term for millimicron, as used in UV and infrared measurements.

Natural light Daylight.

Near point The closest object to the camera in focus for a given distance.

Negative Photographic image in which the amount of silver present is more or less based on the reflectivity from the original object. Black appears white and white appears black.

Nicad Nickel cadmium (NiCd) rechargeable battery.

Normal lens A lens that makes the image in a photograph appear in a perspective similar to that of the original scene.

NTSC National Television Standards Committee that sets the analog video signal standard used by the broadcast television industry in the United States.

Ohm adapter, 300/75 TV antenna wire is either 300 ohm (flat, twin-lead ribbon type) or 75 ohm (round, shielded coaxial cable). TV sets and VCRs can accept both types of antenna connections.

Open flash Method of using flash in which the shutter is opened, the flash is fired, and then the shutter is closed. It is used when the shutter speed is unimportant because existing lighting is poor or nonexistent.

Open up Increase of aperture (f-stop) opening.

Overexposure The result of too much light reflected from the subject.

Painting with light Multiflash or tungsten light movement to cover an area with light during a time exposure.

Palette A specific group of colors used for painting.

Pan-and-tilt head Tripod head with separate locks for horizontal (pan) and vertical (tilt) movements of the camera.

Panning The movement from left to right and right to left of the camera; normally associated with movie and video cameras.

Parallax Difference between the image seen in a viewfinder and that recorded by the taking lens. Most pronounced at close distances with twin-lens reflex and rangefinder cameras. Single-lens reflex and studio cameras are free from parallax error.

Path The specific order of branches of the tree taken by the computer to retrieve the image files.

Perspective The relationship between objects in a scene in terms of scale, position, and shape when seen from one viewpoint.

Perspective grid target A two-foot square (or other predetermined size) target used in the scale mapping of scene documentation.

Photo-electric cell Light-sensitive cell used in exposure meters and for remote triggering of the shutter.

Photo flash lamp An electronic lamp working at higher than normal voltage, giving brighter light.

Photoflood Photographic lamp designed to produce a high output of light during a comparatively short life.

Photogrammetry The process of surveying or mapping through analysis of photographs.

Photography Literally writing or drawing with light (from the Greek words *photo*, meaning light, and *graphos*, meaning writing.

Photomacrography See macrophotography.

Photomicrography See microphotography.

Photosensitive Material that is chemically or physically changed by light.

Pixel Picture element. The smallest unit of information on a computer screen.

Polarized light Light vibrating in one plane instead of in all directions at right angles around its line of motion. The polarization of specularly reflected light produces glare.

Polarizer Two lenses used together to cut off all phases of light waves but one, eliminating glare in varying degrees.

Polarizing filter Filter that transmits only polarized light and can be rotated to block polarized light, cutting down glare from polished surfaces or from blue sky.

Polaroid A trade name usually associated with on-the-spot processing of film for quick results.

Portable VCR Any VCR that can run on batteries.

Positive An image that is like the original. A slide or reversal film is a positive image.

Preset All settings and functions have been determined beforehand.

Pressure plate A metal plate found inside the back of the camera used to keep the film lying flat and to prevent distortion.

Preview button A button or lever on the camera lens permitting the photographer to see the actual light level and depth of field while using an automatic lens.

Print A positive picture, usually on paper, and usually produced from a negative.

Processing General term used to describe the sequence of steps whereby a latent image is converted into a visible, permanent image.

Pushing An extending technique used in conjunction with uprating the ASA speed of the film during exposure. Used to increase speed and contrast.

QUAD Professional 2" reel-to-reel format videotape.

Quartz lens A special lens used for ultraviolet photography.

RAM Random access memory. This memory is available for data storage only while the computer is turned on.

Rangefinder A viewer system found on cameras without a through-the-lens viewing capacity (SLR cameras).

Raster image The representation of an image by colors as a two-dimensional grid of pixels.

Ray tracing A technique to generate an image from a geometric model of an object. For each pixel in an image, a theoretical ray is cast from the observer's viewpoint into the model to determine what part of the model should be displayed at that point in the resulting image.

Real time Continuous motion of the computer system with no noticeable movement between images. Television broadcasts in the United States are recorded at 30 frames per second, at which the human eye perceives no delay. If a computer can keep up with this motion it is said to be in *real time*.

Record/review Automatically rewinds and plays back the last few seconds of videotape recording. Provides a smooth transition from one segment to another.

Reflection The bouncing back of rays of light striking a surface.

Reflex camera A camera in which the image can be seen right side up and full size on the ground-glass focusing screen.

Refraction The bending of a light ray when passing obliquely from one medium to a medium of different density.

Remote An action originating from another location, as in a surveillance situation.

Rendering Generating an image on a computer screen that is a precise scene.

Resolution The fineness or coarseness of the computer screen image designated by the number of pixels vertically and horizontally (e.g., 512×480).

Reversal A positive film such as slide film (either color or black and white).

REW Rewind.

RGB An abbreviation for video primary colors: red, green, and blue.

Roll film A strip of film wound on a spool or reel.

Root directory The "trunk" directory of the tree, which contains the subdirectories and files.

Scale The enlargement or reduction of an object or texture.

Screw mount A lens mount threaded to fit the camera.

Secured A traffic, crime, or fire scene under control of the appropriate authorities.

Self-timer A timing device permitting the photographer to delay shutter function.

Sheet film Individual film with a heavier base, which is loaded into a film holder (e.g., 4" × 5" or 5" × 7").

Shoot A slang term for taking a photograph.

Shot sheet A form for recording all pertinent photographic information on a particular roll of film.

Shutter Mechanical device that regulates the time in which light acts upon film.

Shutter preference An automatic exposure system in which shutter speed may be selected and the aperture is adjusted automatically to give correct exposure.

Shutter speed The action of the shutter that controls the duration of an exposure. The faster the speed, the shorter the exposure.

Silhouette A photograph that shows only the mass of a subject in black against a white or colored background.

Single-lens reflex Camera system utilizing a hinged mirror between the lens and the film which swings out of the light path when the shutter is open, allowing the taking and viewing functions of a lens to be combined.

Skylight filter A pale pink correction filter used on a camera when taking color slides to eliminate blue casts found in dull weather or when subjects are lit only by reflected blue sky light.

Slave unit A photo-electric device that, when activated by light from the main flash, fires one or more auxiliary flashes.

Slide A positive film mounted in a slide mount or a positive print on glass for projection upon a screen.

Slide film Direct reversal film; usually color film used in cameras for full-color projection positives. Sometimes called *color transparency film*.

Slow The relative speed of a lens, shutter, or film in capturing the photographic image.

Slow film Film having an emulsion with low sensitivity to light. Typically such films have ASA ratings of 32 or less.

Slow lens A lens with a relatively small maximum aperture, such as f8.

SLP (Super long play) The slowest VHS speed.

SLR Single-lens reflex.

Snapshot A casual picture taken by a amateur, usually with simple equipment.

SP (Standard play) The current industry standard for prerecorded VHS tapes. Also the fastest VHS speed available.

Spectrum A colored band formed when white light passes through a prism.

Speed The sensitivity of a photographic emulsion to light. ISO, ASA, or DIN numbers indicate their relative speed characteristics. The higher the number, the faster the film reacts to light.

Spotlight Lamp unit with reflector and lens that can either focus light into a small, concentrated circle or give a wider beam.

Sprocket hole The perforations on sides of a roll of film that permit the sprocket mechanism of a camera to advance or rewind the film.

Still A photograph lacking motion; a single frame.

Standard lens Lens whose focal length is approximately equal to the diagonal of the film format with which it is used; also referred to as the *prime* or *normal* lens.

Static streak Light streak that appears on photographic film, usually in cold weather when film is advanced too quickly. Static streaks interfere with development of clear photographic images.

Stop A lens aperture or diaphragm opening, such as f4, and f5.6.

Stop down Change to a smaller aperture (f-stop).

Strobe Electronic flash unit. An electrical power supply charges a gas-filled flash tube emitting light between 1/1000 second and 1/50,000 second. A strobe can be manual or manual and automatic.

Subject The person or object photographed.

Surveillance photography A secretive, continuous, or periodic visual documentation of activities involving persons, places, or objects of importance to an investigation.

S-VHS Super 1/2" home system videotape.

Sync-cord An electrical power cord used to connect the flash unit to a power source.

Synchro-flash A term applied to flash photography in which a flashbulb is ignited at the same instant that the shutter is opened.

T-120 Most popular videotape; allows one, two, or three hours of recording time, depending on speed used.

Telephoto lens A lens with elements placed to produce larger images at a greater distance.

Texture map A section of a two-dimensional (2-D) raster image of texture that is "mapped" onto a 2-D or 3-D surface automatically by the computer.

Thin A weak negative that lacks contrast and density.

Through-the-lens metering (TTL) A system built into a camera body that measures the amount of light seen by the lens and provides this information for the photographer.

Time exposure Manual opening and closing of the shutter.

Time lapse A timing device that can be set to take a photograph every few seconds, minutes, hours, and so forth.

Tint A color made lighter by the addition of white.

TLR Twin-lens reflex.

Transmission The ratio of the light passed through an object to the light falling upon it.

Transmitted Light Light passed through a transparent or translucent medium.

Transparency An image on a transparent base which must be viewed by transmitted light. Also refers to the light transmitting power of the silver deposit in a negative. The opposite of opacity.

Tripod A three-legged stand used to support a camera or lens and camera.

Tungsten light Incandescent light; light from a bulb having tungsten filaments, usually of lower wattage, 15 w to 500 w.

Tungsten light film Color film balanced to suit tungsten light sources with a color temperature of 3200°K.

Twin-lens reflex (TLR) Camera having two lenses of the same focal length. One is used for viewing and focusing, the other for exposing the film. The lenses are mounted vertically.

Type A color film Obsolete type of artificial light color film balanced for light sources with a color temperature of 3400°K.

Type B color film Color film balanced for artificial light sources with a color temperature of 3200°K.

Type D color film　Obsolete designation for film balanced for daylight.

3/4 U　Professional 3/4" videotape cassette.

Ultraviolet (UV)　Part of the electromagnetic spectrum from about 400 nm down to 1 nm. It is invisible to the human eye. Most photographic materials are sensitive to near-UV bands, down to 250 nm. UV light records as increased haze, particularly in distant views and at high altitudes, and may give a blue cast to color images.

Ultraviolet filter　A filter that transmits ultraviolet light; as used in photography, refers to the reflected ultraviolet light method.

Ultraviolet rays　Invisible rays with lengths shorter than the visible rays of light.

Underexposure　Result of insufficient light during film exposure.

Unipod　A one-legged support for a camera.

Variable focus lens　Alternative term for *zoom lens*.

VCR　Video cassette recorder.

Vector graphics　Computer-generated images represented as points in space interspersed with line segments.

VHS　Video home system 1/2" tape format.

VHS-C　Video home system compact 1/2" tape.

VHF/UHF　Frequencies used by televisions and VCRs to receive programming. VHF (very high frequency) channels are 2 through 13; UHF (ultra high frequency) channels are 14 through 83 on most TVs/VCRs or 14 through 60 on newer products. Cable TV channel programs are also transmitted on VHF frequencies.

Video　Visual; when applied to a television system, the picture portion of a signal.

Video cassette　A plastic container used to hold videotape.

Video dubbing　Replacing portions of existing video recording with new video material.

Videographer　A person who produces videography.

Videography　The recording of visual images electronically on magnetic tape, usually accompanied by a recorded soundtrack.

Video image capture　The securing of an image from a videotape source, storing it in a computer as a still image to be retrieved later in photographic format.

Viewfinder A viewing instrument attached to a camera that is used to obtain proper composition.

Warping Mapping the texture onto the object in perspective.

Washed out A negative or print lacking detail and contrast.

White balance A procedure used to tune a video camera's color by setting it to perfectly reproduce a white object.

Wide-angle lens A lens with a short focal length covering a larger area and condensing the subject matter.

Window A boxed area smaller than the computer screen in which images appear.

Wireframe A three-dimensional computer image represented with single lines.

Wratten filter An Eastman Kodak trade name for filters.

X-rays Electromagnetic waves shorter than visible light and ultraviolet rays which have the capability of passing through certain objects.

Zooming Moving a variable focus lens during an exposure.

Zoom lens A lens that can adapt to varied focal lengths while maintaining focus on a particular subject at a given distance.

Index

A

Accelerants, 51
Accident(s)
  boating, 131
  hit-and-run, 127
  Investigation Units (ACIUS), 105
  motor vehicle, see Motor vehicle accident
    scene
  scene documentation, 111
Accidental injuries, 190
ACIUS, see Accident Investigation Units
Activation methods, 240
Aerial photography, 137–151
  aircraft positioning, 149
  choosing of aircraft, 141–142
    fixed-wing aircraft, 142
    rotary-wing aircraft, 142
  equipment, 138–141
    accessories, 141
    camera and lens, 138–139
    film, 141
    filters, 139–141
  hiring aerial photographic services, 150
  safety and choosing of aircraft charter
    service, 142–147
  shadows and time of day, 149–150
  shutter speeds and F-stops, 149
  weather and atmospheric conditions,
    147–149
Aircraft
  charter service, choosing of, 142
  fixed-wing, 142, 144, 147
  positioning, 149
  rotary-wing, 141, 142, 145
Amateur photographers, 48
American Standards Association (ASA), 12, 72
Aperture, 8, 139, 156
Aqualung, invention of, 151

Arc lamps, 201
Arson
  /crime indicators, on-scene, 49
  possible indicators of, 51
Artifactual evidence, 223
Artificial lighting, 158, 159
ASA, see American Standards Association
Assailant, 224
Assault, 191
Atmospheric conditions, flight safety and, 147
Atmospheric haze, 140
Attorneys, professional photographers
    retained by, 106
Autofocusing problems, 139
Automatic camera functions, power supplies
    for, 162
Automatic iris, 84
Automatic white balance, 83
Automatic winder, 24, 25
Autopsy, 37, 191, 225
Auxiliary lighting, 111

B

Background radiation, 217
Backlight, 98
Balloons, hot-air and gas-filled, 141
Barrier tape, 53
Battery(ies), 33
  charging manual, typical log sheet from, 34
  electronic flash, 26
  nonrechargeable, 29
  packs, 90
  /tape removal, 101
Black spot fires, 42
Black-and-white film, 27
Black-and-white filters, 140
Blizzard, 36